America
on
Five Valium a Day

America
on
Five Valium a Day

★　　　★　　　★

LINDA BLANDFORD

METHUEN

First published in Great Britain 1983 by
Methuen London Ltd
11 New Fetter Lane, London EC4P 4EE

Copyright © 1983 Linda Blandford

British Library Cataloguing in Publication data:

Blandford, Linda
America on five valium a day.
I. Title
082   PR6052.L/
ISBN 0-413-51840-X

Phototypeset by Wyvern Typesetting Ltd, Bristol
Printed in Great Britain by
Richard Clay (The Chaucer Press) Ltd,
Bungay, Suffolk

Contents

Acknowledgements

One of the nicest things about a book is this chance to thank in print those who might, in conversation, brush aside such expression of gratitude.

Shortly before I left London to live in New York, Suzanne Lowry asked me to write a weekly American diary for the *Guardian*. Her patience and encouragement will always be appreciated.

To Liz Forgan, I owe a special debt for her unfailing kindness. To Frances Cairncross, Andy Veitch, Brenda Polan and Aidan White, I can say only that those cheery phone calls stopped me feeling as though I were merely casting messages in bottles out to sea. The editor of the *Guardian*, Peter Preston, has been a stalwart friend for whom I have been proud to work.

There are others, such as Katharine Whitehorn and Anthony Smith, who have always been ready with advice and enthusiasm. Christopher Falkus of Methuen has not only been the publisher that journalists dream of, but it was he who suggested the title. Cathryn Game, my editor, has been especially understanding.

George Seddon, the 'father of Fleet Street' to all of us who have been lucky enough to work for him, helped me with this as he has so much over the last ten years.

Above all, there is Lynn Harrell whose sense of humour underpins life in New York. To all, I would like to say thank you.

L.B.

Prelude: bad beginnings

It feels like an omen: the door of my husband's apartment opens on a horde of roaches stampeding around the kitchen. After three months' absence, the roach motels ('they check in but don't check out') are crammed with their dead. Three furnished rooms and a kitchen with a dishwasher but no cooker – all taken over by these prehistoric relics.

There are seventeen apartments on our floor, most of them the homes of old women living alone. The next-door neighbour comes out into the dingy corridor. She is tiny, bent almost double, in her nineties. By the time all our luggage has been moved inside, she has managed to shuffle a few paces. She seems to be deaf. The only sound she registers in the time we are here is that of her son knocking on her door. It happens rarely.

After two days of washing out sooty cupboards and exterminating roaches, a deadening chill descends on this new life in New York. Hope of a new apartment is all that relieves it. Finding a home in Manhattan bears a certain resemblance to finding one in Moscow. It isn't a question of what you can afford so much as who you know. Over the telephone realtors scoff at suggestions of some moderate spread with three bedrooms close to Central Park. An acquaintance suggests calling Rudin Management, one of the island's largest landlords.

By chance, there is an apartment available on West 86th Street. It's large and old-fashioned – an aunt used to live in a mansion flat like it in London. She couldn't wait to move out. But it does have a certain unwieldy charm, two large bedrooms, three bathrooms, a dining-room, living room, kitchen and maid's room (the latter a box, naturally).

I go to visit Rudin Management to hand over a deposit. Rudin envelopes a thickly carpeted suite of offices in a magnificent forty-four-storey skyscraper on Park Avenue which they happen to own. It gives new meaning to the word 'landlord' to one who has just come from London. Jack Harris, supremo of Rudin's less significant buildings, is a nice, friendly man in a small office with no window. It is not surprising to hear that big decisions are made by Mr Janson, a shadowy figure in a larger office with a scenic view.

Mr Harris is delighted we wish to move in. He remembers my husband's father, Mack Harrell, from the Metropolitan Opera after the war. All is going wonderfully well until the question of references comes up. Rudin's want no less than nine – three business, three financial, three social. It's the latter that causes the problem.

We suggest the Dean of the Juilliard School of Music (my husband's on the faculty), the cellist Leonard Rose and perhaps James Levine, Artistic Director of the Metropolitan Opera. Mr Harris looks worried. He asks if we know any important people. Perhaps we know someone who knows Lew Rudin? Mr Rudin, it seems, is very keen on show business. We mention that we know someone who knows someone whose father-in-law runs a major picture studio. He looks happier.

The next problem is even trickier. Mr Janson, it seems, might not like the thought of a resident musician. Over the next week Mr Janson (who is never seen despite the hours spent in the office next door to his with Mr Harris running to and fro like some global diplomat) makes it clear he doesn't like it. One last chance: my husband must take his cello and a piece of carpet round to the apartment for an audition.

The lady in the flat below says the cello won't bother her nearly as much as the previous tenants' children. Mr Harris advises against letting Mr Janson know that she has a subscription to the New York Philharmonic in case he dismisses her as a partial witness. Perhaps it's a joke.

Mr Harris is developing a bad back. It's hardly surprising. We've got to the point of wondering if it's worth it. The New York landlord–tenant relationship is not unlike that between the medieval baron and his serfs. Every serf hates the baron who owns his dwelling but lives in terror of his displeasure. We are at the mercy of Rudin's approval. At last we sign a lease and take possession of our new home.

It feels about as safe as a bird's nest in a tree with Dutch elm disease.

★   ★   ★

The West Side is where the liberals live. The week we move to West 86th Street, posters go up all along this wide street of gracious old prewar buildings: 'Save our Block! Save our Community! The Bridge, a post psychiatric socialization facility for formerly hospitalized chronic psychotics, is scheduled to move into the Brewster.' *(21 W 86)*

The Brewster is at the Central Park end of the street, round the corner from the expensive apartments with their canopies, cavernous marble lobbies and uniformed staff. This is where the richer liberals live. They, apparently, are particularly concerned about the Bridge. It seems wise to find out what is up: tales of drug addicts and psychotics sound worrying.

Fortunately a meeting is imminent of the New York Health and Hospital Subcommittee. The Bridge staff are coming to explain their work. The Committee to Preserve 86th Street are rallying the opposition in force.

By 8.30, the hall is crammed; people are overflowing on to the street outside. The meeting started at 8 and the mood is ugly. Many of our new neighbours are screaming that they don't want to hear about the Bridge – they don't want it whatever it is and, anyway, they know what it is so what is the point?

Chairman Ludwig Gelobter, the picture of a harassed walrus with anorexia, has some trouble imposing order. On top of everything, his chain smoking causes a ten-minute rumpus among the more health-conscious members of the community.

Enter the executive director of the Bridge, Murray Itzkowitz, who leaps on to the stage with a cigar of Churchillian proportion clamped between his teeth. It seems an expensive accessory for a social worker to anyone reared on the image of leather elbows and darned sweaters adorning those called to serve. (Mr

Itzkowitz, it turns out, earns $30,000 a year from the Bridge but also owns a flourishing private psychotherapy practice and a restaurant in Chinatown.)

Listening to the howls from the floor, it's possible to imagine what a lynch mob feels like. Undaunted, Mr Itzkowitz brings forward a plump, motherly-looking woman to talk about the Bridge. At last. Elaine Yatzkan, herself resident of a luxurious Central Park co-op building, is nervous. Understandably. Still, for twenty-five stoic minutes she tries to make herself heard while explaining that the Bridge is a day service centre where former mental hospital patients can go to sit, read and relax. Not many can have heard her repeating that the Bridge does not accept individuals with a history of drug or alcoholic addiction, violence or a criminal record. Their patients are mostly depressed and isolated people, terrified to cope with life, who learn through the Bridge such skills as how to go into supermarkets.

What seems to be going on in the room and what is going on are utterly different. This becomes apparent once the speakers from the floor take over. The row isn't over 'dangerous mental patients who might attack children and old people'. It's about property values; about what might happen to the prices of those marble-halled apartment blocks.

It might be all right if it was a facility for private, $100-an-hour patients, for the nice white middle-class sick – every block along West 86th Street is peppered with those. But, alas, the Bridge is for the poor and, here's the rub, most of them black and Hispanic. If they're rich, the mentally ill deserve sympathy. If they're poor, they're contagious.

Picking among bad moments, perhaps the worst is when the minister of a local church hands out his statement opposing the Bridge. On the bottom of his church's notepaper is printed certain exhortations: 'So that together we may find compassion and courage for the struggles of life: a Christian community gathers in unity to celebrate diversity.' His statement above these commendable ideals is not distinguished by its Christian spirit.

West 86th Street, at this moment, does not seem too inviting.

Nothing to do with the Bridge; it's the liberal neighbours.

        ★   ★   ★

As I am cleaning out the lint extractor in our fluff-free tumble dryer one morning, it occurs to me that life has taken a turn for the worse. Humidifiers go day and night to counter the effect of tropical central heating. The drinking water is purified through an electric Water-Mate. No one can come up without announcing him or herself to the elevator attendant downstairs. I never open the door without yelling 'Who is it?' in the particularly shrill tone that is the call of the New York apartment dweller.

I'm now living the way all outsiders think all New Yorkers live, i.e. under seige conditions, alleviated only a little by the shower with tension-soothing massage attachment, commercial meat slicer, automatic lettuce dryer and similar aids to life. At least there's a sense of other human beings nearby. When we moved in, I acquired a pair of binoculars. Now, I stand in the kitchen, binoculars trained on the twenty-storey block next door. Any neighbours who don't like it, I reasoned at first, could simply draw their nets. Not one window opposite has net curtains; not one has any curtains that close for that matter.

No one knows or apparently cares that I am watching. If you assume the world outside is hostile, you try to shut it out. If you assume that it's merely impersonal, that it doesn't give a damn about you either way, there's no point in bothering.

Actually the neighbours don't do much. I'm living opposite a slump-and-slurp block (slump in front of the television slurping sodas). I've noticed that in spite of the women's movement, every time I look across at the twenty kitchens stacked neatly on top of one another, I see at least fifteen stacked women working away. But recently, I've spent more time away from the binoculars. Central Park is half a block away. For the last few days, it has been magically covered with snow. For once the air has been cold but scrubbed clean. It has been beautiful. Perhaps, after all, there is a life beyond Nu-Soft concentrated coconut fabric conditioner and outside our West 86th Street fortress.

        ★   ★   ★

It is some months later and all over the Hamptons they are

dusting off the occasional tables and arranging, oh so casually, upon them the five volumes of the complete art history of the world. These at least can be trusted to cushion the drips from the iced tea, withstand the annual onslaught of suntan oil bottles and pass the quick-eye test of visitors who keep up with the *Times' Book Review*.

The village store has stocked up with Melita coffee filters no. 6 and next-door the bottles of California's best Chablis are on ice. At the hardware store, they're low on 75 ft sprinkle hoses with Siamese connections, there's been a run on designer doormats and there isn't a $400 runaround jalopy for sale to be found for miles.

Last weekend, the Long Island Expressway smouldered with traffic jams and anyone who couldn't talk about 'going out to the beach' crawled into some Manhattan corner and turned on the air conditioner. We were ensconced on our new wrap-around deck, sniffing the sea in the distance. It is something of a surprise to find ourselves the part owners (together with two or three of the more obliging local banks) of a desirable, plywood-clad contemporary ranch house on a similarly desirable wooded acre in Quogue, a quiet seaside spot eighty miles from the city.

As far as we can tell from the specifications issued by Bill, the moonlighting policeman whose first building venture this is, our stalwart home is constructed of cardboard, wood by-products, tufts of cotton wool and nails that are, one hopes, of a generous length. This Long Island playhouse was the result of a rash whim and a bout of rock fever: the island of Manhattan was growing ever more claustrophobic. A day trip to Quogue to see a friend somehow ended in the acquisition of lot 25, Foster Woods and the news that a local policeman was longing to be in the custom-building business.

The property was finished within three months. No one out here, it seems, lives in a house; everyone lives on a property. And everyone has to know the exact dimensions of that piece of property. 'Where do you live?' I asked a neighbour in the hydroponic lettuce queue the other day. 'On a beautifully wooded acre and a half near the library,' came the illuminating response. The talk is always of size: there's no such thing as a three-bedroomed home – we are now the incumbents of 2,000 square feet of versatile living space.

In the mornings the only sound is that of the racoons rootling through the garbage cans. In the afternoon, the air hums with intruders wondering if they could just walk through to see how we've used the space because they're considering a perfectly situated acre and a quarter in Remsenberg. It is the usual tack of these strangers who have just trampled down the newly seeded perennial rye to remark how 'gloriously subtle' the property is from outside. They mean small.

It will surely be an uplifting experience living here, rubbing shoulders with *New York Times* advertisements, listening to the tinkle of gold Tiffany chains, the whir of the trash compactor and the sound of the high-class bray acquired from years in WASPy private schools and colleges.

Two miles from our house, or rather property, is the reason we're all here – miles and miles of unspoilt coastline with white sand, white transparent pebbles and the rugged, Atlantic ocean splashing on to it. A half-finished letter to London lies on the table beside me: 'New York is not so bad after all,' it reads.

Around West 86th Street

West 86th Street is not a momentous place. No starry businesses see this as their natural home. No celebrities waft across other lives laden with scripts and Mark Cross address books. It is a corner of small enterprises, small joys and people who have learned to fear the unexpected.

In the Lido Bello Hair Salon Alan from Brooklyn wilts over his habitual cigarette. Slight, fiftyish with wispy hair and a scaly scalp, he lives for Saturday afternoons when the Texaco Metropolitan Opera broadcast fills the shop and he can talk to his old ladies of Luciano, Montserrat and Placido.

Alas for Alan, he is in an overcrowded profession. While there isn't one young hairdresser on our corner, there are at least four old-timers, all competing for the diminishing pool of ageing heads. These salons look as out of date as their clients: harsh neon, the occasional flutter of pink voile, fierce dryers and fiercer backcombing. The going rate for a shampoo and set is eight dollars: hard to scrape a living out of that.

One of the great mysteries of West 86th Street is how Alan keeps his door open. (Well, to be exact, he doesn't: the chain is always on. Alan is as nervous as his old ladies.) His rent has gone up again and still he persists. It cannot be his hairdressing skills or his charm that keep his shampoo-and-sets loyal. He has the belligerence of the timid. At his command, whining and arthritic clients shuffle to answer the phone, take the chain off the front door or simply wait uncomplainingly while he tries to cope with the unaccustomed pressure of three heads at once.

To hear Alan at work over some backcombing, however, is to feel part of the glamorous world of the international opera stage – a world he knows intimately from his hours of listening and reading, alone in his salon. 'That must be Siegfried,' an aria starts up on his radio. 'How can you not have heard of Siegfried Jerusalem? He's very promising, don't you agree Mrs Blumenthal?' And a head reared in 1900 Vienna, now washed on to 86th Street, nods obediently.

Most of Alan's old ladies live in rent-controlled apartments, trying to shut out the clamour of landlords lobbying for the removal of all such controls. They shudder at the thought of cash in flight from Europe and South America crowding into their corner of Manhatten. At Alan's, they feel safe.

At Maison Celine, 'The House of Quality & Service', is Harvey the Cleaner. He has been up since 5.30 for the long drive down the Bronx River Parkway to pull up the steel shutters and open for business. He shows up at the Three Brothers Coffee Shop on Columbus Avenue for a seven o'clock breakfast ('coffee and toasted bagel with a schmear, please Sophie'). In winter, pullovers, jumpers and anorak fend off the day-long cold. In summer he bustles around the street in an embroidered sports shirt, bemoaning the paunch of winter, beaming with the freedom of long weekends to come.

On Friday summer evenings, he closes early and drives out to his wife, Del, their motorboat, rowing boat, fishing, swimming and barbecues on the back porch. His sons Steven and Mitchell are there; daughter Gloree comes with her husband.

Since Harvey became a grandfather, nineteen months ago, the family's summer home on White Lake has taken on even greater importance. He has installed a cot and toys for his beloved Sarah ('Expense? What else do you keep it for?') and he treasures his two-week vacation when they all stay put. This is what he works twelve hours a day for.

This is why he lets the old ladies scream at him down the telephone and why he tolerates the monotony of a life composed of spots and alterations. Sometimes, when it gets too much, he daydreams of going back to college to train as a radiologist. At 50, he knows it's unlikely.

Meanwhile, he has his favoured customers to whom he will, in moments of intimacy, show the latest photograph of Sarah. He

also knows that he matters to West 86th Street. He is its notice
board – spreading news of who has left, who has arrived, who
has married, divorced, changed jobs. He is often the only one to
listen and care. Bad news, good news, it's always brought to
Harvey the Cleaner.

Other shopkeepers have tried to live up to his kindly ways.
Somehow it isn't the same. Perhaps the street senses sadness
behind Harvey's smile, his feeling of waste, imprisoned, as he is,
among the plastic-covered rails. No man with a subscription to
Music for Westchester's winter season, who devours every issue
of *Time, Newsweek, Money, Changing Times, Reader's Digest*, truly
wants to pass his life in dry-cleaning, albeit French dry-cleaning.

Alan is given to pointed remarks about Harvey's presence at
the Westchester Chamber Orchestra concerts. 'Suburban music,'
Alan sniffs. Understandable perhaps since Harvey, who has
more cleaning than he has space for, has been trying to take over
Alan's deserted salon for years.

If Harvey the Cleaner is the street's favourite psychiatrist,
George the Greek, owner of AA Florist, is its philosopher. 'So
why do you want to get aggravated?' says Harvey, 'Life is short.'
'Go home, be good to your husband and look after your
children,' says George, presenting a pink rose with a flourish.
'That's all there is, for life is short.'

Polish Mrs Malatzky, now in her eighties, owns the framery
shop, where she galvanises her nervous, anxiety-ridden son with
her sweet and calm determination. An iron mouse from old
Europe, if ever there was one.

The economy is puzzling Mrs Malatzky at present. Too many
people are bringing in their prints and photographs for framing.
'If the newspapers know what they're talking about,' she says,
'people shouldn't feel this secure about spending money.' She
seems to have a point. Up and down the street you'll see people
carrying pictures shrouded in thick, best quality brown paper,
corrugated cardboard trimmings and twine with old-fashioned,
no-nonsense knots – hallmarks of a Malatzky wrap.

Mrs Malatzky has acquired a new neighbour about which she
preserves a conspicuous silence. What could this purist,

craftsperson framer have in common with the bearded enthusiasts next-door who have opened West Side Comics? At four in
the afternoon this intergalactic emporium is crowded with pupils
from the West Side's private schools and Columbus's public one
(about the only ground on which they meet). The off-spring of
liberal West Siders, sporting Madison Avenue haircuts and costly
orthodontic ironware, crowd in with the macho eight-year-olds
from the fringes of Harlem.

Valerie the Fishlady, around the corner on Columbus, has
been trying to make wet fish a warm and wonderful experience
since she bought Powers Fish Market, five years ago. She has
found a supply of torrid romances and westerns for customers to
take away free with their filleted flounder. She lends one window
for community notices: free concerts, play-groups, flute lessons,
lost dogs. For the other, George the Florist has been persuaded to
furnish fresh flowers to bloom among the crushed ice and display
of whole and exotic fish.

Valerie, wan and blonde, sits at the cash desk framed by
holiday postcards from loving customers in Venice, Greece,
Spain, writing to assure her that nowhere is the fish as fresh as at
Powers.

That must provide some consolation as she rides the subway
alone every morning at dawn to pick out her fish at the Fulton
Market. Later Frederico the Driver will set off on his rounds. He
used to sit proudly in a delivery van marked Powers, but
unfortunately Valerie's ex-partner took it with him when he left,
along with her Cadillac.

He left behind $30,000 in debts. That alone would have won
her the sympathy of the street. That he was also her fiancé has
made buying a fish elsewhere almost an act of treason. Imagine
the response, then, when Valerie threw a party one Saturday
night after closing.

She scrubbed out the store, rented chairs and invited all her
customers to hear a would-be opera singer (another customer, of
course) give his first recital standing on the fish-wrapping bench.
No matter that he was partly deaf or that his baritone voice did
not lend itself totally to a tenor aria from *La Traviata*: it was

Valerie's party and everyone stayed till midnight feasting on her cook-up, singing along and making friends. 'This is our neighbourhood,' Valerie always says, 'There is a lot more here than fish.'

It was not thought unreasonable for Valerie to adopt as her store motto a while ago 'The Powers of Love'. It had long been noted that the poorest and oldest customers receive her most personal attention. Deftly she pushes the wrong numbers into the cash register for them. 'You have to be very gentle in giving,' she says. 'If you try to *give* them the fish, they get flustered. If you charge even 50 cents, they can go out feeling independent.'

Nearby, on the corner, is the Three Star Coffee Shop. It is part of a network of Greek coffee shops in which dark and glowering men, bred to the sea or land, waste away behind plastic-covered mountains of prune and cheese Danish. Growing ever more pale, they dream of the islands where men are men, not servants of unemployed actors, building staff and old ladies fussing over the exact consistency of a breakfast egg.

The Three Stars' are the first lights to go on in the street. Long before dawn, Tommy, the once-handsome Greek from Athens, opens the doors to get ready for the 6 a.m. breakfast special – orange juice, two eggs, bacon, toast, fried potatoes and coffee, $1.35. Until 11.00 when the price goes up and custom slows, he performs amazing feats before the crowded shop.

The American breakfast is a wonder of nuance, and Tommy remembers it all: who wants double potatoes, who wants none; whose eggs go over, whose should be crisped; who takes bacon, who prefers sausage; whose western omelette goes with white toast, whose with wheat. And all this is for the dubious pleasure of a 25-cent tip and being trusted on the till while his face grows thinner until even his moustache seems no longer to fit.

Sometimes Tommy disappears, presumably to make better use of his prodigious memory and black-eyed charm. Then the Three Star lapses into chaos and its atmosphere grows mean. The short-order waiter is a two-bit gladiator – the slightest sign of fear or insecurity and the crowd turns. Tommy's replacements, flustered and uncertain, have never lasted. Sooner or later he reappears, leaving behind yet another crushed dream, and the show goes on.

Sometimes, if there's a street party, Tommy turns up at weekends and his regulars, eyeing his soft suede coat and careful elegance, sigh for his future. He's 32 now and may never escape the life of scrambled and a side order of sausage.

The Three Brothers along the road is owned by the same Pete the Greek who owns the Three Star. The problem with Pete the Greek is that he never talks, unless it is to discuss the rare $100 bill. He examines it meticulously in the light but always decides to reject it. He is a careful man, both with his business and with himself. He is not a true West Sider.

This is not East Side, mid-town lunchtime with its rushed frenzy of office workers shouting for service. ('Sorry to cut this short but I must get back.') West Side lunch starts at 10.30 and goes on till four. Eating out is a social occasion, an interruption of the unavoidable or self-imposed isolation of apartment building life. It's about talking to strangers at the next table and having the owner remember that last week your arthritis was terrible. Pete the Greek is not of this ilk.

Moe Greengrass, though, is another question. For forty-three years he has worked in the store his Russian father founded on the corner of 86th Street and Amsterdam Avenue. Barney Greengrass, known to all as 'The Sturgeon King', has, it seems, always provisioned the street with its Nova Scotia salmon, cream cheese and onions on bagels.

Half of this establishment is a delicatessen with sawdust on the floor and Moe, fat and cheerful, ensconced behind the till. The other half is a restaurant in the possessive care of Tony the Waiter who has worked here for twenty-seven years and still can't always remember the English word 'onions'.

Moe's sons come in to help on Sundays but his wife, Shirley, is there all week. The street calls her 'the brains'. She knows how to be firm but charming with those who try to queue-jump during those perilous hours on Sunday when the shabby, familiar dining-room is packed with gold jewellery and Florida tans.

They are the customers, imperious and demanding, for whom

Tony the Waiter is as likely to throw down the scrambled eggs and lox as pass it. So renowned is his temperament that those few for whom he reserves a shy, sweet smile are as gods here. Moe, on the other hand, smiles at everyone. Nothing makes him happier than a few free moments in which to demonstrate his unexpectedly dazzling card tricks to all and sundry.

Moe belongs. He lives across the street and has grown into middle age with many of the faces that pass his till every week. When the store celebrated its fiftieth anniversary by offering its menu at the original prices, there was a queue out into the street from morning until late afternoon.

This was no publicity stunt. Moe didn't even bother to advertise. It was a party for his friends on the block. No one came that he hadn't seen often here before. Thus everyone knew to admire the gold-embossed letter hanging conspicuously above Moe's head. It was a happy birthday note from the Mayor, paying tribute to 'the ambrosial tables' of Greengrass. (The Mayor knows the West Side: this was not a moment for emotional understatement.)

Louis Lichtman, by comparison, is almost a newcomer. He has run his bakery over the road for only thirty years. As you might expect from a man who hails from Szatmar, his Hungarian strudels (apple, cheese, cherry, nut, poppyseed, cabbage) are his *tours de force*.

West Siders are partisan about their bakeries. They have tried them all. Some swear by Bernie Katz's chocolate eclairs, others by Herb Grossinger's and his mother's *rigojancsci*. Magda Honti's chocolate cream and caramel cake has its enthusiasts while others still will touch only Miss Grimble's cheesecake.

But 86th Street is faithful to Louis Lichtman. He has handed over the business to his son, Harvey, but still comes in every day, fussily supervising the baking and boxing up of single slices of strudel for his oldest customers as a jeweller would present a diamond to a queen.

And down the long block of our street between Amsterdam and Columbus Avenues, the ladies of West 86th Street make their way home of an afternoon: walking stick in one hand and

Lichtman's tiniest white box dangling by its string from the finger of the other.

★   ★   ★

57

Most of the shopkeepers of our corner bank at Chemical Bank. It probably has something to do with the branch manager, the unfortunately named Mr Faust. Against considerable odds, Mr Faust tries to run a friendly, neighbourhood bank. On the counter by the door he has placed a large notice saying how we all want to get to know one another and as a start let's call each other by our first names. It's signed Jim.

From his desk at the back of the open-plan bank, Jim keeps a benign, paternal eye on the day's proceedings. Of course, everyone has learned to hate that bogyman in mid-town Manhattan – the Chemical Bank head office – but the street feels that Jim is on its side, even if, in these hard days, he is always having to turn down requests for loans.

Within this peaceful Upper West Side village, there are no fewer than seven establishments offering photocopying services and, indeed, in one there is even a day-long queue. The Quick Copy Service, a charming misnomer, is the aristocrat among them. This rendezvous is the favourite of those seeking a hundred or so copies of their latest professionally laid-out résumés necessitated by yet another creative career change or, more often these days, redundancy. Here, those in the queue welcome the chance for a quiet chat, and possibly a tip or two.

Quick Copy is the centre for the paper addicts and their output – novel proposals, film projects looking for non-profit funding, the week's dreams for distribution at the next gathering of the group (strictly Freudian with Jungian leanings), the everyday New York sort of thing.

This is only the beginning. The Puerto Rican real estate consultant/income tax specialist/immigration lawyer and notary public also offers photocopying. His, he declares, is 'a community service'. A large, happy man, he casts sheet after unacceptable sheet into the waste can searching for the perfect balance of ink and paper for his 25-cents-a-copy customers.

The other lawyer around the corner is avoided by those in the know. It is his dour but doubtless realistic view that whatever the machine spits out counts as a photocopy regardless or whether or not it can be deciphered. Poor Mr Smith of the Lido Pharmacy, on the other hand, longs to bring satisfaction and happiness to his photocopying clientele even he can't interest them, as they wait, in a pot of special organic 14,000 I.U. Vitamin E cream or a little Mace spray for the handbag. It is simply his lugubrious belief that photocopies come in only two shades – dark and black.

Chemical Bank sensibly conceals its photocopier somewhere. This is a free service for customers and there's a long enough queue as it is of people wanting elucidation as to how they could possibly have been writing cheques on an empty account. The loan house round the corner that has a special line in the movement of funds to relatives in the Dominican Republic is also said to offer free photocopying. To take advantage of this service, however, requires fluent Spanish.

Thus regulars along West 86th Street have their closest photocopying relationship with the machine that Big Harold has recently installed just inside the entrance of his Talon Pharmacy. Since it commands a direct view through the glass-panelled door of the news-stand and telephone booths, it is possible, while waiting, to catch up on much of the street's business. Indeed, a regular *Kaffeeklatsch* has evolved here led by Harvey's Fred and George the Florist's elusive delivery man.

Not only does Big Harold stay way back in the shop, leaving the photocopying clique to their own kind of rough democracy, and the gossiping pundits undisturbed, but he charges only 10 cents a copy, which is a veritable bargain. The disadvantage, alas, is that often half an hour can be whiled away before noticing that the machine has attached to it Big Harold's notice announcing that it is out of order – again.

Even then, all excitement is not lost. Those accustomed to the life of photocopying know to peel back the lid. How often has some novice walked off with the copy forgetting that the riveting original is still in place. Once this heart-rending plea, carefully written out on lined paper, was uncovered:

Dear Sir or Madam, I have written you twice before telling you I did not get the stocking and you still keep harrassing me you will put my name on the Credit Bureau but let me tell you Something if you dare put my name on the Credit Bureau you will be sorry. I don't owe anybody and if at any time I want to credit and you put my name there, I will 'sue' because I have witnesses to prove I did not get the stocking. Ira Taylor, 1240 Sulter Avenue, Brooklyn NY 11208.

Big Harold's group could not let this rest. They wrote to Ira Taylor, tried calling her, eager to offer encouragement in her indignant stance. Is there one among them who has not fought as she but finally paid up for fear of the same shadowy Credit Bureau that threatens us all? Ira Taylor, regrettably, did not respond even after the cable despatched by the excitable waitress from the Three Star. So, Big Harold's may never know what happened to her, her stocking and her witnesses, but the adventure around the photocopier continues.

★   ★   ★

They have been digging up the road on Columbus Avenue, an activity that has caused unusual enthusiasm among bystanders since it is not a sight most New Yorkers expect to see in their lifetime. A crop of wheelchairs has appeared on the sidewalk as elderly residents flanked by companions in white uniforms make the most of this unexpected diversion.

There is an air of 'amateur hour' about. The roadmen, a colourful bunch in jeans, baggy sweaters and woolly hats, seem as new to the task of filling in the craterous potholes as the spectators are to the idea of a street smooth enough to be crossed rather than clambered over. Those at work busy themselves with exaggerated gestures and dialogue as if aware at all times of being centre stage. The skinny teenagers deputed to take charge of traffic control rush around in a frenzy, waving their red flags ferociously in all directions to the fury of cab drivers and delight of the admiring crowd.

This is a neighbourhood event. So much of life takes place on the street that its reconstruction is a celebration to be shared. It has also greatly increased afternoon trade at the Three Star, which happens to have picture windows overlooking the arena of tar and bulldozers. How thoughtful of City Hall to suddenly remember us this way.

The famed Columbus Avenue 'renaissance' is creeping up town. Everyone on the Avenue now has a story. Valerie the Fishlady was chained to the till (some say the deep freeze). The chemist from 69th Street was shot in the arm. Will Barry from Woods Nest ever see his Silver Skill toolkit again?

Kelly, the sensitive soul from Rough Rider, who has hardly recovered from his own smash-and-grab raid, reports that they're hitting dentists now for gold. Frank from the Rocking Horse Café complains that they're always after his liquor. They storm up from basements, tunnel through walls, or just walk in through the plate-glass windows.

Columbus Avenue, the new Camelot on the West Side, has turned into a thieves' turf. The old-timers wearily clear up the mess and try to forget about it. Among the newcomers, there isn't a store owner who hasn't some meaningful burglary experience to share. But even against this competition Joy Dicker, of One Woman vintage clothing, is the acknowledged Avenue princess. Seven attempted break-ins in four months – and not so much as an old beaver gone.

Dicker ('I'm spooky in a way but I believe in all this') puts it down to having a wonderful, wonderful karma. Police officers from the 20th Precinct suggest her alarm system played some part. That this system is regarded with awe by the Avenue at large is perhaps some indication of the nature of Camelot's shopkeepers.

All the newcomers have past lives. Barry Jones, who makes custom furniture at Woods Nest, was an export executive with Burlington Industries. He got sick of corporate life and now expresses himself in stained plywood. Jane Bloom from Tianguis Folk Art was in publishing but 'none of it was real'. She now offers very real Peruvian wall hangings ($400 to $1000), quilted Guatemalan jackets ($65) and hand-knitted Turkish $12 socks to the Upper West Side.

Frank Garofolo of the Rocking Horse turned 35 and fancied a restaurant. 'This is something I wanted to try, I'd like to live all my dreams if God doesn't take me first.' Admittedly, twelve years as a Connecticut school-teacher and a stint as vice-president of the Hartford Opera Association might not seem ideal qualifications for the tortuous café business – still, the Rocking Horse has survived.

'My only strength,' says Garofolo, tossing a sculptured head covered in tiny curls, 'is my creative feeling and my instinctive reactions.' It is almost entirely due to these qualities and Joy Dicker's relentless enthusiasm that Columbus is finally acquiring a merchants' association. (Not that the old-timers are greeting it very warmly. 'They'll want money,' said Alan from Lido Bello, tearing up his application form. 'I'd rather have my chain.')

The idea came to Dicker the last time she was called out by the police at four in the morning to turn off her alarm and clear up the intruders' crowbars. She takes up the story: 'I'm a Pisces with Scorpio rising; I'm into yoga and I'm a vegetarian. The force is with me now but my life hasn't always been great. Some days I didn't have five cents in my pocket. Three years ago I had nothing. This whole shop is a fluke; one day I just went down and signed the lease. I was waitressing then; I never was in business before and I worked real hard to make this into something. The day after the last alarm I made forty-five phone calls and said, "You get your asses down here, this is serious".'

Forty-four shopkeepers turned up for a meeting. Captain Marty Feltman of the 20th Precinct was hauled in. The captain has his own problems. The population of the West Side has increased nearly a third in five years while the city in its fiscal embarrassment whittles away his force. 'I can't make men out of dust. I don't have enough people to patrol adequately,' pleaded the good cop.

A committee took shape meeting weekly. The five men on it thoughtfully admire one another's merchandise and are over-whelmingly personal with one another. No one mentions the tension between Tianguis's Jane, so bookish with her granny glasses and reflective regard, and One Woman's Joy, black hair, scarlet fingernails, a clatter of vintage diamante. 'I've always had a lot of trouble with women,' explains Dicker. 'Jealousy.'

Even these *frissons* have sweet excitement. The talk may be tough, of police protection and value for the tax dollars; but what's happening is the forging of village life. It's gossipy, tinged with malice, competitive but also generous and quizzical.

Kelly lends Joy wire for her window display. Frank borrows sugar. Jane acquires a 'buddy buzzer' linked to the shop next door. And Joy even takes whole afternoons off from One Woman to sign up the newest shopowners. No one says no to her.

'I put my heart and soul into my business.' Joy tries on a newly-acquired $800 monkey coat and glosses her lips. 'When I opened, I'd be in Brooklyn at six in the morning, running around warehouses for the clothes and still up at three in the morning washing them in the tub and ironing them all myself.

'Don't let anybody fool you, you can make lots of bucks if you're not greedy. I have fabulous quality, terrific prices and good karma. I love this shop and let's face it, no one gives you anything. So no one but no one is going to walk in here and try to take it away from me. Here I stand all in one piece and I'm telling you I'm tough but tough ladies are the only ones who make it.'

There are 200 known burglars around Columbus Avenue. They had better stop messing with Ms Dicker.

West Side seasons

This morning, as predicted by the WQXR weather bulletins, there was precipitation and the wind chill factor eased. In short, it has been wet and warm. With the last vestiges of yellow-stained snow and grime-encrusted ice washed away some weeks ago now, the denizens of West 86th Street have emerged from hiding to greet their corner of the world.

It is not nature that decrees the seasons in Manhattan but the wardrobe of its inhabitants. And so this year there was no spring. One moment it was chilly and then overnight the limp, humid heat of summer sank into the city. On West 86th Street the old ladies have changed their pebbly coats for jersey knits and at Maison Celine Harvey the Cleaner heaps the winter blankets in a corner and dreams of summer by the lake. Any day now his garments, swathed in pink tissue and plastic, will bear the notice: 'Closed Saturdays during July and August.'

Sunshine makes him restless. He can be seen through the window of his store poring over holiday brochures for Aruba and Guatemala. As he gently folds sweaters into pink tissue and plastic bags marked proudly 'every garment a masterpiece', he gives an unaccustomed sigh.

A torn coat lining brings him up short. Nothing offends the proprietor of Maison Celine more than the neglected wardrobe. 'Divorced men.' He wrinkles his nose. 'They bring their things in falling apart.' No details of the street and its inhabitants pass him by. 'Put that fur away,' he calls to a wayward customer outside. 'You will not see Mrs Astor wearing her mink after 1 April.'

In the Lido Bello Hair Salon, Alan from Booklyn sits waiting for customers, dropping ash and distress over the latest copy of *Opera* magazine. Business as usual here.

But during the months of hibernation subtle changes have crept over the Columbus Avenue corner of 86th Street. George the Greek has refurbished his florists shop so that the $1.89 specials (a handy $2 with tax) stand in buckets on a bright new plastic floor. Improved lighting glints on George's elegant silver hair and on his chunky jewellery.

Now summer is here the old timers are back on the street setting up shop. Ouside Ramirez Travel, the 80-year-old Russian with his sooty, lined face scrapes and chips at the blocks of ice stored in his rickety trolley. For 25 cents he offers crushed ice poured over with coloured, sugary syrup to those passing the time watching their neighbours. What does he do in winter, this old man with his bent and calloused hands? 'What do I do? I do,' comes the inevitable New York answer.

His is a desperate trade. By three o'clock when the hot and smoggy air hangs over the corner, his ice starts to melt, running down over his boots and into the road. At the very moment his trade would be briskest, his chances trickle away. Still he stands, ringing his small bell, calling again and again in broken English, 'Strawberry, orange, coldest here.'

His best moment is lunchtime when he trades a drink or two for a few of the burned kebabs that the old food vendor forgot to turn during the busy morning. This corner is not really the kebab man's territory – he belongs to a fleet of carts that ferry to and fro the Central Park softball field from a Columbus Avenue kitchen – but he likes to spend an hour or so here swapping stories and racing tips.

The most lucrative kebab business is done by the young and eager who run with their trolleys to the Park to bark their wares across the sea of picnickers. The old men, the ones who have been doing it for years, are too resigned to boast about the wizened bits of meat they sell, too tired to move fast and, anyway, couldn't – hampered as they are by the thick, heavy coats they wear no matter how hot the day. Given the New York winters, these coats are their most prized possessions too valuable to be left in the hostels and one-room walk-ups where they live constantly fearing the worst – as if it has not already happened.

Not all the street hawkers are full-time. On any day there are at least three or four trestle tables set up along the sidewalk spread out with the results of some seasonal cleaning-up. The writer is selling review copies of unremembered titles. The lawyer is getting rid of his record collection. The housewife has finally decided to part with clothes that fitted her once. They haul it all out into the street, set it up meticulously and then settle down to wait out the day.

There again some are not even selling anything. They bring their chairs and wooden boxes and just sit for a day on the corner. They admire the fashions, eavesdrop on the rows and try to guess how long the cyclists will survive with their 'sounds' plugged into their ears. This is the only difference between this latest summer and those that have gone before it. The blaring tape decks are fewer. The big black noise machines gave way to Sony Walkmen. Now each person skips and dances along to an unheard, inner tune. It would be a welcome relief were it not that the thunder of traffic goes on, the blast of exhausts continues. Now and again, though, in a quiet moment, the high sound of the iced drink vendor's bell rings across the corner.

★   ★   ★

Now it is fall and Manhattan is getting ready to move indoors. Sloane's Clearance Centre on East 84th Street is completely out of bedrooms. The fifth-floor furniture department, crammed with marked-down chests and wardrobes all summer, is bare now.

Harvey the Cleaner has closed up his cottage by the lake and is working his usual seventy-hour, six-day week again. In one corner of the shop on West 86th Street Lino of Alterations is stitching through the mountain of winter-weight rising daily by his sewing machine. Since Harvey is the street's community centre, it is through him that we catch up on our neighbours' summers: who went away, who stayed home, who split up, who lost 40 lb. Harvey is astonishingly patient considering that he gets by in a haze of Bufferin and pain. His slipped disc again. It hates the fall.

It is always a marvel to find wispy Alan still in the Lido Bello

Salon at the end of summer. With the coming of fall, his ladies start fussing again about their hair colour which can deceive no one. One of the street's joys is to observe Alan with his rubber gloves and apron, daubing on pungent concoctions, expounding at length on the summer's productions at Salzburg.

Meanwhile, over the road, Chemical Bank advertises special 'Back to School Loans' to help with all those fees, books, extramural lessons and goose-down parkas without which there is no fall.

This is the time that the building superintendent has his moment of stardom. He who normally shrinks along the street avoiding notice ('Where's the hot water?' 'When are you coming to fix my sink?') swells with pride as a leader of men, engaged in matters of importance. Harried handymen rush to and fro beneath his direction, washing down hallways, replacing floor tiles, painting the basement laundry room and workshop battleship grey as befits this military operation.

Jealousies, submerged all year beneath a haze of cigarette smoke and bonhomie in the corner coffee shop, come to the surface as supers stand outside their apartment buildings eyeing who is acquiring what. There are twinges of resentment as a beautiful new burnt umber awning appears over one doorway. Supers on either side of it set their lowliest maintenance men to scrubbing the faded, dirty grey canvas that still stands over their own entrances.

The super from number 51 takes on a smug air as the front of his otherwise nondescript building is painted an elegant shade of French vanilla. Across the street one super responds with a vigorous show of brass polishing while another makes much of cleaning his strip of hallway carpet.

The super, after all, is a victim of the landlord who owns the building in which he toils and lives. Once all the rental buildings along the street had brass accessories, upholstered armchairs in their downstairs lobbies and thick, rich carpets leading to wood panelled elevators. Now but one carpet remains, cherished by the proud super to whose care it has been entrusted, while the rest must accept a life of plastic-covered banquettes, rubber mats and bare stone floors dictated by those who gather the rent.

The stature of his tenants is also, alas for him, beyond the super's control these days. Once, in the golden days, the way to a new apartment was through his heart – or, perhaps more often, his pocket. It was the super to whom would-be residents applied, dropping a few dollars hither and thither, in the hope that he would smooth the way. Now power has been returned to the desk of the landlord's agent.

This bodes ill for the army of supers. Once they wielded great power in the land with promises to replaster crumbling walls and resuscitate ageing plumbing. Now New Yorkers are satisfied merely to have living space, so grateful indeed that they will spend weekends working on it themselves and the more Eeyoreish supers bemoan the day when they will be mere bustlers in the basement confined to the care of old and ailing boilers.

The passing of the super should not be prematurely mourned though. As West Siders pile back into Manhattan from summers by lakes and seashore, fatigued from the strain of house care and the responsibility of property owning, they greet the uniformed and braided super with generous warmth. All houses, they sigh, should come with three Hispanic superintendents in the cellar. The relief of being able to call to have steel pipes fixed, electric wires unravelled, bookcases put in place, expresses itself in the soft sound of hundred-dollar bills changing hands.

In the cool September nights, the noise of air conditioners extinguished for another year, windows thrown open to catch the breeze from the Hudson River, West Side apartment dwellers engage in the time-honoured rite of fall cleaning. Shaggy, long-haired, cream carpets are torn up to make way for the fashionable beige industrial of today. Rattling venetian blinds are pulled out so that preppy Roman shades can come in. Table lamps, armchairs, dining sets, last year's hi fi, forgotten designer sheets – all find their way to the back door. And, in the morning, the super sets off on a grand tour of each floor's garbage to pick over his booty.

The best is carted down to his basement workshop to be fitted up with loving care by his minions before installation in his already crowded apartment on the ground floor. What's left is offered, in strict hierarchal order, to the elevator operators, handymen, maintenance personnel and finally, Miguel the Sweeper, he of no English who is today's scullery maid.

★ ★ ★

The letter from the Parish of Trinity Church was waiting on the doormat with the Christmas cards. An appeal for the needy, perhaps? 'Dear Fellow New Yorker,' it began, 'A letter from a cemetery doesn't exactly make your day, I know. None of us, including myself, like to think about death. But it is unwise to avoid this subject until it becomes a tragic reality.'

Thus began our seasonal greeting from Mr Frederick H. Roberts of the Cemetery and Mausoleums Office. ('The last available burial grounds on Manhattan island.') How sensitive of him to point out, in these weeks of expense, 'the financial wisdom of taking advantage of the 20 per cent pre-completion discount'.

It is the season of goodwill. Harvey the Cleaner is clipping shiny shocking pink rosettes to his plastic bags. Over at Chemical Bank, Jim Faust has presented each of his women tellers with a tinsel corsage and arranged for piped carols to entertain the waiting masses.

Every shop and diner has its tree and on the sidewalk of Columbus Avenue mighty pines are up for sale. It is a time of artistic challenge. From the kitchen window, binoculars trained on the next building, there is the sight of one tree after another glittering with decorations and careless splendour.

This year ours is a Cinderella building. The blush pink lobby may be Lysol clean but it is bare of Christmas cheer. Last year jovial Joe Medina, the then superintendent, trimmed a tree by which tenants could warm their hearts, so glowing was it with angels and coloured lights.

Joe was everyone's favourite, with his talkative wife and teenage daughter whose every waking moments were spent dressing for midnight screenings of *The Rocky Horror Show*. It was no surprise when Rudin Management, our esteemed landlords, promoted Joe to the East Side. To a super, serving on the West Side is like spending the last war in Aldershot.

In his place, arrived Mr Hernandez (and it is always Mr Hernandez). He's a no-nonsense organization man who in no time swept the lobby clear of Joe's tasteful arrangements of plastic flowers and the basement clear of the stray cats Joe sheltered amid the exercise equipment and cosy mess. Where Joe's Sunday garb was his hunting gear, Mr Hernandez can now be glimpsed in a blue suit with snowy shirt and silk tie. His is a classy act.

The brasswork in the elevator gleams, the sidewalk is spotless, the elevator reeks of furniture polish – and the cheer is gone. Mr Hernandez is physical fabrics' man; he doesn't see himself as a nurturer of tenants. And, therefore, no Christmas tree. Nor has he given time to printing those yuletide cards that Joe always cranked out in his basement empire listing the staff expecting seasonal tips. This omission may endear him to many of the tenants if not to his army of underlings.

Well, you might wonder, surely the residents of sixty-four apartments could cough up for a communal tree? That is not the way New York buildings work. There is to be no knocking on a door unasked. The last hawker (for some church charity) got only as far as the second floor before Mr Hernandez heard about it. If an Englishman's home is his castle, a New Yorker's apartment is his fallout shelter.

Take the case of the man who lives in the lobby on the red leatherette couch. He sleeps in the building somewhere, but from early afternoon until long after midnight he sits silently and morosely downstairs. No one so much as nods at him, let alone asks whether he is all right (which he patently isn't). Sometimes he wears shoes, mostly carpet slippers. Every now and again he shuffles out into the street with only his thick toupee to keep him warm. Only Daniel the youngest elevator operator shows concern.

Admittedly, Daniel is unusual by any standards. His family is in Puerto Rico and he rents a room on West 87th Street. He has been putting himself through college which often means working nights and then going straight to school. He believes that a college degree will be his 'open sesame', an understandable but unrealistic mistake. In the meantime, he amuses the elevator with his good-natured musings and constant worry about whether he can afford to maintain his $35 Grecian perm.

But Daniel's jollity is no longer the building's. Perhaps it is the undercurrent of worry as everyone prays, in this wolfish rental market, not to attract the attention or disapproval of the landlord, the mighty Rudin on Park Avenue.

'Dear Santa, for Christmas can you send me some thoroughly happy Rudins. Signed A Tenant.'

Omens of disarray

On the corner of West 86th Street the Blue Star Coffee Shop, reeking of fried grease, loud with the cries of the perenially exasperated Greek cook, was a particular favourite of felt-hatted old men and building staff. There was something masculine about its chipped Formica, torn lino, harsh lights and disdain of comfort.

Imagine the horror of its regulars peering anxiously through new windows to see two enormous gold chandeliers waiting to be put up. Carriage lights, tiling, padded stools: it was an omen.

At least across the road, under a ramshackle tin and cardboard shelter, there was always Olga the Newslady. She cowered there in winter and sweltered in summer. Olga was a tiny Puerto Rican of 48. She wore scarlet lipstick that had a blue tinge in winter when she was frozen to the bone. No one noticed then, of course. Her smile was quick and everyone assumed that she had some trick, some extra stamina with which to work from five every morning till seven at night without so much as a whimper. Perhaps she didn't get tired like ordinary people?

Sometimes, when it was not too cold or, in summer, too hot, her husband would come down to her news-stand to pass an hour with his pavement cronies. Sometimes her five children looked after the stand over lunch when it was quiet so that she could have coffee or sit down for a moment. Olga was proud of her family – of her eldest daughter, a beauty, of her grown son, a handsome young man. When she closed up the green wooden stand she would go home to cook and wash for them.

One day, over Christmas, she went home and died. Her children ran the stand then, shivering in the cold, perched on newspapers to ease the ache. Those customers who never dreamed that Olga suffered from asthma, who saw only what they wanted to, felt ashamed. They remembered that they never gave her a Christmas offering because, unlike everyone else, she never asked. And so, to avoid unpleasant memories and bad consciences, they bought their newspapers elsewhere. Who, now that Olga was gone, would fight for the children for whom she worked and died?

When she was alive it was somehow understood that no one would try to steal her business, meagre as it was. Now Shim Si, the Korean grocer, stocked newspapers too. Her children opened later and closed earlier than Olga. Shim Si, who like her was not born into the American dream, was there before and after them. His business improved; Olga's shed grew shabbier by the day, and the children abandoned it.

Shim Si had his own problems, it should be understood. Until that winter it was understood that this formal and impeccable doyen of late-night shopping would stock groceries and leave fruit and vegetables to Hyun Ki Chin across the road. Trouble started when an ambitious Kyun Ki Chin thought of presenting Walden Farm all-natural, low-sodium salad dressings to enhance his array of mange-touts, bean shoots, hand-picked asparagus tips and five varieties of lettuce. A venture into organic breads was inevitable and now, to Shim Si's dismay, he has a full wall of groceries.

Shim Si countered with a greengrocery department; Hyun Ki Chin with a freshly-squeezed orange juice machine. It was of this war that Olga the Newslady's children were the hapless victims. The Sunday *New York Times* was Shim Si's answer to Hyun Ki Chin's Haagen Daz ice-cream display. Hyun Ki Chin moved ahead by introducing his nieces, giggling, smiling maidens, to the cash register. They certainly overshadow Shim Si's parents who look like wisdom-embodying ancients from *National Geographic* magazine.

No one knows where Olga's successor came from. A thin, mangy man, with long tangled hair and matted beard, he appeared one morning. He hid inside the old shed, black eyes glimmering in the darkness, shooting out a skeletal hand with claw-like nails to take in coins or hand out change. Occasionally, some unknowing passer-by would hand over a $10 bill in return for *Apartment Life* or the *Times*. The bearded recluse drew back, silently shaking his head. Street life had made him wary; he preferred to go home with his jangling bag of quarters that no one would waste time trying to forge.

Picture the commotion, then, when this half-seen being was to be found one morning standing beside his small empire of papers and magazines, excitedly sweeping the sidewalk in preparation for the great endeavour of rebuilding the shed. His ubiquitous black coat had been removed and folded tenderly to stand by the stack of *El Diario*. He bustled about clearing up the mounds of empty beer cans, brown bags and soggy boxes that are the natural furnishing of our corner.

Wood arrived in a battered truck, evidently the booty from some serious building job elsewhere. Higgledy-piggledy, it landed on the sidewalk, every shape and size, no two planks the same. From the chaos, the news-vendor obviously expected wonderful things to arise. It was soon clear that he had no inkling of how to influence such a happening. Three friends appeared as he was squatting on the concrete trying, in a desultory way, to sort his prize into almost matching sizes. Impatient at the delay, they seized whatever was on the top of the pile and started to bang things together with great gusto.

So it continued throughout the week. A crowd gathered around, offering advice and seizing small, stray patches of wood from the gutter to nail over holes and cracks. To some onlookers it was a comic show; to others it stirred memories of the early pioneers and the old log cabin. To others still, it was a reminder that Olga is gone and that the five children she left behind have simply vanished.

The hut now suggests the work of a maniacal quilt-maker let loose with plywood. It is hard to believe it will withstand the first strong storm of fall, let alone the blizzards to follow. The thick black and red flourishes of New York graffiti have already been daubed across it and soon, no doubt, it will have its share of notices from suicide counsellors, dog walkers, psychics and other such street professionals.

Meanwhile, to everyone's concern, the unthinkable has happened. Overnight, on the opposite corner, a neat, prefabricated metal shed was placed on a concrete foundation outside the Three Star. No one saw it happen; no one knows how it could have happened. It was once a rule that a man's tiny patch was his own. Scraping a living from the street is battle enough.

★   ★   ★

Our corner is also in disarray because of the gentrification stealing along Columbus Avenue. Dry-cleaning stores closed; hearth furniture shops opened. The watch repairer disappeared; Shinera, the Japanese bed shop, fluttered into being with its promise of athletic nights and Italian sheets. It is the tyranny of the rent; the seduction of the singles' scene.

The gay young men in their Calvins, the preppies in their strawberry pink polo necks, the waitressing ballerinas in their pointed western boots, drift by the windows of the old-timers who hazard their way down their street wondering what's left, who's left – and for how long.

It was a sign of the times. First came total refurbishment complete with Acropolis mural after the primitive style. Then came a grand reopening with freshly-baked, zingy chocolate doughnuts where the familiar, floury pound-cake once stood drying out. And thus the old Blue Star became the new Three Star Coffee Shop. Unbelievably, there was even a display stand for a computer dating service from New Jersey.

This street of European refugees, Isaac Bashevis Singer, chess players, La Leche breast-feeders and consciousness-raisers had been invaded by singles. Those remote beings, who go to night school to study roller disco, who invest $37 in quest of better pivots, hops and mohawks, faster spins and cross-overs, who spend Sunday afternoons in Central Park wearing teeny, coloured-coordinated roller hustle pants and weeny matching radio headsets with twin antennae – those same Ralph Lauren-odourised, Bill Blass-bedded studio dwellers had crept along Columbus Avenue to 86th Street. Alien had happened.

The red imitation velvet and leatherette booths in the Three Star are bereft of yesteryear's doormen guzzling home fries and Wonderloaf toast, tucking into *El Diario*'s editorial columns, telling tales of grandchildren glimpsed in Confirmation snapshots to those same tenants for whom across the road and up the street they bow a deferential head.

On Sundays the singles now swarm over the Three Star, juggling *New York Times'* sections. And the doormen and superintendents, neat in new maroon, put in their best sets of false teeth, stroke pomade on to thinning black curls and set off for the Bronx or Queens for church with the family, lunch with the Americanized grandchildren.

In the old days, before the pseudo carriage lanterns and neo-terrazzo plastic tiles were fastened on to the Three Star, the live-in superintendents would leave their ground-floor 'tied cottages', dark but spotless, and come here for the $1.35 Sunday breakfast eggs, fries, bacon, juice, toast, grape jelly and coffee. Then they would go home strengthened and eager for the ride out of Manhattan.

It was something the old ladies and felt-hatted widowers from Warsaw or Vienna had in common with the supers found across a booth – the grandchildren. The old ladies, in their seventies or eighties now, would show snaps sent from Boston, Florida or California; the supers and their imposing wives, 45, maybe 48, married young, would understand and shiver inside. The Bronx was still not a world away. The children and grandchildren for whom they had scrubbed floors and furnaces had not yet learned to feel ashamed of the too-gold teeth, the broken English and gabbled Spanish.

But rehabilitation has put an end to the village's Sunday parade around this corner of Columbus Avenue. The brownstones and apartment buildings have been ripped open and boxed back together. The 10-foot-square studios with new oak strip floors have been let to those singles who can afford (or, more often, can't) $800 a month.

Where singles settle, Bazaars soon open up. These ten huge centralized furnishing supermarkets have been scattered over smarter Manhattan. In all of them identical, acrylic-framed posters and wicker log baskets can be found nestling by butcher-block tables, bentwood rocking chairs, red plastic hangers, purple extension cords and orange lettuce driers.

Unlike most such establishments, the Bazaar staff are not drawn from that pool of hard-bitten, seen it all before, waddya-want-from-me-I'm-on-commission sales persons. Those who help move merchandise in the Bazaars know for whom the made-in-Taiwan wind bell tolls – for their fellow singles from studio land.

It is very helpful that all singles buy all furnishings from these same stores. When sleep-overs become live-ins they arrive with matching vitamin quotas and bits of decoration. The Vitbe Stress 100 tabs go into the bathroom cabinet and if the statutory Bazaar primary-coloured plastic pill-boxes should later get mixed up there will be no harm done.

Singles with their No Nuclear Future Benefit Concert posters on the wall are not into Valium yet. They are still optimistically taking courses in self-management skills for handling anxiety and depression on an ongoing everyday basis.

These new cadres are not much in evidence during the week. Unlike resting artists and other neurotics, who are just younger versions of the defeated and knowing old, singles have careers. When Monday comes they bustle off downtown on early morning buses and trains or stand on the corner hailing taxis with lovat and beige striped golfing umbrellas, glowering from beneath the brim of pristine tweed fishing hats.

Later the others venture nervously out; the elderly with new snapshots and tales of cheap rate telephone calls from distant places, the building superintendents back in overalls and oil smears, the families, serviceable and machine-washable, all trying not to look into the windows of the new Columbus Avenue Bazaar with its reminders of excitement, adventure and, above all, the threat of change.

Trotters and joggers

It has become quite common on a Sunday to find the restaurants and cafes of Manhattan crammed with the uniforms of a warlike elite. Its feet are shod in Nike trainers. Its sweat-suits are a perfectly acceptable going-out costume. Its talk is of the Wall (of the pain, naturally), of shin splints and of anything the sports medicine department of Lenox Hill Hospital may have done to cartilage. To have shared a knee injury with Billie Jean King is to be the apotheosis of success.

Every day in Central Park some perfectly harmless mother pushing her child is stampeded by a herd of joggers. She is left kneeling in the dust, ineffectually shaking a fist at the backs of countless sweat-suits, while reflecting that there is almost nothing quite as beastly as the average New York Health fiend.

It should be unnecessary to point out that Central Park is a public place. So that the ordinary citizen can more safely enjoy recreation therein, its roads have been closed at weekends to motor vehicles. This, evidently, deals with only some of the danger.

It is the arrogance of the joggers that so offends. There is an assumption that there is some kind of moral superiority in a sinewy thigh and that a toe blister has integrity. Lesser creatures, bundled in cellulite, probably puffing from cigarette consumption, should know to clear the way or be cast aside rather as peasants were by their lordships' carriages. There are those nowadays who interpret the doctrine of survival of the fittest far too literally.

What, one wonders, has happened to tolerance? What has become of compassion for the weak? One no longer gives thanks for health and strength; one disdains those who are infirm or old for allowing these conditions to overtake them.

It has been assumed that young men no longer offer seats on the bus to women as a consequence of the feminist movement. It should instead be remarked that neither do they offer seats to old people, cripples or the blind. With only a few exceptions, if these latter do sit on a crowded route it is through the intervention of middle-aged women still able to empathize and to grasp that where others now shuffle, they may later.

It has yet to be explained how a society so obsessed with getting in touch with its own feelings can be so shut off from those of others. 'But enough about me, let's talk about you . . . how do you really feel about me?' is a New York joke that is wearing thin. And as the driven body shrinks and hardens, it draws even further away from those whose outlines are still blurred. The issue becomes clear – the meek shall inherit the earth, the strong shall inherit all that stands upon it.

So they run, they wrestle machines, they consume carefully measured calorie allowances and they become smaller and meaner. But even more disquieting is the assumption that, somehow, muscle equals intelligence. Once there was brawn and there was brain. Now to be fat and lax and unfit is an admission of mental malfunctioning.

There is also an equation between the states of physical fitness and total independence of others. My body the machine shall need no nurturing, no nursing, no tending, and therefore my soul shall give away no IOUs. To that end, I shall punish it.

The lumpen proletariat is fast coming to mean all who are well and truly lumpy, and in Central Park being downtrodden is coming to mean exactly that.

★   ★   ★

At almost any time of the day traffic along Central Park West is likely to be held up by a motley crew of horse riders clopping precariously out of West 89th Street for a good bolt in the Park.

For those accustomed to the impeccable appearance of urban riders in Hyde Park, their New York counterparts come as a surprise, not to say a shambles. There is, of course, a fair quota of refugee Italian contessa-types sitting straight in slender jodhpurs and custom-made boots, but on the whole the style, if it could be called that, of the Central Park equestrian resembles nothing so much as a day-tripper taking a donkey ride on some sea-side stretch.

Leaving aside such inessentials as the much-in-favour black-berry pickers' garb, there is something in the easy seat and flailing arms that suggests a camaraderie with the horse owing nothing to skill and all to optimism. It quite obviously never occurs to most of these $18-an-hour, wouldn't-it-be-a-lark riders that a horse is anything but an obliging old fellow rather on a par with the average New York taxi-driver.

The idea that riding involves technique is a patent nonsense to those reared on the belief that any green cow-poke can unhitch and mount up. But, above all, this nonchalance in the saddle is made possible by the fact that no one cares. There is no sense of being on show. In a park where ageing, pot-bellied men engage merrily in solitary displays of something approximating to a martial art without attracting a second glance, clearly the whooping exhuberance of amateurs along dusty, cantering trails is not about to impress or dismay.

Those at play in the free stretches of the Park are people without class. On the softball field of the Great Lawn the banker teams with the plumber with no other thought than the blaze of his fast ball, the doggedness of his run, the flamboyance of his catches. On the rocky pot-holed courts below the 96th Street transverse, familiars of Carnegie Hall pick up a tennis game with subway-engineers from the Bronx.

On the sidelines sit the Central Park elite, a dozen or so kings of the mole-hill, they of the fantasy ace, the ripping top spin, the inevitable sliced backhand bestowing on the occasional newcom-ers the much-prized 'Hi.' If anything, an inverted snobbery is at work. Show up in good tennis whites, not sloppy T-shirt, carry a Saks leather bag in place of a well-worn knapsack and the chances of a good game plummet.

It is not the American way to do things by half and in the park built for the common weal we're all common folk. It is a life apart. No last names here, no discreet probing of background or thoughts on acquaintances in common. This is the world of Bill, Bob and Dick, of Mary, Sue-Ann and Jo-Jo, who may or may not be married, rich, vice-president or menial. More to the point, they may or may not be available, but that's another story.

Since the campaign against mess started, dogs' bodily functions and the discussion thereof ('I find plastic bags so much easier when he's loose') have become a major Central Park preoccupation. It is curious how undog-like these one-time animals have become. They hardly bother to chase the squirrels, fat and smug, let alone a pigeon or horse. Resigned to being left from dawn till midnight – or never left at all – they accept only what passes before them as though all Park life were but television.

It is the English who have the reputation for being dotty about animals, but it is the Americans who believe in their proximity whatever the cost, to the animal that is. How else to explain that Gulag near Fifth Avenue, otherwise known as the Central Park Zoo?

What, one wonders, can a small child learn from seeeing a scrawny, morose lion pacing in a tiny concrete and tiled cell without so much as a twig to suggest its habitat? What horror of existence will be conjured up by the spectacle of a gorilla shut into a bare space that shames the viewer for even being part of its humiliation?

Getting into home-making

Legend hath it that there are New Yorkers who have furnished whole apartments from the pickings of other people's dustbins. Wander along the Upper West Side late at night and there on the sidewalk are perfectly good mattresses, sofas and chairs waiting for the dustmen.

It is considered almost smart these days to pillage the East Side pavements about two in the morning. The seventies between Fifth Avenue and Park come particularly well recommended by a merchant banker who has in his living-room a beautiful old coffee-table of rich mahogany. He found it underneath some soggy newspaper outside a brownstone round the corner from the Metropolitan Museum.

The true collectors, however, do not leave anything to chance. They know the exact timetable of the Salvation Army pickup trucks and regularly comb the streets outside plusher apartment buildings the night before they are due. This is one of the benefits of living in a throwaway society.

Some people throw out possessions. Some give them away: except that it is not quite giving away. There is a financial incitement to generosity – it is known as tax credits. You bundle up your goods, carefully adding an address label, and take them down to some worthy charity's thrift shop. At the end of the year the shop sends a statement of how much the goods have raised. The total figure is tax-deductible so even the best people are doing it now. As a result, hunting about in thrift shops for that special bargain has a social cachet in New York. Older women clutching voluminous bags are often to be seen down Third Avenue at the Sloane-Kettering cancer thrift shop casting a knowing eye over the china and trinkets.

All of this, however, is very amateur stuff, as dedicated recyclists are quick to point out.

Robin the Recyclist was once a New York amateur. Now he lives in Miami dividing his time between playing in the Miami Philharmonic, teaching tennis and lecturing on the humanities to college students. ('I asked them to put down ten important dates in history. Most of them put down their mothers' birthday.') He shares his bungalow with his 10-year-old son Linus, who collects boa constrictors, Michael, who is a chemistry professor, and Bob, a mathematics professor. Their home is almost entirely furnished from the local dumps.

The chintz-covered oak six-seater convertible sofa was a special find. The electric sewing machine and six-foot General Electric refrigerator with separate freezer compartment were found on the same night, as good as new. The six dining chairs might not match but they are sturdy. The pink-patterned carpets in the bedrooms and wall-to-wall champagne-coloured woollen rug in Michael's 1965 Ford Fairlane V8 stationwagon ('rebuilt almost from scrap') did not even need cleaning when they brought them home.

One Wednesday evening, as Michael was browsing through the complete set of Solzhenitsyn, found the week before, cooled by the electric fan (one of Bob's trophies) and Robin was practising by the light of a silk-shaded table-lamp (Michael again) it was decided that it was time to 'hit the dumps'. Somewhere between S.W. 136th Street and Old Culter Road, near the mangrove swamp by the ocean, large notices pointed the way to the neighbourhood trash centre. Michael plugged his 12-volt sealed-beam spotlight into the dashboard cigarette lighter. Hitting the dumps is a night-time occupation; during the day paid guards sit in salvaged armchairs taking first pick themselves and saving the rest for the county incinerator. It was deserted as they drove up but then it was nearly one o'clock. Early in the evening business is brisk.

Robin toyed with a redeemable washing-machine; but he already has one and it is against the dump hitters' creed to take more than you need. He once found a clothes hamper that had belonged to a woman who had been a strict Baptist. Halfway down was a bottle of unopened Seagrams Seven Crown whisky, carefully wrapped in tissue paper. He left it there. Michael was turning over a carton of files and photographs – mementos of a high school graduation, summer of '62. He has gone home before now with boxes of personal effects dumped after a death in the family.

'I once found all the letters that a man had kept since 1909. There were letters his father had sent to him as a boy in 1912 talking about his future life – and now he was dead. It makes you very thoughtful when you drive up alive and alone with only the wind in the trees and find a whole person's life gone to the dump.'

★   ★   ★

Such is the present dearth of rental accommodation, the cost of renewing leases and the burden of fuel surcharges, that New Yorkers are being forced to explore what are challengingly known as 'alternative living arrangements'. Serious articles analyzing these new urban frontiers of interpersonal experience are already creeping into print. Generations of English landladies might identify these new arrangements as that old standby: 'taking in lodgers'.

Lodger, however, is not a word that could pass the lips of any dweller of a Manhattan building with uniformed personnel. It has distinctly tacky overtones. (As a guide, cheap plastic luggage is tacky, especially when coloured Florida citrus; so, too, is slipping taxi money into the purse of a sleep-over.) Lodger, spoken out loud, is very tacky. Those who would admit to taking one in might just as well move off Manhattan to half-price, lodgerless Flatbush.

The unnamed reality, however, is something else. There are many justifications for offering a refurbished maid's room or erstwhile den to A.N. Other. The rent he or she pays (never to be mentioned out loud, naturally) is not among them, although $350 a month, electricity and telephone excluded but with kitchen privileges and bathroom privacy is the minimum going rate. A need on the part of the leaseholder to work out a one-on-one, sharing relationship under non-stressful conditions ('I've always had this problem with isolation') is acceptable, containing, as it does, the promise of inner growth.

Those who move in must not be complete strangers or that destroys the notion of apartment sharer as kin-substitute. For the same reason, former lovers are absolute no-nos. Sharing is about being cosy, not about incest.

The profile of the perfect lodger (if you'll pardon the expression) would go something like this: he should be out from early morning till late evening competing harshly and successfully in some field functional to the landlady. (Landladies, for some reason, comprise 95 per cent of the species.) Law will do: 'Should I sue?' Banking's better: 'Should I roll over my supersaver certificate?' Students, shop clerks (even when called assistant buyers), hairdressers, would not satisfy, hung around, as they are, with a mantle of ordinariness that any self-respecting doorman would instantly recognize and disdain.

The lodger is a social statement. He must be well dressed; clean would not suffice. His shirts, handed in twice a week to the Chinese hand laundry, should be Brooks Brothers Special Order. His suits, which will be in and out of the French dry-cleaner, should be dignified as befits one who looks Reagan and wants to vote Kennedy. A green Loden overcoat (picked up on a business trip to Munich) or regular Burberry completes the weekday image. Lovers can look shabby, husbands may sag but the lodger must be *New York Times* fresh.

He should subscribe to *Fortune, New Yorker, Economist* and receive regular communications from such organizations as the German Information Center. Lavender letters from his mother in Buffalo would not do – anyway, they would immediately draw the attention of the doorman whose job it is to sort mail and snoop for the landlord. The latter could not give a damn about social statements; any form of sub-letting beyond the blood group is subject to a 5 per cent rent surcharge.

Lodgerdom is one of the sexist bastions. Choosing a woman is, perversely, as politically inept as having a male gynaecologist. Or allowing the cleaning lady to wear a white nylon overall. Like everything else in New York, sharing is about power and one isn't supposed to lean on the sisters.

Telling the male lodger to clean windows/scrub the omelette pan bottoms/wash his closets out with Top Job is an act of kindness. It corrects years of sexist upbringing. What does he know from cleaning? To dump it on a sister is to be controlling, compulsive, an emotional heavy and an ideological misfit.

Besides, the sisters would put up too much of a fight for their identity. In the case of sharing that means the right to put out photographs of the family on Daytona Drive-on Beach, Florida or similar knick-knacks that would destroy the apartment's theme: the celebration of the I that signed the lease. To be a lodger in Manhattan is to be a spy behind the lines; not even the merest scrap of background may show through the assumed identity. The lodger is courtier, there to dance around the monarch and provision the feast, i.e. keep the refrigerator well stocked.

Since this is not Blackpool boarding-house-land, the lodger is ostensibly encouraged to bring home sleep-overs. The hope is that he will be utterly unable to do so – so unmanned will he be by the endless pushing and squashing he has received in the name of 'honest communication'. Having had the last detail of his life examined and rearranged, he should be unwilling to expose his sexual preferences to scrutiny over the Zabar's fresh-ground Blue Mountain coffee he has learned to buy in place of his old Nescafe. A man who has been forced to embrace Arm and Hammer phosphate-free, non-pollutant washing powder instead of Tide ('You can't mean it: using Tide is like voting for Nixon') is not likely to bring home a living hostage.

Why then does he do it? Surely any cockroach-laden fourth-floor walk-up on West 108th Street would be better than this servitude in the name of alternative living? To be a lodger is to know that when you get knocked down by a car, someone will care that your underpants came from Saks not Gimbels. Such is security in Manhattan. 'See you later, Ms Portnoy. Have a nice day.'

★   ★   ★

The notion that all relationships must be equal is throwing a bit of a dark cloud over those who want other people to do things for them – those people, that is, who used to be called servants. Today's liberals can't have cleaning women and they certainly can't have maids. What they have instead are 'support systems'. They come very expensive, these systems, and some of them live in. But it is extremely difficult to pay other people to do an old-fashioned, out-dated job like being a servant, while calling it by a more acceptable name and trying to pursue it in an emotionally more enlightened way.

Cleaning ladies, alias household technicians, are a real problem to the liberals. Do not believe everything you read about labour-saving New York. Someone has to polish the microwave oven; someone has to clean the pasta maker. Most family apartments are old and awkward with floors that encourage polishing and windows that have been painted over so often that opening them becomes a mighty feat. Should they open, the dirt that flies in is of a character associated with a nineteenth-century mill town. It is a six-hour job vaguely to clean such an apartment.

The going rate for this sort of support system, who will not do windows, clean Venetian blinds, or iron, is six dollars an hour plus fares. But that is only the beginning. Lunch is an ordeal. Since the progressive employer is now on first name terms with her household technician, where should the latter eat? Not in the kitchen, obviously. Should she be left to take her own meal? All those who answered yes, lose ten points. She must have a platter attractively laid out and served to her at the dining-room table where she will sit while her employer gulps a pot of cottage cheese standing in the kitchen.

A typical lunchtime conversation goes as follows:

Liberal Lady: 'Would a tuna salad be all right, Irene?'

Her technician Irene: 'Aw, Shelley, I had tuna yesterday. Is there any ravioli?'

Noises of cupboards opening and closing. 'I'm dreadfully sorry, no ravioli, Irene.'

'Don't bother, Shelley, I'll take that roast beef.'

'But Irene, that's my husband's supper . . . '

'Thank you, Shelley, I'll be ready in ten minutes.'

Of course, not all household technicians enjoy their new

position in life. Some hate to be stuck in the dining-room and feel desperately uncomfortable at the one-on-one relationships they're expected to have over the pail of diluted Clorox. Others don't like being asked to come in on a Saturday . . . the only day the liberated employer is free to share the cleaning experience with them. These women leave in search of reactionary employers, usually older, who'll leave them alone and let them wear their nylon uniforms again.

The wife who has somehow negotiated her cleaning problem may still stumble badly over who will look after her first child once she's back at work.

Where should the secondary care-giver sleep? – that's a big dilemma. Old apartments have a tiny room off the kitchen, known as the 'maid's room'. Obviously she can't sleep there, even though it does have privacy, a bathroom ensuite and has been redecorated in wall-to-wall Laura Ashley. No, the baby must move in there and the secondary care-giver must take the large spare bedroom.

Since the baby is now, logistically, sleeping in the most inconvenient spot of all, the cot must be wired for twenty-four-hour instant sound. Fine when the mite is still inarticulate but some parents get used to bugging their child. It is not attractive to go to dinner with people who have a microphone snooping on their five-year-old children relaying their every secret over the stuffed courgettes.

In time, of course, the children go to school and learn about the Invasion of Privacy laws. But by then the parents are also aware that a child who has been 'environmentally displaced' by a paid outsider might grow up damaged. Since the secondary care-giver still can't be asked to move into the 'maid's room' she must be replaced by a 9 to 5, five days a week, $200 a week housekeeper, presently known as a 'governess' to distinguish her from a 'housekeeper' which is what a live-in dogsbody is called these days.

This relationship, it goes without saying, is also doomed. There is nothing more extraordinary than to be in an office and watch a tough, pushy New Yorker suddenly change into a cringing wheedling wreck. She is telephoning her excuses to the governess, desperately seeking dispensation for not being home until 5.02.

The situation is fraught: the tyranny of today's non-servant is infinitely worse than guilt over yesterday's servant. Some liberals do find other solutions. Friends have finally parted company with their long-standing support system. They could stand the way she called their house 'hers': they could put up with the complaining when they took 'her' car at weekends: but it was too much to be asked not to invite their guests to stay because of the mess.

They've taken on an impoverished public schoolteacher. In return for room and board, he'll clean the apartment each evening and teach their two-year-old to read over weekends. By the time the child's five, he'll doubtless be well into Freud and R. D. Laing, which is probably just as well.

Time for mothering

New Yorkers are not nice to mothers. A pushchair is an invitation to let a door slam. The merest suggestion of a pram leaving a kerb is enough to spur the distant motorist into acceleration. The woman who produces yet more competitors does so at her peril.

These are not the stuff of our immortality. These small people will grow to take our jobs, our sons and daughters, our self-respect. Merely by existing, they will eat away our youth; their hair will be thicker, eyes brighter, stomachs firmer. Let them learn, say those who eye them coldly, that life is hard and that we are to be reckoned with.

And the wretched creatures who brought them forth for their own weak gratification, let us make it clear that there is no approval. Let them stand on crowded subways, clutch in vain at groceries that spill and scatter, queue in long lines with a fretful child and be given no quarter – lest they forget and think fondly of another.

It is no coincidence that, like the heirs to the courts of the Middle Ages, and for many of the same reasons, the young of Manhattan have no concept of childhood. They are small men and women who learn early to be watchful, suspicious, quick to spot enemies and expect betrayal from friends. Being sent to summer camp for weeks or months is to ride to war; from the campaign comes self-reliance and allies for the future.

These princes and princesses have what is called, with some admiration, 'street smarts'. They connive to be kept in comfort and to be bribed with 10-speed bicycles and whatever is recommended by their closest intimate, the television set.

There is a distance about the child of upper Manhattan. There is no desire to be smiled at, no invitation to share the moment. At four a boy will sit implacably in a bus eyeing the frail old woman standing before him. Woe betide the mother who tries to invade his territory, to pull him towards her. Is she her child's keeper?

But babies; babies are another matter. Not infants squalling into the day but the unborn babe, listening in the womb, learning to be tranquil or, more likely, cultivating an early anxiety attack. This is the only time of infancy that Manhattan appreciates. It hovers over the pregnant woman.

It is a time for theories, for the latest conclusions of the latest studies culled from in-flight magazines, for the newest ideas found potted in some book digest. Not a soul but knows and offers thoughts on 'Birth without violence' (was Jesus a Lamaze baby?) and the dangers of a social glass of wine.

For a while this woman has been rendered harmless; she has fallen into a state of disrepair, suffering the pangs of creation and the withdrawal of nicotine, caffeine, alcohol and tranquillizers; all the weapons of modern-day living.

Today's pregnancy is yesterday's nervous breakdown. It makes all the rest of us feel so much better. There but for the grace . . . She's out of it now, poor dear, and therefore can be indulged and succoured. Soon she will know the true bleakness of motherhood in Manhattan where the only consolation is the new quilted lining of Pampers.

Certain things will protect her after birth, most of them to do with money. Most, but not all. As the pond was once the testing ground of the village witch, so is the office the place of ordeal for the woman who has acquired a new, living , tax credit.

If she cannot face leaving home, creeping back reluctantly after six weeks or – suicide – drops out for two years, if she returns wearing the one Gimbels' dress that does up and 14 lb still hanging loosely around her – yea, she is a mother, a non-being. But let her be back at her desk within a fortnight, stomach flat, her pre-pregnancy fighting weight and wardrobe regained, mentioning the baby with the nonchalance of a recipe for moules – this is a New Yorker who has a place in the world.

Incidentally, she has a child (as she has a summer home) but preferably one and one only. There is no time for a brood. The hand that creams the diaphragm rules the world.

If the one is a girl there can be no suggestion of wistfully contemplating a boy. A son has no mystique. The daughter can grow up to be a stranger just as satisfactorily. Perhaps that is why this city is so careless with its mothers, so impatient of them. It expects these small inconvenient children that she fusses around to grow up and discard her. It's taken for granted that children will drift away cutting off all contact.

The idea of investing time, effort, self, in a child is discredited. New York is a place of business, not a nursery. To give up work for children is as feckless as building a life around a husband – another prize piece of ephemera. New York is a giant orphanage. Most of those who come here have lost or, purposely, mislaid those parents they once had. At Thanksgiving they gather friends and talk of having a real 'family' holiday, meaning the peer group of the moment and a home-made, freshly frozen Mrs Smith pumpkin pie.

But fortunately there are fathers; they will be our salvation. Those innocent beings, hitherto shut off from parenting and locked away from feelings, are awakening to peanut butter and jelly sandwiches, playground muggings and no-more-tangles shampoo. See the world smile on the father and his young child.

★   ★   ★

If one is to believe all one reads, New York even now is aloud with the sound of little gold pumps beneath festoons of cashmere and wool in all the colours of mystery. Butter-soft boots in delicious aubergine are reputedly gliding around the city beneath phantasmagorical midnight-purple shawls and capes swept across silky shoulders of rich loam. On West 86th Street, however, the same old sweat-shirts and beaten-up jogging shoes are much in evidence.

Whoever dwells in that mythical world of high fashion encapsulated in page after page of *New York Times* display ads – they do not inhabit this corner of late motherhood and cheap semi-permanents. In a city in which the illusion of its advertising is mistaken for its reality, those who muddle along in the unkempt and ordinary way know themselves to be failures. The problem with Manhattan is that there is no acceptable way of going to seed.

There are no established guidelines and patterns here for the woman who lapses into domesticity. There is no equivalent, even, of the old Laura Ashleys in which, once, ouzo was consumed beneath the Greek stars. The English Earth Mother, sitting in her basement kitchen surrounded by whole-wheat bread and honey, Ribena and rows of Penguin paperbacks, serving fingers dipped in boiled egg to her children and mugs of tea to her friends, lives as she knows others do. There is a valid point of reference – the country kitchen with the wellies by the back door – for the untidy town nest that she has created.

The New York mother, dousing the Fischer-Price toys nightly in disinfectant, rushing thrice daily to the behavioural baby books, scrubbing apple juice marks from the French beige fitted carpets, does not know of a world in which disorder is not only tolerated but even welcomed as an order of its own. Given no ideal of an old-fashioned farmhouse life (who knows how they do things in Nebraska?), there is only the conviction that a home should look sleek, thin and utterly perfect.

And what shall she wear as she spends her days on the floor experiencing a deep and honest relationship with a toddler? In the end, it makes no matter. The jeans go baggy, the sweatshirt fades but who takes notice of a houseperson with small children anyway? A city that believes a woman should be sharp, successful, bright and wrapped only in fat-less muscle does not put much value on qualities such as being jolly, especially if they come poorly packaged.

The truth is that very few New York mothers are jolly. Habituees as they are of such expressions as 'my feelings of conflict', 'expressing my inner anger' and 'what about my needs?', they tend to suffer *Weltangst* about the sugar content of breakfast cereals.

Given this level of compulsion, a mother's lot is not a happy one. Most of the time is spent feeling inadequate; the rest is passed in a sense of martyrdom. But the worst of all seems to be the feeling that somewhere everyone else is having a wonderful time in all that silk and cashmere.

New York's nickname is Fun City. In today's thirty-two-page *Times*'s news section, twenty-one of them were taken up with advertisements for the accessories of a life of looking gorgeous. Those who walk down Madison and Fifth Avenues, envying those who can afford the clothes and go to the parties, forget to notice that in this rich town there are also those whose only clothes come out of garbage cans.

★   ★   ★

Time was, about two years ago, when a tiny advertisement in the *New York Times* household help wanted column yielded never fewer than 200 telephone calls. At least fifty reasonably qualified 'warm-hearted, intelligent child lovers' would turn up to audition and the children would soon reel from the poking, tickling, cuddling and general exhortations to 'show mummy how much you like me'.

This notice was, therefore, inserted last month: 'Student to help busy mother with 2 yr old twins. Live in Manhattan.' No one called. More up-to-date friends advised a new insertion to include such goodies as own room, Park view, colour TV.

This produced five replies. One woman spoke only French, another only Spanish. One said she wouldn't 'touch a job where the mother was at home'. Another said her terms were $200 a week, Monday to Friday 9.30 to 5.30 and $6 an hour overtime for 'evening duties'.

The fifth set a time for an interview. Never has an arrival been so avidly prepared for. Rosamunda ('My mother named me Rose but I think Rosamunda is more me') pronounced herself charmed. The salary, $150, was acceptable. She talked at length of her 'perceptions of the job-description as being positive' and thus she arrived to try out for a day. That night she helped herself to some fur boots and was never seen again. Her reference, when contacted, said she wasn't at all surprised. 'The trouble is you can't give anything else than a glowing reference these days in case they sue.'

The English network came well recommended by some. For a $250 fee, a housewife in the Bronx finds a 'cheerful, home-making, unspoilt school leaver' from the north of England, who will, apparently, fly over to work for $100 a week. More than that, however, has to be spent on the preliminary telephone calls, coaching her in the lies she is to tell the American immigration officials. ('What me work here? I've got a wonderful job in England and I'd never leave my sick mother.')

The drawbacks are many, not the least of them being that it's illegal. The English network, alas, has a reputation for either going wild in the heady atmosphere of Third Avenue or pining away from homesickness.

The Swedes are known to have an efficient ring going too. These are mostly young men who have tried bumming around in Australia for six months and now feel like a bit of America. They are, it seems, marvellous with children but allergic to any form of household chore.

It seemed sensible to go the agency route for an American or foreigners with legal papers. 'Oh dear,' said the lady from the Overseas Customs Service in Connecticut. 'I had so many lovely jobs on my books and so few suitable girls. Your salary isn't very generous, of course, and my girls can pick and choose from so many lovely homes.'

The indomitable Mrs Fox from East Sixtieth Street simply refused the listing. 'It's not up to our standards.' Miss Rose of Arit on West 72nd was longing to help. 'There are so many jobs,' she lamented. 'So few good people.'

Columbia University Placement Service regretted that students these days wouldn't work such long hours for such little pay. A notice on the New York University Student Board produced one response: a Greek-speaking Cypriot would like to be taught English and would help for two hours a morning: 'Room, food, $80 a week, very good for me.'

A friend called last week. 'I've found someone,' she cried in triumph. 'She's yours for $150 a week, she's from Minnesota and she's lovely. There's just one thing, she wants you to pay for an hotel room for her every other weekend when her married boyfriend comes to town. Would you have a problem with that?'

★   ★   ★

Maisie had answered an advertisement that read: 'Experienced, responsible child care wanted for loving family.'

At 9 am and 1 pm precisely, on that Friday, she had pushed the children through Central Park. At 2 pm they were put into their cribs until 3.30 while she washed the kitchen floor. All was on schedule. For six days a week, from dawn until dark, her every minute was ordered by her employer who called her one of the family – as long as she didn't sit down to rest.

It was after Maisie had drawn up the three-year-old's menu for her employer's approval and before she started the ironing that her grandmother's call came through from Jamaica. Her mother had had a stroke; it wasn't clear whether she would survive it. That evening the employer, felled by strain, telephoned her friends. 'You won't believe what's happened to me,' Mrs Jennings began.

It was Mrs Jennings's very own disaster. 'How can she do this to me?' her cry wailed down the line to friends, whose Janes, Hyacinths and Doreens were even then clearing away the dinner dishes. And the young woman whose mother lay unconscious somewhere in Kingston sat in her bedroom behind the kitchen, alone with her sadness and fright.

'Naturally, you'll stay for two weeks,' Mrs Jennings said next morning, while combing the grocery bills lest the woman had been spoiling herself with secret coffee yogurts. 'You can't just walk out and leave me. You owe me more than that.'

Mrs Jennings turned off the telephone and started what she termed 'the harrowing business of interviewing'. Irene from Guyana, she hoped, would last longer than Mary, Yvonne, Prudence and Maisie. How she lamented the necessity of hired help.

They have no surnames, these women who leave home, family and friends in the Caribbean Islands for the grey, cold life of the maid's room off Manhattan kitchens. They slip into New York on visitors' visas in search of a 'sponsor' – an employer who, by virtue of signing their green card application, will control them completely for the eighteen months or two years of their dependence. The bureaucracy grinds slowly and uncertainly.

It looks like an ordinary piece of plastic: Alien Registration

Receipt Card Form 1-151 (Rev. 7-1-72) N. In truth it is the golden ring around which fairytales are spun. With its possession go dreams of a nine-to-five, five-day week, of a $250 weekly salary and a life where children need not be left in a grim Brooklyn flat under the fitful care of sister, brother or neighbour. 'I think it's dreadful,' pronounce the Mrs Jenningses, 'the way these women just leave their children alone. I mean, how can I trust them with mine?'

Sometimes, to hold the family together, they hold out. They have savings to buy their independence. They go from interview to interview in their best cream trouser suits apologizing that they won't live in and they can't sleep over. And when the reality of winter coats and electricity bills, of boots, scarves and gloves for children reared in sunshine, devours what they have put by, the fiercest and most protective of matriarchs are forced to teach the 10-year-olds how to get dinner for the smaller ones and then go out to stay in homes where their employers cannot imagine the anxiety of separation.

She cannot win, this dweller of the maid's room, for she is never allowed to weaken. Being treated well means being given hand-me-down party clothes. It does not mean being given time off to go home to care for a child alone with 'flu. If she shows concern for her own, she is seen as a betrayer of that other's. She is paid not only to dress the toddler in his $45 Baby-grow but, once in it, to love him unconditionally, provided she teaches him to love his inaccessible mother more. If she hides the longing she feels, it is assumed that, animal-like, she has no feelings. A passive face is interpreted as a passive heart.

Some of the women, despairing at this half-life, send their children back home to be reared by grandmothers or aunts. Some of them, knowing what lies ahead, never bring them at all. Their babies grow up unknowing of their love or sacrifice. In cheap plastic wallets they carry pictures of tiny, smiling girls in sun-flower dresses and mourn the moments of their growing that they will never see.

From a salary of $150-$200 a week, they take $40 for that bleak bolt-hole in Brooklyn – a necessity for the night off but, more important, lest they are dismissed with a few hours' notice. (Guilty mothers are quick to jealousy and suspicion.) And every week $80 is sent home to Port-of-Spain or Kingston. Occasionally a friend or brother comes up from home and then they may be seen struggling home on the subway carrying bags of rice, washing powder and small plastic toys to be sent back for the girls in the sunflower dresses. 'Why don't you treat yourself to a taxi?' suggest the Mrs Jenningses, all thoughtless concern.

From the money left over come clothes, food, soap, everything. ('She's so messy,' says the employer, 'she always has holes in her tights.') And over the eighteen months of waiting that pass so slowly she must save at least $1,000, sometimes $1,500, for a lawyer. Without his expertise, his skill with the telling phone call to his contacts in the immigration department, her green card would probably stay a dream. It may be a racket but who will cry out against it? Without it there would be no hope at all.

For the moment, there is only this twilight world of illegality. There is no social security, no unemployment pay and no medical insurance. The most generous or pragmatic of employers would pay a doctor's bill. A healthy woman works harder. For the most part, there is only complaining at the results of anaemia, high blood pressure, bad backs and all the myriad of damages wrought by stress, worry, diet and simply overwork. The cheapest back street doctor charges $20 a visit, then there are drugs to buy. And what would he prescribe in any case? Rest? A nice holiday, perhaps?

And so it goes. Once in the morning and once in the afternoon, the helps push their charges around Central Park. White babies swaddled in snow suits, fluffy blankets and French ski hats. Black women patched together with flimsy coats and leaking shoes. And in offices and drawing rooms the mothers count their burdens.

★   ★   ★

The Household Help Wtd. Female column of the *New York Times* is an interesting guide to the changing patterns of middle-class Manhattan. 'Single parent (father)', for instance, is a newly-met advertiser. More women are leaving their children behind with the Cuisinart and more men are fighting for custody.

'Warm-hearted and loving babysitter' has almost disappeared. 'Fluent English essential' is the call of the day. Summerhill is no longer the apotheosis of education; Neill's works have vanished from trendy bookshelves. The talk is now of verbal acuity and structured schooling. The word homework has re-entered the vocabulary of parents. A good cuddler was yesterday's requirement; today we are into order and regulation.

But of all these shifts in small type, none is as poignant as the increasing demand for 'grandmotherly person'. Those who spent years in therapy defining themselves as individual beings now feel bereft and desolate in the freedom of their independence. Too late, they long for the reassurance of the generations. This being Manhattan, a totally made-over rock with barely a patch of what is natural left upon it, it is taken for granted that what does not exist can be spontaneously created. The mother who was discarded years ago in Iowa, Missouri or Brooklyn can be recast with a dear, grey-haired soul desperate for work.

She will fuss over her surrogate grandchildren and their mother with never a complaint about her poor varicose veins. If there were ever others she loved as much, she will tactfully keep her mementoes in a drawer of the smallest bedroom in the apartment to which she can cheerfully be relegated. No others compete for her attention; she is the perfect mother of a child's dreams. For many the paid fantasy figure will do as well, if not better, than the original.

But this longing to be fathered in government, mothered at home, is not only to do with whose hand is on the kettle when the working woman rests ('Sit down, dear, and I'll make you a nice cup of 99 per cent caffeine-free coffee'). It is about reassurance and protection but it is also about belonging. Where there are no ties, neither are there bonds. Where there is no obligation, neither is there a community of memory.

Who else will remember or care when her child walks, let alone recount the days of her own faltering steps? Who else will hold her child through a fevered night with the love that comes of being part? And who will comfort *her* in moments of grief and joy? A husband can be many things but not always nor all at once. And who will bear witness that this strong and conscientious provider was a small boy himself once who stoned the neighbours' goldfish and cried for a lost tooth?

A generation of American women looked at their mothers and turned away before their differences. Sisterhood became a family; the peer group stood in for kith and kin. But now that they come themselves to motherhood and middle-age (not necessarily in that order), they look back at those who gave them life and find what they have shared to be stronger than what divided them.

In the meantime, though, they have moved across a continent. Embedded in Manhattan, they reconstruct the families they so carefully and relentlessly destroyed. 'Reach out and touch someone' – a Bell telephone commercial. 'I miss grandma,' says a freckle-face. 'So do I,' agrees her mother – and American Airlines shows how it bring families closer. But closeness across a continent is an expensive business, fitful at best.

Often there is nowhere left to go back to, and that is another fantasy to reweave. The old family home, swing hanging by a frayed rope from the big tree in the yard, was traded long ago for a condominium in some adult leisure village. Houses are a stage parents go through – like school fees or measles.

Few live where they were born; few know where they will be buried. To live for the moment is to be closely surrounded by obliteration. And so these independent women slowly gather up comfort against its cold. The move towards country homes was part of it. The hills, valleys and seashores around New York are dotted by weekend places with old fashioned quilts on the bed, hammocks on the porch and pine dressers in the oil-lit kitchen. First came nostalgia; then came home-sickness.

Tentatively, they reach out to Iowa, Missouri or, for the lucky ones, over the river to Brooklyn to make amends to those whose only crime was in bringing them up as best they knew. All over the country mothers are coming in from the cold. It is a miracle of patience and nature that they are still willing.

Growing up in New York

This year it is embarrassing for any 18-month-old New Yorker not to be in possession of a genuine, miniature Cosco potty with authentic working loo seat, a three-storey garage with diverse parts, at least two examples of large muscle equipment, a Gloverall duffle coat imported from England and a nursery school reservation for 1984. Keeping up is tough for a middle-class Manhattan toddler.

Small New Yorkers are expected by the mothers of other small New Yorkers to have acquired a vast amount of objects. Children with less than four varieties of pedal bike (push chicken, Mickey Mouse car, Chips motorbike, bubble truck, etc.) cannot expect others to come to tea.

Certain toys are taken for granted: a Sesame Street playhouse with furniture, typewriter, cash register, lawn mower, light-up cooker are to be found in every nursery. It is the little something extra that will encourage Jacob/Jason/Amelia/Amour to find time in their busy social calendars. A videotape of the Muppet Movie? Not again. A $280 Brio train set might just do. Toddlers do not come to play with their friends; they come for the challenge of their friends' toys.

The wardrobe of the pre-twos receives its share of scrutiny too. This year's toddlers are into a look that can best be described as preppy-workmen's chic. Polo necks with adorable strawberries fit snugly beneath muted Osh Kosh overalls. Purple is not in this season although no toddler can go wrong in timeless navy with white trim. Emeralds, royals and scarlets are in evidence. Pastels and cute embellishments, of course, are a social misfortune.

Insecure primary care-givers (the current non-sexist label for parents), snooping for tips on the well-dressed toddler, are to be found lurking in the aisles of fashion emporiums. It is an axiom that where shopowners seem to hate children, and especially their primary care-giver of the female sex, there must be the true temple of high fashion. In such places the impatience unleashed upon any customer who cannot tell her Lacoste from her Lauren is enough to convince any ordinary New York masochist that this must be the acceptable place to shop.

In the end, clothes are easy. They are but a uniform – a costume, rather – in which to prepare for the many costumes to come. It is the problem of the toys that never goes away. Old, loved battered teddies with squashed faces are a sign not of heirlooms but of financial embarrassment. All must be spanking new and socially and psychologically up to date. Dolls must display an ethnic mix and be engineered for such reality that there is nothing left to hug but movable joints and battery casings. It is all right to drive out to the suburbs to shop in discount warehouses. That's street smart. It is not all right to frequent Gimbel's department store sale.

Those with aspirations to Yale or Princeton for their toddlers can also relax at Pennywhistle Toys for it is owned by the wife of a famous television newscaster and therefore worthy of a *People* magazine feature. It is also one of the few places in America stocking Madame Alexander dolls, about which there is nothing particularly remarkable except they are hard to find thereby creating a black market in this teenies status symbol.

While it is certainly NOSD to take, let alone need, hand-me-downs from friends, it is now enormously clever to buy used toys from Play It Again, a second-hand store in an East Side townhouse. Here is Adele, the owner, in her strawberry-dotted polo neck; her children appropriately go to Dalton (Manhattan's Harrow) and she's the very sort one would want to procure from the park bench if only her children still had a vacancy for new acquaintances. 'I was very big as a toy buyer. People used to come to my house and say, "My God, you're in the toy business!" and I thought, "Why not?" ' As she points out, it is so satisfying to recycle.

But even equipped with a roomful of cars, slides, puzzles,

planes, trains, whatever, there is still the necessity to break into the magic circle of peers. Organized play groups are the answer – at $14 a morning. Is it not absurd to have to fill in an application form that includes father's and mother's occupation in order to enrol one's children in a group of two-year-olds? How does one dress to pass the rigorous standards of an interview for a toddlers' group? Designer jeans? Silver fox? Down?

Above all, it is the competitiveness that is so daunting. Heaven forbid that a 20-month-old child is discovered idling with a puzzle marked 'one to two years'. Hear the sharp edge at a friendly, informal gathering when someone's child simply will not recognize that 'Fer is for Frog'. Imagine the shame of she, whose two-year-old is still in nappies (we of the eighties are no longer into mess).

At two, we in Manhattan are big boys and girls and we ask for our potties and we sleep in beds not cots, so that we shall not be a bother when we go to Vail or St Croix with our primary and secondary care-givers.

★   ★   ★

On Tuesday Katy and Eben have their first graduation ceremony. They will each receive a certificate of efficiency and dates will be set for a class reunion. For the last time, they will wend their way through the school lobby, catching whiffs of an exotic substance which, like true New Yorkers, they seem to take for granted. After one term and $250 spent, they can now climb through a tunnel and over a bar. Eben and Katy are two years old.

By the standards of Central Park's playground tribunal (composed of mothers and babysitters), their end of year report is not entirely satisfactory. They do not know all their alphabet, cannot count beyond ten, prefer chips to *nouvelle cuisine* and do not understand what is Bermuda (as in 'my mummy and daddy have gone there'). When asked what they are doing this summer, they do not answer 'Going to Aspen/Europe/Mummy and Daddy's house in the Hamptons' but 'Go away in sky.' This is not a suitable response. They do not even always boast an alligator about their person (Izod being the first word the better Manhattan toddlers can recognize).

For this, they can blame their mother – and probably will when they go into therapy. (In New York, Hispanic children get confirmed, WASPs go to camp and the middle classes get shrunk.) She does not, as a start, belong to a mothers' support group. These groups meet one evening a fortnight to help members deal with guilt feelings and compare paediatricians. They are not composed of friends – such soul-searching is too intimate for New York friendships to bear.

They are mostly gatherings of strangers collected from various playgrounds, checkouts of supermarkets that charge at least 10 cents extra per item (hence Gristides but not Sloan's), and bank queues. Banks are by far the most favoured by mother-collectors. It is generally assumed that anyone who can talk knowledgeably about six-month certificates of deposit versus money market funds can be relied on to have an adequately stimulated child and to bring a decent present to a party.

The ritual for going to and giving two-year-olds' parties is not so much refined as expensive. It is thought tacky not to be prepared to purchase an entire costume for Halloween, a miniature ball gown or three-piece dancing suit for Christmas, a bunny outfit for Easter, organdie for birthdays. The children bounce in, dripping designer labels, tossing locks touched only by the six stylists at Michael's Children's Hair Cutting Salon on Madison Avenue and behind them, all too often, droop their over-stretched mothers, racked by inadequacy, creased and washed-out.

Old hands, who have had a child or two before, recommend giving parties on a Saturday afternoon. That's when the working mothers can come. The housekeepers, with their notions of cheap dolls and plastic cars, will be off duty, leaving behind these bundles of conflict, excluded all week from their offspring's world. Bankers, lawyers, executives, with their two-income ideas, fervently wanting to be liked by the nursery set, can be trusted to turn up bearing nothing less than Absorba track suits and boxes of Petit Bateau T-shirts.

A party is an investment. On top of the $1,400 pre-school school fees coming up, the routine $50 doctor's visits, those $12

Michael's haircuts, there is now this $150 party to give. There's the statutory bouquet of helium balloons with coloured ribbons, the complete set of Sesame Street disposable tableware, the videotape rental, pâté and smoked salmon for grown-ups – and, of course, the 'loot bags'. All children must be given bags of presents before leaving; training for the *quid pro quo* of Manhattan starts early. It is a city where money is never too far away.

But all this is coming to an end. Memorial Day marks the official opening of the summer season, the emptying of New York. The Y Parkbench programme has finished. The mothers have marked the last of their report cards on the toddlers' group leader. ('Do you consider she has helped you with your anxieties about your child's development?') This is not a town where teachers judge but where they are judged. Parents who lay out fees are the ones whose expectations must be satisfied. If the children do not learn fast enough, it is the teacher who must try harder.

The toddlers are off to summer homes by the beach and near the lakes. There their parents will be working the cocktail and dinner party circuit trying to find sponsors for country clubs so that their children will have acceptable playmates. Picking up parents in Manhattan playgrounds is one thing. In summer resort areas there are but those hidden, elusive spreads where only the approved may roam and meet.

Manhattan's children learn early that life here is but a series of fragments. Continuity means Big Bird, Bert and Ernie – puppets, not people. How can you explain to two-year-olds that their friends vanish, that Liam has gone to London, Sara to Fire Island and, especially, that Kathleen has gone to Quogue but can't be seen when they're out there because Mummy and Daddy don't belong to the Field Club?

'Children are just a question of management skills,' says an acquaintance from the park. 'You go out and train new friends for them.' In fall, the headhunters will stalk again.

★   ★   ★

The old gang is back in the sandbox. It is wonderful, everyone says, to be home at last. Picking at splinters of broken glass, there is a feeling that all is right with the world again. There's no place, it is agreed, like New York.

The 86th Street playground year has begun. Housekeepers fall on one another, exclaiming over their new Ralph Lauren tee-shirts that were the gift of some grateful grandparent in St Louis or Milwaukee to whom they were despatched, wards in tow. These yearly summer visits, dreaded and avoided by daughters-in-law, are beloved by the housekeepers sent in their place. It is the one time when they're asked what they would like to eat, not merely set for forage among the children's leftovers.

They return from this Mid-west paradise with ready smiles at their eyes and these bright, sleek tee-shirts of which they are so proud. The life of the maid's room will soon still those smiles as rough washing will fade their treasured shirts. 'Just throw it in with the children's things; it'll be all right,' say those whose wardrobes are jammed tight, thinking only of the electricity bill.

Tan is the colour of the new year; it is everywhere. Rich, golden tan creamed in place with gallons of gooey Arden and Lauder, that speaks of months in another place. Here and there a pale, haunted face intrudes that knew a different summer in this same playground when it was hot, heavy and deserted of playmates. These wan survivors are fox-hole buddies now, bonded by the memory of their endurance. 'How was the week with your folks?' they ask one another quietly while the others, covered in tan, call out to the world at large. 'How was your summer? Mine was great!'

Some old faces are missing. They've moved away, never to be seen or spoken of again. This move may have taken them only as far as the East Side, but across the Park or across an ocean, it is the same. Even the deepest friends of the playground cannot expect to survive such inconveniences as the cross-town bus. Over there, by Fifth Avenue, are other playgrounds, other mothers.

Over there, too, are other schools. A toddler destined for Episcopal on Madison should not waste time on one destined for Trinity on Columbus. And getting into the 'feeder system' for the right school is a major preoccupation of mothers of two-year-olds. Any moment now they will start filling in endless forms, spending hours on the phone to early childhood specialists and covering sheets of yellow legal pads with their research.

The canny, leaving nothing to chance, already have their tiny children enrolled in school. Three mornings a week, these early starters will be noticeably absent from the playground. Aged two years and three months, they will be staggering around some room somewhere, trying in vain to keep up with classmates who are months, sometimes a year, older than they. 'I wanted to give Lily an edge,' says mummy, regarding this said 'edge' as worth the outlay of some $1,200 after tax.

Anyone unaware of the ritual of starting at a New York private school might have been taken aback by the appearance in the sandbox, one morning, of a mass of three-year-olds dressed as if for the fanciest of parties. In the most intricate of smocks, most elegant of dainty dancing dresses, they were marked by the large name-tags pinned to their chests. If was the first day of school, the moment when beady-eyed mothers would be picking out prospective friends for their darlings. Oh, the horror of being a wallflower at three.

But in the littlest sandbox, the small safe one with its miniature slide and not a Smurf bucket in sight, the real new girls were getting acquainted, swopping names and phone numbers. The mothers of seven- and eight-month-olds, making their first visit to the playground, were nervously looking around for help, advice and support.

Knowing nothing of park-bench hierarchy, they bestowed radiant smiles on the big, unflappable housekeepers from Barbados or Jamaica who came to their aid. Innocents that they are, the new girls still think any child is a thing of joy. They coo at every toothless mouth around them, not noticing whether it opens above a body clad at Cerruti or in handouts. They'll learn, alas, soon enough.

★   ★   ★

On East 85th Street, a mere peep from the fashionable reaches of Park Avenue, a dapper old boy of Kilburn Grammar School and Wadham College, Oxford, clips along the pavement in his Gucci loafers exuding that particular atmosphere of a man well-pleased with himself. Ronald Stewart, known to admirers at Wadham as 'The Kilburn Flash', currently owner and headmaster of Manhattan's York Preparatory School ('$4,500 basic tuition a year and say 300 bucks for shrapnel–you'd get change out of five grand'), is nearing the end of another satisfactory term.

In his small office on the ground floor the final draft of his Christmas letter to parents, including the obligatory mention of tax-deductible contributions to the school fund, awaits his approval. Beside it stands a pile of college application forms, for it is also that time of year for seniors. Stewart treats them with his habitual air of casual confidence. 'Frankly, I can get your cat into college.'

A copy of Delderfield's *To Serve Them All My Days* is wedged into a nearby bookshelf. This weepie about a dedicated Welsh schoolmaster seems an odd selection for a head who held his school's tenth anniversary party at Studio 54. But, presumably, to prospective parents of this exclusive private school, Stewart seems the archetypal Brit.

He himself has no such illusions. His finer points (teeth, hair, engaging personality) are not, traditionally, the first thing one notices about a custodian of learning. 'I would have no problem with being described as a bright opportunist,' he says cheerfully. 'A pushy, aggressive son of a bitch would be worse.'

This is, after all, still the clever grammar school boy who won a scholarship to Oxford at 16. 'I walked up and down the train full of young people going to take the exam and it was pretty intimidating. And then I looked at one and thought, "Hey, I'm brighter than him." By the time I got there, I'd convinced myself I was brighter than all of them. Is that bad? Is that good? I only know I've never thought there were any excuses for failure.'

The difficulty in terms of New York private schools is in defining failure and success. In a situation where the proverbial cat can get into some kind of college ('a triumph of tenacity, not of capacity'), the rate of those admissions is no guide. In short, a school is successful because word-of-mouth has it so and people invest amounts of after-tax dollars to educate children there. Stewart opened York Prep in 1969 with $75,000 bank loan and 138 pupils. Today he has over 400 pupils. Therefore it's a good school.

'Americans love to play games. For Americans, schools and children are very interrelated in terms of status so it's very important to them how competitive even the nursery schools are that their children get into. There is a feeling that schools are more important than they are. People actually come to me and say, "We're thinking of getting divorced, what do you think?" It's none of my bloody business.

'Things have happened to American parents. During the sixties they developed serious feelings of inadequacy and guilt. Because of them, they so elevated children that now they're considered almost more than equal because they're young. In a culture that values youth so highly, who's the youngest of all? The children. When I was young, whoever asked a kid his opinion?

'A child of 11 comes to look at this school and four other schools and then someone asks the little one which one he chooses. There are children in New York City who've been to six private schools in six years. "You didn't like it? They weren't nice to you? Yes, darling, of course, you can leave." There are kids looking for the perfect school. Precociousness now means an ability to self-direct their lives almost to the exclusion of their parents.

'It might not have occurred to us, for instance, not to do our homework as often as it does to these kids. "I didn't do my homework last night," they say, as though that's a reason. "Sorry, I didn't do it because I went to a Stones concert." Is that a reason? Still, I've never thought academic brilliance by itself is exciting. An original thought is rare in 14-year-olds; I'm not sure I've ever had one. So the kids who excite me are the nice ones – and the ones who do something different, who have some pzazz.'

Like he had. When he left Oxford with an upper second ('Some do well, some do it with spirit'), he went into criminal law, chambers in Middle Temple and practice at the Bar for three years. His last major case was as junior defending Charles Kray. ('I rather like Charlie; he used to give me tips on horses.')

He was 24, married to an American teacher, his father-in-law owned schools and summer camps – York Prep was the result. 'They won't come if we run a rotten show but no one can fire me and that's really the bottom line. Believe me, it's not necessarily happy days for private schools but it's enough to pay for bread, and butter and a little jam.'

Stewart lives on a ninety-acre farm in Westchester, breeding thoroughbred horses – so much for the little jam – and hunting with the Golden Bridge Hounds. ('They always assumed I hunted when I was young. I explain that around Brondesbury Park we do not have the Kilburn Hounds.')

It is hardly the stuff of which Mr Chips was made but, at 37, Ronald Stewart is a contented man. 'Idiots like me never make a mark on anything. They just end their days in Palm Beach in comfort and elegance.'

★   ★   ★

Angelo Evans is sitting in a cafe, holding forth. One arm rests expansively on the back of a chair. He has his feet up on another. Now and then he turns to the mirror behind him to check on his beautiful brown hair.

'My brother and I go out a lot to a discotheque. I put on Jordache jeans, a nice tie, the latest boots and a double-breasted jacket and we go to Magiques on First Avenue. I used to dance like Travolta in *Saturday Night Fever* but I've learned more steps so now I'm better than him.

'Of course I'm good-looking. If I'm not, why do all the girls come over and ask me to dance with them and kiss them? It's because they know I'm sensitive and I'm smart. I can trust myself with them and they know they can trust themselves with me.' Angelo Evans is 11 years old and a movie star.

He is a New Yorker. Naturally. 'My new place is on 74th Street–it's nice and quiet, nice people and not rough.' He would rather meet in the cafe, though. It is more in keeping with the image of one who had a bodyguard to take him to the set, who is the pet of such as Diana Ross and who takes calls from the Coast.

At home there are two rooms. The bedroom is for his parents; at night Angelo sleeps in the living-room on the little couch, his brother takes the large one and his sisters sleep on the floor. His family are Gypsies. They give him freedom–he can go out at night and live on the streets – but expect him to honour traditional Gypsy ways.

'My brother was married at 14 but he's divorced now. His wife never learned anything my mother tried to teach her–to get up early to make my father's coffee, to respect people who come to the house–so we gave her back. I think we paid $8,000 for her and I don't know how much we'll get back.' He used to see himself as the king of Columbus Avenue where he spent his days attaching himself to friendly shopkeepers. He worked in their stores, served customers, ran errands; 'I didn't get paid – they were my friends, I wouldn't want their money.'

The shopkeepers called him 'a good kid with a good heart'. One of them tried taking him to school. It lasted three days. He never went back. 'Other kids like to do too many childish things. When you want to be smart you have to hang around with smart people. You have to be with grown-ups and remember everything they say and get it in your head.'

His memory is prodigious: since he can neither read nor write, he needs it. 'I'm calling up a friend of mine and telling him to come over and by this summer I'll learn how to read. Definitely. If I have time . . . '

Being a star is busy work. Robert Duvall, the actor and his mentor, has been teaching him to play tennis and introducing him to other stars. Mr Duvall found him on Columbus Avenue when he was six and wrote a film around him, *Angelo, My Love*, which he financed and directed himself.

When it is released, it should make of Angelo an event and his friends on Columbus Avenue worry what will become of him. Showbusiness does not shelter its young. There is no premium on innocence within it, only a need for what is newer and fresher. Strangely for a boy with no regular childhood, he has dreams and innocence. It is hard to believe his parents will be able to protect him. 'Proud of Angelo? No, I am not proud of him,' says his father. 'The boy's nothing but a nuisance and a knuckle-head. I get 500 calls a day here for him. He's a nuisance.'

And what if nothing happens to Angelo? If the chic crowd that presently finds him so adorable move on, leaving him behind– another New York enthusiasm of a moment? Will they care that they have built him up only to be dropped when they tire of what they have spoiled? In the magical world of his young mind, nothing bad is thinkable.

It certainly doesn't bother him that not one penny of his film money has been saved. 'I bought myself a diamond and gold ring and a lot of clothes. I gave my mother a thousand dollars because I love her for giving me birth and for watching me. It was nice of her. I gave my father a thousand dollars for helping me. How did he help? He said I could make the movie and I made it.

'I think I'll always be a success because if things go wrong I'll just keep on trying until I get it right. And there's a lot of people that can help me. Mr Duvall: see how he's helped me. I never had an acting lesson in my life but he just wash-brained me, saying, "Be yourself," "Act yourself." I'd rather be myself than anyone.

'I might make another movie, I might. Or I might go into the oil business or whatever else will make four million dollars. But definitely I'm going into the discotheque business. I want to be a businessman and not work for anyone else and the best time to start is when you're young like me. I guess I dream a lot but you can have more things while you're young–a new car, a new wife, happiness and love. That would be enough for now.'

On Saturday nights, when Columbus Avenue is quiet and the police cars trundle heavily by, the kids come to hang out. The star team from the junior high play ball by the bus stop. There's salsa from a large black tape deck around which a crowd of boys huddle and giggle with that special excitement of the dark. At home the folks watch sitcoms and soaps, swilling Lite beer, and on the streets the young prance and let off steam to the dismay of severe black matrons in white polyester uniforms who have just tucked their old ladies into bed and are hurrying home with the week's wages.

Soon the girls arrive, high heels clipping on the sidewalk, hair curled and piled above make-up that is the work of hours. They slink along puffing on cigarettes, shivering in low, gossamer-thin shirts, setting a flutter of excitement as they pass. It's Saturday night, time for the 13-year-olds to try once again for Paul.

In the Jackson Hole, Paul Kovalevich is mopping tables, taking orders and dominating the small, steamy hamburger joint. This is his stage. When he is behind the counter surrounded by 120 lb of raw beef, onion, bacon and all the other trimmings with which he concocts seventeen different varieties of hamburger, he sees himself as in performance. On a good night, when the energy is flowing, he can have the whole place laughing.

It's hard to say exactly how he sets off such an atmosphere of good humour in this grubby hole reeking of old fries. He doesn't tell jokes or do imitations. It must be that Paul himself is contagious; he's working six days a week, noon till 10, running the place and being 17 years old. 'This isn't hard work; this is fun. My first job, that was hard, lifting heavy bundles of newspapers, going out delivering them at four in the morning–that was hard for a seven-year-old.'

He's young, good-looking and full of hope. 'I don't want to be just another person in the world. Either I want to make it or have nothing. To me making it means you can have whatever you can see if you really want it. I'd like a beautiful wife, a couple of kids that respect what I give them, the cars and two homes.'

In some ways, he has boundless imagination, in others none. (His high point was an invitation from a talent scout to read for a prime time soap opera.) He knows only this small enclosed world of home and hard work, where rewards are measured in what can be bought. Where would he have learned of more?

His Ukrainian father is a maintenance man for the city, so is his older brother. His mother, thin and drawn, wears on her face the message that life isn't easy. She comes into Jackson Hole every day. 'He's my baby and I'm very, very proud of him. It's tough here, but we live round the corner and, God forbid, anything happens he can pick up the phone and I'll come running.'

It's hard to imagine anything he couldn't handle. It can be no coincidence that this is the only store on the street that hasn't been held up. It's always the ones who are most afraid who get hit time and time again – the timid old man in the liquor store over the road has been robbed twice in four months.

Paul takes for granted that it was all right to work nights at the age of 13 – New York is not a city where people ask questions – and, anyway, by then he was a veteran. 'When I was 10, I went to work for Tom in the Pizza Parlour, running deliveries and helping prepare the food. I helped him a lot, I really took a lot of pressure off him, and for three nights a week I'd get, say, $75. That's good money for 10.'

The girls on the high stools are giving Paul their most eager attention. Over the strains of WKTU 92 FM disco, they sigh for his gleaming black hair, his broad shoulders, the cowboy moustache. He kids them along and sends them away; they're too young and too easy. At 17, a guy has to know better. 'Listen, it happens here all the time. I've had offers from both men and women to go to bed with them. To both the answer's no.'

Near closing time, the dudes from the street roll in to the Cokes and noisy laughter. The neat West Siders freeze: Paul just sees customers. 'I don't mind what anyone does . . . I know that running around and dope can hurt you. One of my cousins died of an overdose last year so I know. I never liked the life on the streets, it didn't accomplish anything. I'd rather be inside making money. I don't want to be just another kid.'

At 10 o'clock another Saturday night is over. No, he isn't tired; he never gets tired. He's taking his 21-year-old girlfriend out and then going home – her mother has a midnight curfew. 'Sure, I still live at home because I'm only 17, and outside of here I'm only a young kid and my ma's a doll and my father's old and he's been in the hospital for his heart.

'Let me tell you about my father. When I was eight, I bought some golf clubs on the street for $50 and I sold them to my father for $75. But he heard about it and he wasn't sore, he was just sympathetic because he understood about my being young and wanting money. But I vowed never to beat anyone on a dollar again because it wasn't a nice thing to do. Now I have my own money and I don't have to beat anyone. That's okay for 17.'

      ★   ★   ★

Lauren Rokosny and Michelle Ina Block are friends. They are not best friends and, indeed, there are moments when they swear they will never talk again. Such moments are likely to occur on a Saturday afternoon when Michelle calls Lauren to see if they can meet at Michael's house and Lauren says she has to phone Robert, who might want to get together at Scott's. Michelle is then likely to say she is bored with them all and Lauren says she would rather stay home to watch television anyway.

But most of the time they are friends. They share that puzzling condition of being 19 years old, middle class and New Yorkers. They are the ladies-in-waiting. High school is behind them; life has yet to begin. They live in what is supposed to be the most exciting city in the world. They can't think of anything to do.

They watch *Gone With The Wind* on Michael's father's video. They ride around Central Park in Michael's father's car. After her advertising, journalism and fashion classes, Michelle scoops ice cream for $3.75 an hour. Lauren babysits for less but gets to sit down. And the rest of the time they spend on the phone talking about what they should do.

On Saturdays they meet in Central Park to watch Michael and Robert play softball. Lauren is usually hot. In the preppy style, she layers at least three shirts with a jumper and an occasional navy blazer. Michelle is usually cold. Her shocking pink and black butterfly shirt doesn't fit under anything else she owns.

Sometimes they go back to Michelle's parents' home to sprawl in her purple bedroom calling their friends on Michelle's private line. Sometimes they go out for cake and coffee. Cream cake is their weakness. Michelle gave up drugs when she was 14. Lauren never took them up ('Grass. Yuck. I hate it'). What they really like is playing Scrabble and talking.

In fact, they love talking. All the restless energy of the waiting pours out in hours and hours of talking, bickering, confiding and supporting.

For Lauren and Michelle, leaving school is far from a momentous occasion, a milestone, a watershed. They are not joining the world outside for, in truth, they have never lived apart from it. They have not grown up in some special garden shared with others of their own age that must now be left behind. Like all middle-class, apartment-dwelling Manhattan children, they have always lived in their parents' reality.

'Maybe it's nice for kids to have a backyard and ride around the suburbs just being kids,' says Michelle. 'But I'm just not crazy about the suburbs. My parents took me to museums, to the Park, to shows, to restaurants. I was a good kid. I didn't throw up in the middle of nowhere. I was cool. So they took me places.'

These are not the children of parents who saw themselves as guardians and upholders. 'When I was 15,' continues Michelle, 'I lost my virginity and I couldn't face telling my mother – I thought she would hate me for ever. But I finally told her at dinner one night and for an hour and a half she was on the floor laughing. I mean that really hurt. My mother could accept anything but stealing. She isn't into stealing.'

Such moral generosity, however, does not work both ways. In January Lauren's 41-year-old schoolteacher mother left home to live with her boyfriend. Lauren moved into Michelle's purple room for a while and then took a live-in job as mother's help. 'I have turned my back on it all and tried to ignore it as much as possible.' No one is allowed to give her new phone number to her mother. 'At this point I have nothing but contempt for the woman for being so selfish. I don't need her.'

For her father, trying to rebuild his life in a small, new apartment, there is uncomfortable sympathy – the hero of her early years has been felled. She marks time, wondering where her summer clothes have strayed in the morass of packing boxes and whether her girlhood toys and books have disappeared for ever.

The separation will make no difference to her college plans. She already worked out how to find loans, grants, scholarships to see her through the next six years to her master's degree. 'I wouldn't have wanted to ask my parents for money anyway. I'd rather do it on my own. I've been working for my own money since I was 10. If I need it, I suppose I can have it. It has just never occurred to me to ask.'

In September Lauren and Michelle will set out together for

Rutgers University in New Jersey. The future will be underway.
They look back over a long career waitressing, working in
dry-cleaning stores, shoe stores, popcorn stores ('got burned to
bits for $2 an hour') and the old standby – babysitting. ('I sit three
nights a week for this kid of eight – the kid's weird, the father's a
wacko but it's $3 an hour so who's complaining?')

And in ten years time? 'We are going to be very successful
businesswomen living in Manhattan and unmarried,' says
Lauren. 'I think we'll always be friends, though. It's nice to have
someone to talk to.'

In the evenings, when New York is alight with excitement,
Lauren picks up the phone, draws on a Salem Light, picks at the
alligator on her sports shirt and calls: 'Hi, Michelle, so how're you
doing?'

'Oh, God, Lauren, I'm so bored . . . '

★   ★   ★

New York is not a romantic city. It does not choose to be.
Romance is soft; so are Paris, Venice and lavatory paper and that
about sums it up. New Yorkers wear the softest lambswool and
silkiest fur as though they were breastplates. In a city where
success and power are prized so highly, the velvet glove means
nothing without the iron fist.

It takes its toll first on the ambitious young, especially the
women. To be intelligent here is the equivalent of being a starlet
in Los Angeles. It is an invitation to be used. Watch them walking
down the street early in the morning, their college majors and
masters tucked behind confident eyes. Those are the newcomers
before they realize that they are but some of hundreds of
thousands hungering to succeed.

As they get passed swiftly from hand to hand, from lunch to
dinner, to hotel room and back, they acquire a look that is
misunderstood for sophistication. Back home, in small towns
and modest cities, friends send news of marriages and births.
And in their studio apartments amid the Japanese paper lamps
and pull-out sleep sofas, the used ones ponder the romance they
have made their own. The one-night stand, the office flings, the
passing celebrity handing out his hotel key – is this what little

girls dream of?

It is no wonder then that Valentine's Day cards in this city are rarely about hearts, lace and flowers.

Ask any primary teacher in a private school. Two-thirds of the class will be children of a divorce who think love is not sloppy but fleeting. At least half will have been in therapy for 'emotional difficulties'. Is there some inherent selfishness abroad that conveys the message that loving is painful? Either way, it does not suggest an adulthood that will believe in the magic of a gentle meeting – and is this not the nature of romance?

Listen to an acquaintance offering an opinion on another: all that is there for the eye and ear will be summed up as if the outward details were the reflection of a being. 'Bright smart, amusing, sharp, well put-together' tell nothing. Wait forever for one to say of another: 'She/he is such a good person inside.' Inside is not an American concept.

The image of a hidden garden is not part of a culture that had its beginnings in the hold of an immigrant ship. When the past must be forgotten, it is as if some secret reach of the soul must also be walled up. It's why so many Europeans find Americans not just hard to accept but hard to understand. They cannot imagine what it means to walk on a street where there is no common body language, where eyes must constantly be on the alert to see whether a man means well or not, or even which way he will step.

Romance needs a moment of peace, a still world in which to be cherished. The touch of a hand, the memory of a look, a breath held in a second of silence, there is no room for these amid raucous babble and noise in a city of constant movement and journeying.

And so Valentine's Day becomes an excuse for another commercial flurry. Hand-dipped chocolate shops turn to the business of costly hearts. Florists hoard red roses and push prices up a dollar or so. Novelty stores dust off last year's inflatable plastic heart headrests for the bath and the largest emporiums sigh at the chance to have yet another heavily advertised, one-day only, sale.

But even now, while admitting that all this is true, it must be acknowledged that there is also another truth. Those who sit in the square on Broadway staring at Verdi's statue, hearing in imagination the echoes of his music, are savouring a moment of love. The Greek shoemender who insists on unwrapping intricate brown paper parcels to show off the precision of a new sole is also in love with his craft.

The child frozen in delight at the appearance of a lone winter squirrel will probably carry that memory for years. The sunrise over a cold street as a young boy scurries off to work, impatiently following his dream – the city has a romance of its own. It is only that it has nothing to do with the tradition of the past. But, then, neither does New York.

Being old in New York

Residents of West 86th Street rarely give a glance to Mrs Hartfield, an elegantly turned-out woman in her seventies, hailing a cab on the way to her regular bridge game. Hers is obviously not the elegance of money: it owes more to an innate pride, a sense of how things should be done. Her foreign accent places her as another of those who fled a different life a history ago. The street, wide and almost European, is full of such as she.

There is a story told of the childhood of Joan 'Hanni' Hartfield née Flesch. One day it was announced that there would be no staying up for supper – guests were expected. 'But who is coming after all,' replied her eight-year-old brother, contemptuously, 'Just Kreisler, Schnabel, Nikisch . . . ' The only daughter of Carl Flesch, the great violinist, scholar and teacher, she grew up taking for granted the presence of a century's musical heroes.

Now, only small touches betray that other life: the homemade cake and napkins kept at hand in case of visitors; the heavy silver wrapped away for dinner parties there is no longer room to give; the corner table of photographs – faded ones of the past and colour snaps of curly-haired grandchildren, full of American vitality and humour.

Perhaps it is not surprising that she does not pine for her childhood. She has memories of a house filled with music but there must be memories too of standing backstage ('And do you too play the violin?') and of the constant comparison with favoured pupils.

'My father wasn't really interested in his children. He was not a "daddy". My mother was also more wife than mother because my father was very demanding. He wanted to be waited on hand and foot. I was his secretary, you know. When I was about 17 I typed the manuscript of *The Art of Violin Playing*. He even mentioned me in the foreword – but that was only in the first edition. After that he left it out.'

Then in 1929 came the crash. Her father had to hand over his Stradivarius to his banker. ('The man was a friend but my father owed money to his bank. What could he do?') In 1934 came the Nazis. Her parents, under Furtwangler's protection, left for Switzerland.

She, her banker husband and small son crept away to France. ('We didn't think the French would lose.') They were there until 1943, living under false names, listening for the knock on the door. 'My husband stood at the window all night every night because we knew the Germans came then to collect the Jews. For my son it was a difficult time. It was not a childhood.'

They escaped at last to Switzerland. ('I don't remember how much it cost but it was a lot. You had to'). They escaped to a life of camps and prisons. 'We slept there on straw. Ach, that straw – it walked. But at least the Swiss didn't send us back to Germany as they did thousands of others.'

Their visas to America came through in 1946. Her father was dead, her son was 24, her husband was 50. 'He didn't make much money here. He wasn't in such good health any more and those years of excitement and anxiety didn't help. But we were so happy that we made it. It wasn't a question of liking America or not liking it. So many didn't make it; we did.

'When we got married, we didn't think we would ever leave Germany. We had a beautiful apartment – there was a room upstairs just for ping-pong. We had a cook, a maid, a nurse for the baby. It all came little by little. I had never worked in my life but when my husband died in 1960, I had to go to work because I had no money. I speak three languages and I became a secretary. I still work sometimes if they phone; I always say I am a call girl now.

'I get a little bit from Germany, a little bit from social security. I don't splurge and it's not bad. In New York there is everything and lots of things you can have for free. The concerts are so expensive but I can go to the New York Philharmonic rehearsals for only three dollars. That's not bad. No, I don't think of what used to be because there comes a day when it is finished. My life is not that interesting. It's nothing extraordinary. A lonely widow lives in a small apartment. What is there to say?'

★   ★   ★

Now and again there are glimpses of Mrs Hartfield from 15C at the front door. Occasionally Mrs Goodman from 3B is seen getting into a taxi. Mrs Brill from 3C, though, hasn't been spotted for some time. Mrs Brill wouldn't open her door to an unknown visitor: 'Who are you? I'm sick. Go away.' Mrs Goodman unlocked her door to reveal that she was leaning on a walking frame, her knees strapped into whalebone leg corsets.

Last week she fell over in her hallway but managed to crawl into the bedroom to the telephone to summon help. Brushing this mishap aside, she relayed the information that Mrs Brill had broken a hip and couldn't leave her flat. No, she hadn't been down to see her. 'I've lived in this building since 1939, I think Mrs Brill has been here since 1936 and I've never called on her. I don't believe I've met her in the lobby twice a year.'

About 11 million people live in New York; 1½ million of them are over 65. Six hundred thousand of the city's senior citizens live alone. Three of them in our building.

Mrs Goodman and Mrs Brill have acquaintances in common. They have occasionally played canasta together at the homes of other ladies. They don't visit. Mrs Goodman is 75, she has been widowed for thirty-seven years. Her only daughter, who lives in Maryland, has been trying to persuade her to move into a smaller flat. She has no intention of doing so. When the time comes that she can't look after herself, she intends to move a resident companion into one of her spare rooms. Mrs Goodman's income softens her existence.

Lucy Rowan's mother lives alone in Brooklyn. She has a one-roomed flat (rent: $125 a month) and her only income is her social security cheque for $196. Lucy's mother is 86; she has cataracts and arthritis. Until a few weeks ago she could still get about; she shopped, visited, went for walks. Her arthritis is so bad she can't move. Lucy would take her to live with her family but daughter Lisa would have to sleep on the sofa. Is that a fair long-term solution? Sister Bernice talked briefly of moving her into a nursing home. The fact that only 3 per cent of the city's elderly live in institutions tells all about its nursing homes.

So that was the situation last month. One day, on the way home, Lucy noticed a dramatic poster in the bus. It showed a mail box stuffed with letters. 'The lady in 3B is dying,' ran the headline, 'only her mailbox can save her.' There was a telephone number for something called Early Alert run by the city's Department for the Ageing.

Not expecting too much (making contact with officialdom often seems as easy as making contact with outer space), Lucy telephoned the number. Early Alert is a project specializing in stuffed mail boxes. However, a patient and understanding official gave Lucy a whole string of phone numbers to try and much encouraging information.

Lucy's mother, it seems, has not been getting all the benefits she is entitled to. Ninety-one per cent of New York's elderly base their income, as she does, on social security. Getting even that isn't easy.

Anyone retiring now who has worked consistently for the last forty quarters and has paid exactly the right contributions is entitled to a minimum of $107.90 a month. Since that's patently not enough to live on, there's Supplementary Security Income. Combining the two: a single person receives $248.65 a month unless he or she isn't entitled to social security, in which case, and for no discernible reason, the SSI income is only $228.65. The official poverty level in New York is $250 a month.

Of course there's a catch with SSI. Being destitute isn't enough: it's essential not to be worth *anything*. Savings over $1,500 (including redeemable value of an insurance policy), a car worth more than $1500 or a house with a marketable value of more than $25,000 (where is there a house worth less in New York?) – any of the above and there's no claim. The official wasn't sure about a colour television set. 'If she has say $2000 of life savings,' said the forward-thinking official, 'friendlier social workers usually advise taking a holiday.' Getting a bit of redecoration done was also suggested as a way of getting rid of the excess.

Then, of course, there's Medicaid providing all manner of home help and paying medical bills. And food stamps and even welfare from the city, if there still isn't enough. Being entitled to all this is not the same as finding out how to get it. As the official put it: 'The trouble is that no one knows how the whole thing works.' Still Lucy felt encouraged that she could work her way through the red tape.

She rang the Brooklyn office of the Department for the Ageing. Indeed her mother should be getting more money, visitors to help her with 'household chores, money management, personal care, laundry, meal-planning, nutrition, shopping, seeing a doctor'.

Unfortunately she would have to be seen by a welfare worker to make an inventory of her health and worldly goods. Someone should be able to come and see her in a few weeks. But what about now? This was an emergency, Lucy explained. The official offered the telephone number of a private employment agency: household helps, $7 an hour, six hours daily minimum.

Lucy moved her mother into her apartment the next morning: daughter Lisa took to the sofa.

Despite cut-backs, the city does everything it can think of to help the old. It sets up centres and projects. Most of them disappear before people can find them. Others complain they can't find the shut in, isolated old to help. But every time bureaucracy comes up with another way to tackle one problem, it runs into yet another problem.

Early Alert is the perfect example. It's available to anyone over 65. This is the theory: nearly all the city's mail is delivered to boxes clustered together on the ground floor of each building (except for those that don't have boxes). Through a tie in with post offices, Early Alert arranges for the postman to put a red dot inside the relevant box to remind himself it belongs to an old person. If he notices a bulging wad of letters, the postman remembers and works out that something might be amiss.

One day Benny Blume noticed that Gretel and William Meyer of 1145 Woodycrest hadn't picked up their post. He told someone in the office who telephoned someone in Early Alert who telephoned the resident superintendent at 1145 Woodycrest who broke into the Meyers' apartment after first finding the landlord for appropriate permission. Two burglars had beaten up the couple and locked them in a closet. Husband William died of a heart attack.

By the time the superintendent let 75-year-old Gretel out she had been locked in the wardrobe with her husband's body for three days. Anyone wondering why the superintendent hadn't noticed something amiss for himself misses the point that it wasn't his job to worry.

Not surprisingly, only 11,000 people have registered so far with Early Alert. Most old people are afraid to. Breaking open mail boxes is so common that people don't want to alert criminals to their vulnerability. Besides not many old people get letters.

Undaunted, the Department for the Ageing came up with a brand new scheme. They opened a pilot Senior Citizens' Crime Prevention and Assistance Centre. Bearing in mind that 40 per cent of the inner city's elderly poor have been the victims of crime, the centre wanted to teach the other 60 per cent to protect themselves. It offered booklets with such tips as 'If awakened at night by an intruder, lie still'.

It would also help people after they have been mugged. Social workers will offer counselling to help post-mugging trauma and, on a more practical level, make the necessary telephone calls to get stolen ID cards replaced and to find emergency financial and housing help if necessary.

The problem? The office is on the sixth floor of an unguarded, almost deserted building in a rough street off Broadway. There is no elevator attendant. The Crime Prevention Centre always advises the elderly not to get into empty elevators.

Lucy Rowan discovered that to get help for her mother, she had to contact seven different agencies. Her mother has since died.

★   ★   ★

It is a well-known fact among those with access to a broad spectrum of bank statements that the widows of Manhattan are in possession of its money. Thus there is one place in New York where little old ladies can be assured of warm welcome, where there is always a chair to rest quivering and wrinkled legs, and always a patient smile as voices wander to, from and around the point – and that is at the bank manager's desk.

Stranded away from family, left behind by friends, ignored by the world at large, the little old ladies are to be found taking refuge at their bank as they once did at the doctor's in the days before each visit cost $50. Here there is still concern and attention. This is the one stage on which their imperious or tentative acts can still be played, their will imposed or cries for help heard.

Faces caked in powder and rouge, eyes for once alight, they progress gloriously past long queues of the young before whom they must normally step aside to the seat of privilege by the bank manager's waiting hand. There are those who regret the open-plan arrangement of New York banks, those who might like an inner sanctum in which to confess in private their useless excuses. But for the little old ladies, what triumph would there be in merely passing behind a door?

Straightening their backs, pursing their mouths on which lipstick is approximately placed, they delight in this public display. Envelopes stuffed with stock certificates are brought forth from cavernous bags in which, as often as not, are crammed a lifetime's papers, so strong is the conviction that apartment buildings are all staffed by burglars and thieves.

'Perhaps you would be kind enough to explain this?'

'What do you think I should do about that?'

'Should I put money in one of your new six month funds? Would that be wise, dear Mr B . . .'

And the bank managers nod attentively, gently answering today the questions that were similarly answered yesterday and probably all the days before. Where else could the bundled ladies go to pass the time so happily? The daily outing to the bank is the high point of so many lonely lives.

Contrary to the myth, it is not the truly-widowed widows who take off to Florida with blue-rinsed hair and the lifetime savings of some erstwhile husband who was the victim of overwork and a fatty diet. Those are the 'lottery' widows who, finding them-selves unexpectedly in possession of a large fortune, settle into euphoria and a determination to marry again both soon and, if possible, this time to a better dancer.

Manhattan's true widows cling with moist eyes and cold hands to the memory of he whose stock certificates and life insurance now ensure them that patch of warmth beside the bank manager. They would not marry again – besides, who would want them with their worship of the past and self-pity for the present? They talk limply of their hardened circumstances – having to go now to symphony concerts on a Friday afternoon, for instance, for fear of being out alone in the dark.

Used as they were to being sought out for a husband's sake, they cannot accept that it is now they who must go out and embrace life without the luxury of being too choosy. Their appearance, of which they were once so proud, grows each year a fraction shabbier. They who lived through another's identity can find no pride in dressing for being alone.

Convinced somehow that they will go on for ever in the silent apartment in which his mementoes and photographs still stand exactly as they used, the widows worry over their principal, fearing to spend one cent more than the interest it accrues. And thus they are the beloved of bank managers who, for younger, lesser souls, bounce cheques and deny credit with ruthless impartiality.

In spite of appearances and 'we're a people bank for people' advertising, it is uncommonly difficult to find access to a person in a bank. Unless, that is, you are a little old lady with such a fear of spending and such longing for safety that it blocks out the knowledge that even banks have been known to make mistakes.

The bank manager's dream woman is 80 years old, well provided for, and she wants to give him her all. Against that, what's an hour here or there?

Women and making it

It has become quite the thing for women of a certain income to take offices. Midtown Manhattan is swarming with newly retired housewives, squeezed into tailored suits that fitted them in another lifetime, venturing from realtor to realtor in search of the perfect broom cupboard with window to call their own.

In this small space, surrounded by send-out coffee shops and rush-hour madness, is to be written the great novel or whatever it is that the former residents of Central Park sandboxes and long-time experts on ring-around-the-collar have decided is welling within. Those who are bored with adultery and sated with sitting at home trying to resist the Bill Blass chocolates from Bloomingdales are now taking tiny office sublets in which, presumably, the Real and Fascinating Me is expected to flourish.

They are not, it is to be understood, going out to work. For a start there is a certain squeamishness about having to take orders from people with whom one wouldn't share a subscription to the Metropolitan Opera. In any case, the mundane task of doing tasks is not what motivates the refugees from nine-room $400,000 apartments. It is not in order to go through the wretched business of work that they are putting down $300 a month in rent and a huge deposit for some complicated telephone system. These are the play offices.

Fathers have dens, children have playgrounds and mothers now have offices. 'Must rush, I have to get to the office' does, it seems, have a more impressive ring than 'Must rush, I'm late for my hairdresser|shrink| course in charisma at the New School.' It is the appearance of leading an interesting life that is being rented, not the spartan space for which the dollars are actually being paid over.

It should perhaps be pointed out that very few women who have dropped out of the work stream in order to keep house, arrange dinner parties, overwhelm children and worry endlessly about when the handyman will come to weatherstrip the windows, could survive re-entry into American office life. Not for nothing do those careerists who also have families scoff at the stay-at-homes.

The average ambitious New Yorker will be up at 5.30 to devour the *New York Times*, consume forty minutes of aerobics exercise and still have an hour with her children before leaving to be at work by 7.30. Being a hard worker is not enough: nothing less than a full-blown case of workaholism will do. (In the park sandboxes, it's always possible to spot the children of successful mothers – they're the ones who, at 18 months, can clearly articulate the word Valium.)

The tradition of the New York office lunch break comes hard to those accustomed to lingering across a table over today's bit of the Scarsdale diet. Working women do not take lunch hours. If there are clients to entertain, they must be accommodated over dinner after a quick call to a husband informing him that yet another Stouffer's gourmet frozen dinner is in the icebox. The lunch hour is the time for all ambitious executives to be on view to passing senior vice-presidents. They should be found chained to their pristine desks behind brown paper bags containing send-in cottage cheese, dealing with this or that urgent matter over which they obviously pored for hours after last night's working dinner without, and this is essential, showing any lapse in a general perfection of appearance.

It is no wonder, then, that those who are now into renting offices are not recapturing past office lives. All they want is to be interesting. They are trying to have an excuse to meet other people who actually are interesting. Manhattan is an island of cannibals. Here people feed on other people for all their stimulation, information and satisfaction. The eagerness to expose all to another is also the desire to be allowed in return to creep into the other's skin.

New Yorkers are huddlers. In streets, on buses, in shops, they crowd together that they may talk and feel the reassuring closeness of other bodies. Even the arguments that break out so fiercely and so quickly between strangers are an expression of that need for contact – that compulsion to break the silence of aloneness.

So those who could not work in deserted apartments, listening to the machinery of life rushing past in the streets below, now move into mid-town Manhattan, to buildings in which offices huddle together. Here, they believe, they will finally do something. They will network themselves, as the saying goes. They will rifle through old address books for contacts who might suggest business deals, gala events to organize, agents thirsting for first novels about alienated housewives. On the strength of a decade's viewing of late-night movies, they will write proposal after proposal for films about amusing women realizing themselves ('I'm working on Candice Bergen now').

And in the evening, as they talk across the dinner tables of all the possibilities in the pipeline, the lights will go on in those deserted offices as the night cleaners move in. At $2 an hour, with husbands unemployed and children to raise, some women don't worry about being interesting.

★   ★   ★

All over Manhattan women are locked up in velveted boxes. Some are called 'homes', others 'offices'. The effect is the same. Freedom is a dream, a soaring seagull swooping over Central Park, glimpsed through sooty glass.

What is there to do for those women who have no offices to go to? No one needs to meet and make new friends. Everyone's lists are full; no one has any openings. 'Call again in a year or so. Someone may have moved to Minnesota.' Women no longer lunch together. They stay home and, while munching through a can of tuna packed in spring water and examining their faces in the looking-glass, chatter down the telephone wire to those they once sat across from.

There are no choices left in life that necessitate going out to meet its challenge. The book-of-the-month-club has replaced the library. Self-help has supplanted charity. No one gives to it or works for it in these dutiless days since one is instead into Causes and then only when deductible, preferably with Sinatra closing the bill.

The poor are no longer with us, only with them, i.e., the federal government. To be accepted as a Cause the poor should be no older than eight and artistically gifted, preferably in dance, which means a good chance of their growing up to be blessedly inarticulate.

Going out to shop is a charming old-fashioned custom still practised, it is reported, in the suburbs. The idea of having to push a cart up and down jostling aisles is as distasteful as that of running on the streets. Mingling is out; privacy is in. Body contact with strangers is to be had only with the battery of doctors or nurses to whom one turns over the machine for its biannual check-up. All must be perfection within the new purdah, in direct relation to the chaos feared without.

It is no longer necessary to retreat into psychological symptoms. There is no agoraphobia any more, there is, simply, no reason to go out. The video tape collection makes nonsense of sitting in a darkened cinema at the mercy of sleepers, snorers, chatterers and flashers on the loose. Umpteen television channels are umpteen windows through the lace curtains of which the women peep.

Of course there is a fad for filming programmes about what are implausibly called 'real people' committing independent and outrageous acts like farming or being a grandmother. It is not in order to make of these nonentities a momentary star. It is to replace the memory of the street, bustling with everyday life, to be snooped on and clucked over from the safety of the parlour. And again on television everyone wins. Out there, beyond the world of the box, and the security of the hermit's shell, is sensed a gallery of losers.

There is no sense of missing anything through this restricted life. It is, after all, a condition of extraordinary privilege. To be able to telephone in shopping lists for delivery suggests charge cards, a background of respectable credit rating. Even sales have been reduced to the level of a gentle living-room distraction –

bargain hunting as Mah Jong.

There are those in the new purdah who can price to the cent every item that has been on offer in every major department store in Manhattan over the last year, such is the efficacy of the colour catalogue. Over on East 86th Street is a beautiful and legendary woman who has not been glimpsed outdoors for years. Nevertheless no one buys so much as a love seat or air conditioner without checking in with her first. She is an encyclopaedia of store sales.

But loneliness, a scratching desire to belong, intrudes eventually. Those independently single women who have been working at home (photographing, putting together a new consciousness, getting into futures or yen) start to crave a job. The world has been withdrawn from, rejected, studied and now is the moment for reinvolvement. It is no longer enough to have two telephone lines and an answering service. There is a longing for a switchboard, a secretary, medical insurance, withholding tax and, above all, a sense of being a part of the game.

All that changes is the costume, the decoration and the tone of voice. The velour lounging suit with scarlet racing trim gives way to the austere tan two-piece with matching briefcase. The bed of cushions gives way to one of thorns. Voices go up an octave. Six months' work with penetrating anti-wrinkle eye cream is put aside under one week's neon. And since everything must be embraced wholeheartedly on Manhattan, office hours start in darkness and end in darkness.

She who was fluid and graceful with time now boasts of being unable to sleep until 200 telephone calls have been made or returned. Somehow it escapes notice that she is carried unseeing by metal tube from her old quarters to the new which are no less of an enclosure. Papers are sent in. Lunches are sent out for. Nothing changes but the quality of the wall-to-wall carpet and the colour of the telephone that conjures the world outside into existence.

Liberation is today's hypocrisy; welcome to the new purdah.

★   ★   ★

Certain situations are guaranteed to make a New Yorker laugh. This was one of them. At the First Women's Bank on East 57th Street an exhibition of women's art opened in celebration of *Helikon Nine*, a new magazine of women's arts and letters hailing from Kansas City, Missouri.

There are at least four Manhattan jokes set off by that announcement. For a start the very words 'Kansas City' are thought to be funny. They're like 'Cleveland' which is hilarious or even, in the right mood, 'New Jersey'.

To say that the First Women's Bank (guffaw, guffaw) in its short life has been one of the movement's custard pies is to put it mildly. It was a great idea; it must have sounded terrific on paper. It was to be the women's answer to banking's discrimination in the matter of credit (without which, as you know, there is no life). It was part of the seventies' assertiveness, set up with sixties' lavishness in a many-splendoured setting.

The bank lost half its $2 million capital in 1976. To lose $1 million couldn't have been easy, but all that sensitive, meaning-ful and expensive interior design certainly helped. You can imagine the publicity; it played straight into the male oppressors' hands (whoever they are nowadays). Not that women rallied around to put their money where their rhetoric was. The bank now has about 5,000 accounts and the majority of its customers are men.

Trust men to appreciate the personal service, the courteous women tellers and officers, the soothing banking hall. Perhaps women feel more comfortable in the harshness of the multi-branch megabanks where they can release their waves of hostility and frustration against male tellers, safe in the knowledge that such rudeness is a political act.

So much for the Women's Bank hosting the show of women's art (next joke: smothered groan). It's no secret that once upon a time 96.5 per cent of all art shows reviewed by *Newsweek* featured men's work, that an exhibit at the School of Visual Art in New York to protest war, repression, racism, and sexism neglected to include so much as one work by a woman or that a treacherous sister-cum-woman-dealer dropped Lee Krasner because her husband, Jackson Pollock, had left the gallery ('It is impossible for me to look at you and not think of Jackson').

Pollock is long dead and Krasner now hangs upliftingly over a teller in the First Women's Bank along with Alice Neel and Miriam ('Vaginal iconography was a true developmental stage') Shapiro. Not that the *Helikon Nine* show has entirely lacked its moment of feminist drama.

It was 11 o'clock and a rainy morning. Customers dripped umbrellas across the forest green carpet and Sally Topoleski, the branch manager, was at her desk, smiling this way and that, patting her blonde, back-combed hair, twitching a backless, high-heeled shoe. The exhibition was nearly in order. And then as the last, delicately untitled, ceramic wall plaque (a Mary Frank) was being hung, Sally saw it for what it was: a naked woman, paddling.

'Oh, dear,' said the motherly Topoleski, chewing her spectacles. 'Because of the exploitation issue, we have a real problem with nudes.' Hang a nude in First Women's and, it seems, hordes of feminists march in to protest. Poor Mary Frank, yet another woman artist who was the victim of prejudice.

At this point, of course, the joke should only have begun. Ann Sperry, the artist organizing the show, should have stormed out of the bank decrying censorship and straight round to the offices of *Ms* magazine. Sperry is not one to cross: an artist who works powerfully in painted and rusted steel, she has even talked of welding as a feminist experience: 'I feel the story of my life unfold, a woman's life, women's lives – one part emerging from another, sometimes ascending or descending, sometimes being pressured or confined, enclosed by felt yet unseen barriers, sometimes unfolding and unwinding, growing quite freely and naturally.' (Page 29, issue one, *Helikon Nine*.)

But Sperry isn't in the business of hysteria. If Topoleski couldn't live with nudes, nudes she would not have. In a trice, the offensive plaque was back in its brown paper wrapping. Another crisis defused.

There is a tendency to believe all women artists in Manhattan have to live in a loft in SoHo, talk of making their art with worship in their voices and spurn men in retaliation for the years that women artists spent as vassals for the macho bohemians' sexual pleasure . . . and so on.

Sperry lives very busily next to Central Park with her husband and three sons: 'I remember when Ethan was born, this rabid feminist came over to me and said accusingly: "Are you at work?" I said: "Work? I've just produced life." ' Her work seems to have survived the fullness of her contentment; it hangs in major museums and exhibitions.

She is also the New York editor of *Helikon Nine,* of which it need only be said that it costs $5.50 an issue. ('It's more than another "little magazine"', editor's preface.) It is a not-for-profit corporation – but of course. Where would we be without foundations and endowments to succour and aid those who seem so convincing when submitted in triplicate?

It deserves to succeed, however, if only because it comes out of Kansas City, Mo., and would therefore be a lesson to those New Yorkers for whom nothing happens between coasts but wasted space. Kansas City was one of the first cities in America to hire a glamorous Manhattan public relations firm. Carl Byoir of Madison Avenue are quick to tell you that the Nelson Gallery there has the finest oriental art collection in America, that there is a public policy to build one new fountain every year and that its 7,000 acres of public park 'is not counting boulevards'.

They are not quite so quick to point out that they also handle public relations for the city of Detroit. Now that is really something to give a New Yorker hysterics.

★   ★   ★

The powder room of the suburban country club is a monument to the discipline of American women in their forties. In the shower rooms gallons of moisturizer are smoothed into bodies as slender as the sticks of celery on which they lunch. Hairless brown calves with ne'er a wobble bear witness to the efficacy of daily exercise routines. Little golden ear-rings peek from under carefully streaked golden tresses on which the sun is never allowed to shine. For the middle classes there need be no such thing these days as middle age.

Here 'we' is the password. For she who isn't half a 'we' (or the daughter of one) life in the powder room can be uncomfortable. Since there are no spare men to speak of in the suburbs, newly divorced women have a hard time of it in the land of We.

At least if they play tennis well enough to make the club's A ranking they can be sure of a game on a weekday afternoon. If in their married days they let themselves slide to a C, well, what can they expect? Just time on their hands to rue their carelessness at losing a husband.

Noses aren't bobbed, wrinkles aren't stitched, breasts aren't made silicone-hard. Such passivity is not for the women of the suburbs. The challenge is to make the most of what you have and by hard work earn what you weren't born with – pectorals and a man being high on the list.

As a result, it's often hard in the powder room to tell the generations apart, although the college-age daughters may be slightly plumper, their laughter a shade less determined. Their faces, too, may be a touch darker. Teenagers and husbands go for tan. As the clock strikes 40, mothers take to total protection creams, make-up and the shade. Here a woman counts herself a success when she can swap clothes with her 20-year-old daughter – assuming they both wear size 8. There's no such thing as 'older fashions' any more.

So they bob around the powder room lending each other French slacks, sweaters and lipstick – these neo-siblings in whom the demarcations of age have been almost completely obliterated. They've all read the same psychology manuals so any slight hiccup in their mother-daughter alliances can be oozed over with sweet reason. Everyone's learned 'how to deal with it'; everyone knows 'how to handle it'. This is the new democracy where parents don't stand on their rights and children don't have any resentments left to nurse.

And yet underlying this familiar Utopia there's still trouble. Now the mothers can't relieve it by squabbling with their difficult, teeage daughters, now they've slimmed and trimmed themselves into a stage of youthful companionship with their husbands – now what?

A few bold free thinkers, finding time on their hands, occupy themselves by visiting hospitals and similar good works. The rest know they should be fulfilling themselves with jobs and earning money. But few of them relish the daily journey into metroland, few husbands would want them to do it, and the opportunities to work in the suburbs are less than limited. The answer is real estate.

Hang around the hair-dryer in the powder room for long enough and you'll hear the gossip about the latest of the ranks to succumb. Selling homes is the perfect refuge for divorced women whose alimony has been found wanting and for the older women whose children have taken off for college. It's a genteel way to have something to talk about, to fill the hours and, incidentally, to make money. Sell five desirable residences a year, and a woman has made the magical million-dollar turnover.

After a six-week, $110 course, a woman can sit the state licensing examination to qualify as a real estate sales associate. She still can't open an office, advertise under her own name or close her own deals. But if she can sell a million dollars worth of property, she can reckon on $20,000 profit for herself (half of her commission goes to the broker to whom she's attached).

Unfortunately, the whole thing's got out of hand. To say the least, this genteel occupation has become a hard-headed business. There are no lines drawn between business and pleasure (i.e. friendship); almost anything goes. Someone hears a friend's getting divorced; she'll be on to her at once asking if she can put her house on the market. Someone hears a friend's mother is dying; she'll be on the phone to see if she can handle the sale of the house. Here and there at supposedly social gatherings you'll hear 'If you ever want to sell . . . '

Some of the more delicate recruits from the powder room aren't sure they know 'how to deal' with that. 'All of a sudden,' confesses one of the latest entrants, 'when I'm at a party I'm having to say I'm in the business. I choke on it but I have to do it.' After all, a woman has to do what she has to do.

★　　　★　　　★

Women are learning to treat other women not as make-does for a fallow time but as preferred companions. The all-women dinner party is supplanting the gatherings of golden couplehood. The most interesting guests and conversations are to be found at the former. This is no bowl of soup affair or left-over cold cuts that women used to reserve for one another. 'Let's eat in the kitchen, it's only us,' is a remark from another state of mind. This is a full-blown best silver, latest *New York Times* recipes dinner. Beware single men of fifty – you who have dined out for years on your spare status ('just to make up the numbers'), frozen meals lie ahead.

How strange the way word spreads in New York. Perhaps when the *Times'* Living section writes up this new phenomenon of the women's dinner, they'll be doing it all over Darien, Connecticut. For the moment, it is something for women of a certain stage to go to and give.

Word has also spread that those women who dress up to eat steamed bass together also undress to steam together at the East Tenth Street Russian and Turkish Baths. It is the latest way to unwind for those women who wear briefcases or who have just dropped their doctoral theses to be typed.

The East Tenth Street Baths are a Lower East Side institution. Once they were a haven for the Jewish immigrant patriarchs, a moment of peace between peddling from barrows along Hester Street and ruling families in airless walk-ups. Six days a week they now cater for those men from corporations who like to sweat away the day's malevolence, gulp a whisky or two and swap jokes before setting out for some suburban, sward-surrounded spread. But Wednesday is different. Wednesday is for women.

Getting to 268 East Tenth is not for the frivolous. The taxis rolling up to the corner of First Avenue are a six-dollar ride away from the Upper East Side studios and Upper West Side homes of those they drop. This is not a neighbourhood to walk alone after dark. Its perfumes are not Cie, Babe or Cinnebar, but stale garbage and staler sweat. The worn steps and shabby facade of the baths are not promising. The crayon sign, '$7', inside the door is an emphatic contradiction to them. Although gay baths in New

York run at $35 (sightseers also risk being beaten up), seven dollars is steep enough to signal that only the privileged enter here.

Al Modlin, whose personality was obviously acquired for the raucous boys-only crowd, stands by the entrance taking money, handing out keys and looking not a little bewildered by the cool crowd to whom he is now host. As owner of the baths, he is evidently used to being treated as a New York character. On Wednesdays the women simply overlook him.

Two long lines of beds run down a darkened room with lockers between them. On these beds women gather to talk before going down to the baths in the basement. Protected still by pale blue, heavily laundered wraps, they talk over the week. From one corner, Iran, International Monetary Fund proceedings, energy. From another, the tale of a New York adventure, the man picked up in a jazz bar and taken home for the night. 'I don't care if I don't see him again. After five years of an el sicko relationship, it was so good to have someone be funny and warm in bed.' Man as a piece of fluff; woman as lone operator.

The baths downstairs are tiled and filled with women's bodies of all colours and not so many shapes. Towels are only for wrapping around hair oozing conditioner. Agnes stands out immediately. Hovering over her massage table, 21 stone of bulbous flesh and cellulite, she wears only plimsolls and a bandage for her varicose veins. Her popular seven-dollar oil massages (forget the words private parts) are interrupted as she ambles over to the door to kiss and greet regulars in broken but expressive English.

'What I love about being with women here,' says a reclining psychologist, 'is that the baths are a great leveller.' Far from it: the slender, lithe bodies with strap marks from Tobago or Jamaica stand in condemnation of those who have fallen into droop and swell. When Agnes started here eight years ago, her customers were old-timers. Today the average age is 30. High earners, out jogging before dawn, down here steaming after dark. The occasional woman with the predatory eye and carrying voice is subtly ostracized. In the steam room and sauna she always finds space around her. The nuances are those of a cavalry officers' mess. Everyone knows who is not 'one of us'.

How ironic that those grandmothers who came here once long, long ago knew instinctively what these MAs and PhDs have only now learned – that women need fellowship too.

'I went to see my grandmother over the weekend,' announces Michelle, 'and I told her I'd found these great baths and how good it is to hang out here. She said,"Michelle, leave me alone; I was going to the East Tenth Street Baths seventy years ago and believe me, we talked about life then too. So what's new?"'

Heroines

There are, or so it seems, two kinds of American heroine. There are those whose very gestures have magnitude, who reach out to touch the lives of others and, by so doing, change them. Leontyne Price, Bella Abzug, Barbara Jordan, Shirley Chisholm are among the names that come to mind.

This is the story of Patricia Panarella Rebraca. She is the other kind of American heroine, the woman who protects her own and goes unnoticed by all except those few to whom she devotes herself. She works eighteen hours a day, six days a week to build a life for her family. Hers is a heroism compounded of countless small deeds, of patience and love. The issues of the day have no place in the enclosed world for which she cares and fights.

Now it so happens that Panarella, as she is known, has recently become something of a celebrity on Columbus Avenue because she and her husband Nikola opened the latest and one of the best of those cafes so beloved of New Yorkers. There are akin to Viennese coffee-houses, a meeting place for endless, searching conversations, sweetened by a dozen or so kinds of cake. Chocolate, chocolate-chip layer cake, mocha Viennese torts, Black Forest cheese cake, La Bombe de Marron – rich, creamy confections washed down with as many different coffees and teas.

For those who can no longer afford to go out to dinner and who shrink from cheap, bare diners, this is a chance to have dessert in style. At Panarella's, each table has a pink linen cloth and a vase of fresh flowers: gladioli here, some tulips there. Downstairs in the corner is a large, refrigerated display case with banks of fresh flowers for sale. There are plants, too, that stand around a waterfall splashing gently into a pool set into the tiled floor.

There is a feeling of peace and beauty. It is a haven from the street outside, rumbling with trucks and discarded rubbish. The cafe is Panarella's dream, her way of keeping her family close and of offering hospitality to those who may become friends.

There was a time a few years ago, when she was briefly a Playboy bunny and even when she worked nights at O'Neal's Saloon, that Panarella was a typically pretty New Yorker. Stylish, slender, with an unlined face that spoke of a future, not a past, she looked like any other bright, hopeful West Side waitress taking acting and dancing lessons. At 33 she is still attractive but her face has settled; the 50-year-old woman that she will become is already there to see. The bones show more clearly; so do the patches of tiredness.

Once she lived for herself, now it is for others. She gets up at 6 a.m. to be with her 18-month-old son, Sergia. By 9 she is at work, buying, planning, cleaning, skimping on pennies as she has since she met Nikola eight years ago. They are at the cafe from noon till midnight six nights a week. (Monday is 'family day' – they shut the cafe and stay home with Sergia.) Usually they go to bed at 2 a.m. after doing the books and four hours later the day begins again. She washes, mends, tidies and tends these two worlds that are her whole world. So does youth pass.

It was just this way with her mother and, probably, with all the women of her family stretching back into the villages of Poland and southern Italy from which her mother and father's people came. 'You don't get anything without working for it,' her father used to say. 'The first thing is to love each other and to work hard together and that's how you are happy.'

When she was born, her father worked in the steel mill that owned their Pennsylvania town. Her uncles and cousins had jobs there too, as did all the men of the town. One year it closed. The men waited. And waited. It stayed closed for two years. Those were especially hard times.

'I remember waking up at 4 one morning because I could hear my parents downstairs in the kitchen. I went down to find them in old work clothes getting ready to go out. They were working as janitors in an old pool-hall so that we'd have clothes and food and we children didn't even know. They took me with them that night because I was so upset and frightened that they were leaving us. I remember helping them to scrub the floor and being ashamed that I had not known. My parents were so proud.

'When the mill closed it was difficult for everyone. We all sat down at the kitchen table and agreed that we had to make our own way. I was 13 then and got a job as a short-order cook in a diner. I worked from 6 in the evening until 4 in the morning. It wasn't very nice and I got burned a lot. I earned 60 cents an hour and it helped.

'Both Nikola and I come from hard-working people. Neither one of us has any money in our families. We know no one is ever going to give us anything so we put as much of ourselves as we can into our business. We save every cent we can and don't buy anything unless we can afford it. It isn't the modern way but it's the only way we know.'

★   ★   ★

Reports vary about exactly what happened at Mozart Hall, East 86th Street one night in May 1978. According to Louis C. Sanzo, he called the meeting to order at seven or five past. By 7.30 the eleven officers of Local 29 of the Blasters, Drillrunners and Miners Union had been nominated and elected strictly according to the constitution.

Ten of the officers were incumbents. Sanzo, president, business manager and trustee, was re-elected unopposed according to the minutes kept by his colleague and childhood friend, Adadio 'Sonny' Petito. Sanzo, 42, would continue to enjoy his $700-a-week salary, 1978 Cadillac (insurance and gasoline paid) and the responsibility of heading a small construction workers' union with only 400 members but an $8 million pension and welfare fund. Not bad for a man who started building work at 16 as a powder monkey on the New England Thruway.

The problem was Charles Smith, a patient man who has been fighting his union leaders so long that his copy of the constitution has grown dog-eared and yellow. The election, he claimed, was fixed; the meeting over in minutes. For the first time since 1955, his protests took effect. On 28 December 1979, after months of investigation, the US Department of Labour took the union to court and the election was declared invalid. The case succeeded through the tenacity and courage of those concerned – not least, Joyce Cole.

Not every bookkeeper, a woman – and a black woman at that – would take the stand as a government witness against a union. Cole testified that Sanzo had told her of his 'arrangements' for the election, revealed details of the union organization and confirmed a pre-meeting meeting that took place on 4 May 1978: Donny Jnr. and Bobby Maglione came with their father Don Maglione Snr., Louis Messina, Sam Caveliari with his uncle, and Sanzo's brother-in-law, Ed Brenta. With her testimony, the pattern of conspiracy took shape.

Charles Smith is in the American Tradition, the loner battling for his rights, standing up to organized power. Joyce Cole doesn't fit in. She was a bystander; it wasn't her cause, wasn't her fight.

She lives by herself in an old East Side apartment that has become her private kingdom. It is a mass of objects; a huge colonial mantelpiece, plants, crystal ashtrays, art books, brandy balloons, pink damask armchairs, floor cushions in silver lurex, fur and satin. In a corner stands a Venus de Milo.

Cole seems an unlikely heroine. She has the presence of a knowing rock star, working her false eyelashes, bright eyes and long hands for their full worth. She is an unusual woman indeed, and this is her story.

'I was born in Quitman, Georgia, in 1937, the youngest of seven. My mother died when I was two; my father was an alcoholic. I first remember living with a girlfriend of my father but after a few years, my grandfather found me and took me away.

'He was half Indian, my grandfather, with white hair that blew in the wind when he walked. He was about seven feet tall and took size 16 shoes. He was a giant in every way. When he ploughed the fields I'd walk with him and ask him about the soil and all that grew in the fields and what made life. I always wanted to make my steps as big as Grandpa's.

'When I was about five or six, I worked in the fields picking cotton. Living in a small southern town like that, being poor and black there was only the fields. Most of the times you'd start at sun-up, five or six in the morning, and go till sundown. We made 25 cents a barrel and I was just a little kid so it might take me all day to fill one. If Grandma decided today you went to school, you went to school but if Grandma decided today you went to work, you went to work.

'My grandparents were getting old so I was sent to New York to my sister. She and her husband lived on 7th Avenue and 120th Street, three of us in one room. It was a big apartment and each room was let out to different families. I was ten. I started having sex with a lot of the men there. I would assume now that I needed affection. It wasn't for the sex; I didn't like it then and I still don't.

'I stayed with my sister until I was 13. It was hell. We didn't like each other at all. I ran away and I've been on my own ever since. I had $20 to my name when I left so I lived in one room in Brooklyn and worked for a bakery part-time after school. After about a month my sister had me picked up by the police. She wanted me put in a home but the manager of the bakery took responsibility for me so I could go to school and work.

'I started modelling then which was pretty gruesome. I was grabbing at everything I could, grabbing at surviving. But I must have been okay inside because I still went to school and kept the job at the bakery and I never got into trouble. My grandpa always said to me, "Never accept just existing, always hold on to living."

'I graduated, and had a job as bookkeeper to a wholesale grocer for seven years. I taught myself how to run an office and then I knew, "Now, I can look after Joyce." I've done a lot of things since then. I've made some fantastic money and I've lost some fantastic money.

'In 1974 I had cancer. Can you see this scar on my abdomen? Or this on my throat? No, that's how lucky I've been. Illness is an attitude and I'm over it now. But I was getting old anyway. I went to an agency to find a job and the agent had this one with the union. "You won't like it," he said, "it's all men." I thought that couldn't be bad and the benefits were good. So I started as bookkeeper at $200 a week.

'From the moment I was hired, I didn't ask any questions. I was too smart. It was really nice in that office. The president, Sanzo, trusted me and talked to me and the men liked me because they didn't have to watch their mouths – the kind of men who run unions aren't churchgoers. We were a good group. I loved the job but when it came to it, I had to tell what I knew. Here were the members being ripped off by the people they were paying to help them and I resented that. There were just things I thought were wrong.

'Sure I was frightened when I got home and found a message on my machine, "If you don't stop testifying against the union, you're going to find yourself in a box." But if you're going to kill someone, I reckon you do it, you don't leave a message about it.

'Everybody asks why am I doing this. Why does there always have to be a why if anyone ever does anything? There's destiny; why should there also be a reason? Why is it not acceptable that this is what I want to do? And if doing what I want to do is my definition of right and wrong and I get killed in the process, so be it.

'My life hasn't been tough; it's been inconvenient sometimes. But in my lifetime I've done an awful lot for myself, I think I've done magnificent things for myself. Just being and turning out the way I am is fantastic. I've lived to be 43, I like myself and I apologize to no one for what I am, have been or might become.'

The federal case continues.

New York moods

It is wonderfully hot in New York in winter. Temperatures of 75 and 80°F are not uncommon. There is no need for flannel nightdresses, woolly dressing-gowns, or even slippers. The flimsiest polyester will do for dinner. Outside, of course, it is miserably cold. But after November, the outdoors is merely something one crosses en route to some other indoors. New Yorkers and the squirrels in Central Park understand each other very well.

In London, people walk around, look in shop windows and catch buses with a hole in the back. The slightest suspicion of wintry air is enough to send a true New Yorker straight to the kitchen to reach for the 1000 mg Vitamin C bottle. New York buses have sliding windows that do not open in summer because of air conditioning and cannot be opened in winter because of heating. There is a certain yellow, white and green complexion that can be seen every night around 6 o'clock, swaying and faint on the Madison Avenue bus. It is the face of a physically and emotionally overheated society.

It is divisive, this heat. People who work in warm offices and go home to warm apartments meet only those who exist in similarly warm boxes. In winter, the middle classes hibernate. It can be no coincidence that in summer there is much talk of the wretchedness of the South Bronx and Harlem, while in winter hardly a word. They are forgotten and left cold with neglect, despair and rage. The energy crisis means nothing to those with no heat and nothing to those who take that heat for granted.

When day breaks after a heavy snowfall, Manhattan wakes up to the clanging of shovels on sidewalks and the splatter of salt on newly cleared and shiny concrete. By 11 o'clock as luminous snowbanks line the roads, the neighbourhood creeps out to inspect the wonder left behind by the dark night.

There is nothing like a good snowfall to make a New Yorker feel pleased with life. Nothing cheers like the thought of all those wheels turning helplessly out in the suburbs, that land of watered lawns and summer pools. Here in the white, hushed city, everything the heart desires is but a shuffle away along those sidewalks which shopkeepers and doormen are required by law to keep spanking clean.

It is the moment for settling old scores. Gruff restaurateurs and stuck-up brownstone owners may find the slightest streak of ice left before their building to be an excuse for an outraged phone call to the necessary authority. It is amazing how people somehow sniff their way through the labyrinth of City Hall to find exactly the right place for a complaint.

New Yorkers love to call down the wrath of the law. When a roof tank water pipe freezes in an apartment building, half the tenants are bribing the staff to carry buckets of water for them to and from the basement supply while the other half are phoning their lawyers to see whether they can withhold rent and sue besides.

For all that they are supposed to be 'crisis-orientated' and boast of living under perilous conditions, New Yorkers actually fall apart under the slightest strain that has not been planned for. It is only to be expected, perhaps. How much pressure can be withstood by those who swallow Vitamin C and B Complex stress pills just to manage the everyday routine?

The interruption to the building's water-supply has been revealing indeed. It has not, after all, been that terrible. True enough, at such moments there's not much to be done about a dishwasher, washing machine, Jacuzzi fitment or massage shower head. The art of bucket flushing took a while to master although health club freaks have been crowing about not having to bother. ('Thank heavens for muscle control.') But the rides to the basement are snug and, by way of compensation, the super has at last turned on the heat at night.

Talk in the elevator, however, has been mutinous. Some have

deputed lawyers to research the possibility of suing on the grounds that men are not working through the night in the driving blizzard on the roof. ('If you pay, you can get anyone to do anything,' the New York gospel.)

Some tenants, of course, have simply vanished. 'How can I be expected to live like this?' whimpered more than one faintheart, as if a frozen pipe was a personal betrayal by the landlord. 'How can this happen to me?' cried other egomaniacs, most of them on their way out to hotels. Some have adopted hardship costumes, wandering around in battle fatigues and voluminous scarves. Others have had the vapours, trailing down to the basement in dressing-gowns all day as if life itself has frozen. This latter approach has not been encouraged by the super. Unloved at the best of times, he has known not to show his face too often. When he has, it has been conspicuously covered in thick bristle as though Mrs Super has not been boiling water like everyone else.

And amid all the carryings on, histrionics and mutterings at the Front, it took a while for the real news to get around – that Irving had reappeared at the corner stationery store. In the years to come, when survivors of the neighborhood look back, they will surely remember the particular smell and feel of Irving and Henry's Park Stationery.

On the wet mornings when brown cardboard goes down to protect the smudgy grey and black floor and the air is thick with the smell of damp coats and scarves, there is always someone in need of some curious-sized envelope or type of refill that only the owners can find amid the jumble on the 400 or so shelves lining the walls.

Here amid the candies, papers, books, cards, toys, pads and dusty Halloween masks, Irving and Henry have stood and bickered and scurried together for twenty-two years. Irving is thin now; he sports a succession of jaunty hats instead of the long silver hair he lost with chemotherapy. Henry watches the shops. His sons, one a teacher, another a psychiatrist, come in on Saturdays more to show love than to help.

Henry, brusque and suspicious, has a sadder, gentler air. His eyes follow Irving with affection behind his thick glasses. 'What can I tell you?' says Henry, taking the change from the old cash register. 'What can I tell you?' echoes Irving, reaching for some special prize high on the wall.

They come here from the water crisis to buy papers and cigarettes before going to breakfast next-door. They bring their woes to Henry and Irving as they have for so long. What can no water mean to Irving, back for an hour or two just to be with Henry? What can it mean to his partner who came through concentration camps in Europe to build a new life for his family and with his friend?

★   ★   ★

Now that the days are warm again, sex is back on the streets of New York. Outside is no longer a mere conduit for woolly-bundled travellers scurrying between over-heated boxes hoping to achieve some miraculous arrangement of face and form in trundling elevators at their destination. Street life has resumed with all its buzzing and excitement; sex has made its annual reappearance.

In New York, in summer, people do not dress for those whom they are off to meet but for those whom they might get to know along the way. It becomes a city of bright plumage, of exotic creatures dipping and diving along the sidewalks, each flashing colour and consciousness. If there are any drab, mousy relics of good taste, garbed in discreet and sensible cottons, they vanish into concrete undergrowth. Summer in Manhattan is a neon moment that dazzles and delights.

All those cut-price winter subscriptions to health studios, aerobic classes and movement groups, all those well-thumbed paperback copies of *How to Flatten Your Stomach*, lead to this feverish instant in May when smooth and slender thighs suddenly escape outdoors beneath scarlet shorts and royal-blue mini skirts.

Let it not be thought that Ralph Lauren with his layered, understated preppy elegance is a 'New York' designer. He is for those who have already started their flight to weekend nooks or are looking forward to an August spent in Maine with its icy Atlantic waters and aristocratic hauteur. His is just not a look for hot Saturdays in the park, for roller skating, steel drum bands, salsa on Sony Walkmen. Clothes go to Maine, costumes are for New York during these months of carnival.

Summer is the great equalizer; there is no way to buy stage presence or a sense of theatre and that, after all, is what street life is about – it's a gigantic theatre without walls. Those dinky shops on the East Side, with their skirts and shirts that are but a stab at colour and cut, cannot put together a syle that is basically rooted in another, alien culture. The look of the street draws its vibrancy from the Caribbean, from those steaming islands where all is drama – legacy of so many in this city.

There is a beautiful irony in the fact that those who can afford to spend most can probably pull it off least successfully. All those Muffies with their Palm Beach winter tans and Locust Valley lockjaw, rushing into Laura Ashley to stock up on $80 tropical skirts, simply cannot emulate a look that is instinctive to those for whom Haiti means something more than the latest amusing hideaway. Heartening as it is to see the once-deserted Laura Ashley shop on Madison Avenue aflutter with American Express gold cards, it is not exactly the stuff of life in New York fashion terms.

The clue is in its changing rooms where a 'decorator's touch' bentwood hat-stand and linen-covered knick-knack table add a certain lofty look to the tiny, overcrowded space. Here strangers dress and undress with the exquisite etiquette that dictates that at moments like this, others do not exist. Body space is carefully apportioned so that even elbows never jar, bare flesh is never thrust before another's eyes which, in any case, would be carefully averted.

It is no mean feat to slither in and out of clothes here without giving offence to some nearby island of privacy. Silence is the rule, apart from occasional mutterings from some mama hovering in a corner over her braying, debutante daughter: 'The purple one is my birthday present and if you want to use aunty's birthday money for that other one, I'm sure it will be very useful.' Useful? The very word gives all away. What place is there for the merely functional in the heady celebration of the seasons that is taking place outside?

The look of summer is first and last to do with sex at its most immediate. In the various discount emporiums where the hot and funky shop, this sense communicates itself immediately. Here there are no cool and competent salesladies watching over their commission tally, only those who are themselves engaged in the dance and its fever. It is perhaps the one arena in the city where the much-vaunted sisterhood, all that linking across racial and economic lines, actually exists.

Faded white middle-class mothers, bulging over their C-section scars, college students with allowances from daddy in Cleveland, sassy blacks forgetting the ever encroaching menace of welfare cuts – old, young, fat, thin, firm and wobbly, they all come together in a kind of sweaty, locker-room camaraderie comparing breasts, cellulite, backsides with careless and open curiosity.

It is a constant puzzle to frequenters of such stores that all stores are not like this. Why would anyone who could on Columbus Avenue pay $40 for the latest Bis of Paris and Beverly Hills blue denim prairie skirt, be prepared on Madison Avenue to pay $90 for the exact same item? Take Liz Claiborne jeans: $50 in Saks Fifth Avenue, $20 in Nice Stuff on Columbus. Same label, different shopping bag. There are fewer clothes where it's fancy, of course, but plunging into a jumble of rails where Daniel Hechter powder-blue lounging knickerbockers are packed against outrageous jumpsuits of diaphanous turquoise is all part of the performance.

In the changing room lined with harshly-honest mirrors – no subtle backlighting here – the chorus puffs and giggles and shares its all. 'Baby, baby, not the yellow.' 'That's hot shit – take it and don't eat for a month.' 'Honey, you can't – those pants are stuffed up your ass.' Those who cannot stand the instant intimacy flee, never to return, but then they were never meant to be here. Barriers drop, niceties fall away. Janice, the manageress, jewelled bandana momentarily curled around her head, sails in followed by a swarm of quivering attendants bearing garments for a still diffident mouse in the corner. 'Forget everything you've picked out – these are what you need. Try them. Trust me, baby. I just want to see you happy.'

Bags bulging with cottons from Paris, silks from Korea, muslins from Mexico, they pour out of the door onto Columbus as dusk folds around the sidewalk and sirens wail past. 'Hi, honey, how are things?' the calls go out. Things are hot. It's summer on the streets of New York.

★   ★   ★

In summer the magic people come out to play on the streets of New York. The worthy ones, bankers, businessmen, middle-aged sturdies, are shut away behind the throb of air-conditioning, off in the country, gone to Europe or Colorado. This is the special time that young and old come out of hiding to live out their fantasies on hot, hard sidewalks from which they have no escape.

Suddenly the city is covered in chairs. From high walk-ups, old women, faded and parchment-pale, drag down rickety kitchen seats to rest on front steps, watching the children whoop under fire hydrants. The gutters rush with water as children scamper to and fro beneath the illicit torrents that they have released and kindly (or resigned) policemen drive by and pretend that they haven't noticed.

From those who may never see a day by the neighbouring ocean, there are squeals as cold splashes on to hot, dusty bodies. Occasionally some interfering busybody, seeing the city's life-blood drain so carelessly away, will stop to lecture on such selfish acts of vandalism and the old women mutter helplessly in protection, picking at the drooping stockings that they can no longer handle in their infirm loneliness.

But for this moment, they are part of the busy life on the streets, handing out candies bought from meagre savings to small excited children, making believe that they are part of this large, summer family.

Along the traditional shopping roads from Broadway on the Upper West Side to the narrow lanes of the Lower East Side, old shopkeepers rescue dusty chairs from behind laden counters to sit outside bidding a good day to those who pass and browse.

This may be the last generation that will see those small, cluttered New York shops in which a lifetime has passed. The stock on the shelves, some of it as old as the owner, is as familiar to him as the stains on his now gnarled hands. Only habit pushes back the iron gate across his window each morning. What else should he do with his time?

A browser is at least a conversation. For the rare customer, he slowly wraps a substantial parcel of thick brown paper and string taking pride as he thinks of the department stores and their cheap, flimsy bags. There is no room now in the city for the small, old-fashioned shopkeeper, collecting bits of everything without logic and eventually managing to sell some.

Rents double and quadruple; talk is of realizing a six-week turnover of stock and optimum selling capacity per square foot. The one who for fifty years has sold bric-a-brac, an honest pine chest, a teacup or two, has lost to the fanciful boutiques that display and price the same items as though they were works of art.

But a few old-timers linger. What was once a living is now an empty routine. Memories and hopes are buried among the jumble. Wives have passed on. Sitting outside the doorway, looking back over fifty, maybe sixty, summers passed this way, the old shopkeepers remember another age as the young go by in their satin shorts.

The chairs have come out too, along the streets of converted brownstone houses. Yellow and white folding beachchairs appear under pots of scarlet geraniums hanging joyfully from windowsills. ('Someone has stolen our beautiful flowers,' reads one note taped to a sad, bare pot, 'but we shall be back. Smile – it makes the day brighter.') Through windows open wide can be glimpsed framed posters of dreamed-about Greek islands. The sound of Mozart quartets wafts over jungles of exotic green plants in the hope of nurturing new and harmonious shoots. The studio singles persist in their attempts to bring to this fierce city summer some imagined Mediterranean peace.

It is the image of the Mediterranean, heritage of so many New Yorkers, that is behind the recent sprouting of white tables and chairs outside cafes along the West Side. It is as if the long war between cafe owners and planning officials has collapsed in the exhausted surrender of the latter. It is illegal to set up outside tables without a licence. It is impossible to get such a licence. Outside tables must be totally enclosed by fixed glass walls thus, of course, reducing them to inside tables.

But this year, for the first time, it is as if Columbus Avenue has, of one mind, simply decided to ignore the petty tyrants of City Hall. There is no longer a cafe with its summer offerings of $5.95 spinach salad and $2.50 Key Lime pie that does not have its scattering of crowded tables across the sidewalk.

Of an evening, the young West Siders gather over a glass of Perrier – lowly executive suits changed for spanking white trousers and T-shirts. Hispanic families, giggling and chattering, promenade along the Avenue. The building superintendents, in natty straw hats, greet their handymen, transformed in best cream suits. And as the life of the summer streets hums and bustles through the image of dusk, it is possible to pretend, just for a second, that Manhattan is indeed some far away island where all is harmony.

★   ★   ★

At about 5 o'clock on a Friday afternoon it is possible to sense a little something in the air. Those for whom days flow seamlessly into one another will stop in the street and look around wondering whether the wind has dropped or whether some other climatic diversion is responsible for this feeling of change.

Slowly the clues stand out. George the Florist has buckets of roses on special, Harvey the Cleaner is packed with customers collecting chinos and down jackets, Tomasita in the Puerto Rican-Chinese laundry is taking in mounds of shirts for medium starch. The TV guide is the news vendors' hot item. A line has formed by the bank's outdoor cash machine. So there it is: it must be the weekend.

Every city has its own special atmosphere when the week's work is done and the days of rest approach. In New York the weekend is not so much longed for as tumbled across as if by accident. Perhaps because this is a place where so many are out of work or resting, the overwhelming feeling is one of disappointment: two days in which no one will call or return calls.

Perhaps because so many here are lonely, there is a sense of depression. Ahead lie three nights of prime-time TV, *The Incredible Hulk*, *The Loveboat* and *Fantasy Island*. On weekends psychotherapists are not available (there is a Manhattan condition known as Saturday anxiety); paid helpers expect time off; children are out of school. For some it is a reminder that there are no demands; for others it is a time to complain bitterly that there are so many.

What New Yorkers really want out of a weekend is two days in bed with nurturing – checking into a hospital would be ideal. So there is much going away on impulse to hotels where others clean the room and go out in the cold for the Sunday *New York Times*. At this time of the year a lot is made of needing to see the fall leaves in the country. Doubtless Connecticut is magnificent right now in its plump vermillion and yellow plumage, but so too is Central Park.

For those who cannot afford some cheap rural inn or converted baronial spread in upstate New York, there are substitutes. The answering machine is one: 'I'm sorry but we are not accepting calls right now. Perhaps you would leave your name and number and we'll get back to you,' is a common weekend greeting.

And then there is the croissant. The croissant is Manhattan's national dish. It has everything, this flakey piece of pastry. Forbidden calories suggest a riot of freedom for those who all week are accustomed to biting on something thin, hard and ungiving in keeping with the lives they lead. In bedrooms given over to filing cabinets, video machines and metal storage units, the croissant brings dreams of sun-dappled attic rooms in Paris, lovers and romance.

There is no tradition of the weekend joint of beef in Manhattan, of the honest potato and gravy steaming in the jug. There is only this croissant, warm, illusory and oozing butter, suggesting the endless breakfast and a day lost in a haze of orange juice or bloody Marys, with greasy thumb prints on the Lanz of Salzburg flannel nightdress. The croissant is a Me food – to each her own, nothing to share and no one else to demand the best bits.

The weekend is the time for relationships which is what busy New Yorkers experience in place of friendship. The casual give and take of friends, the continuity over time and change become too complicated for those accustomed to shedding lives like skin. Relationships are easy: they exist out of time and place in depths of the inner Me and the new You.

Those engaged in them do not make demands like, 'Will you have my children for the day?' or 'May I borrow your car?' They indulge in intense talk and a chemistry that allows fantasies to bloom and then, fortunately, wither, so that new relationships may be engaged upon with all the mystery of the unknown. Relationships mean being loved and appreciated and sharing an ashtray of low-tar menthol cigarette butts.

Friendship means making an effort reserved usually for those who might be needed later for passing on work or a better job. The office ethic ('I like you until you get fired') permeates a culture that understands but one foreign phrase: *quid pro quo*.

So the weekend is a time when those who are alone wish that they were not and when those surrounded by others talk wistfully of Being Alone. And in the playgrounds in the park the results of this dichotomy are there in all their confusion. These are father's days on the swings and slides when those with visitation rights try to recapture the familiarity of daily life.

Voices are too loud, encouragement too hearty, the newest Marx motorbikes stand out for the bribes they are. On the side benches sit the newest relationships, trying not to look bored or resentful and wondering whether croissants and chemistry were really meant to lead to this. But Monday will come around, telephones will ring again, and everyone will soon be back on hold.

Survivors

There is an advertisement, particularly dear to New Yorkers, that depicts an unnamed personality swathed in Blackglama mink against the headline: 'What becomes a legend most?' Perhaps New Yorkers love it so because it is as much a tribute to survival as to anything else: Lauren Bacall, Lillian Hellman, Barbra Streisand – not necessarily the most talented but among the most hardy, certainly.

America yearns for some at least to stay the course. This must be why an endless parade of fat, divorce-bedraggled stars still parade across the television screen crooning into the soft sentimental patch that is the American heart. Sitcoms and costly series appear and vanish within weeks but Perry Como on prime time is still an event. Mel ('The Velvet Fog') Torme, that 1940s teen heart throb, still fills Carnegie Hall. Tony Bennett, with improbably black locks and tan, endures, and even Rosemary Clooney, encased in a voluminous kaftan that is more than amply filled, still tours to the delight of those who want to remember when.

The point about such entertainers seems to be that they really should look appreciably worse for wear. Those who come to hear them, who come to be moved by memories of an innocence that they fondly imagine once existed, need the reassurance that even long-ago idols bear the marks of time. Why else would June Allyson, once a blonde sweetheart, now in late middle-age, crop up as often on made-for-TV movies in which her character is grateful for any man not actually in his dotage?

Nostalgia buffs, then, who appreciate that America's thirst for the new is exquisitely balanced with its longing for the old, have become used to the posters and display ads announcing this or that name from the past. Alberta Hunter, 87, is at the Cookery. Lena Horne's 'The Lady and Her Music is a Broadway hit. Lauren Bacall and Mickey Rooney have their own shows. And Astrud Gilberto is now appearing at Marty's.

The legendary Astrud Gilberto – a name to sigh over from the early sixties indeed. 'The Girl from Ipaneema', 'One-note Samba', 'The Shadow of your Smile' – tens of millions of records sold all over the world, and always this gentle, guileless voice moving across the notes like liquid.

She was protégé and wife of Brazil's two great musicians – Jaoa Gilberto and Antonio Carlos Jobim. But that was a long, long time ago, and all that lingers is an image of a tiny, shy Brazilian waif standing almost motionless and singing beautifully. How odd suddenly to come across her name plastered to the damp, grey walls of New York between announcements of flute debut recitals and off-off Broadway experiments.

Marty's is something of a Manhattan oddity. It is a medium-priced restaurant on Third Avenue that has a small supper room given over to entertainment. The building is new and the restaurant feels almost worryingly so – not a left-over speck on a tablecloth anywhere, nor a scratch on a knife. There is that utterly instant feeling.

But this is Mel Torme's regular New York club date, and Carmen McRae and Vic Damone come here to sing of long-ago loves across the requisite smoke-filled room. 'Club', of course, is a misnomer: there are no nightclubs left to speak of, except in Las Vegas. The singers became too expensive (spoiled as they were by gambling casino showcases and TV) and audiences stayed home.

Marty's is the next generation: no razzmatazz, no tables for 450 in tux and dinner dresses, just a small roomful of people who look like the contents of a package tour to Aruba. They know value; they don't know glamour. They munch solidly from unblemished plates waiting for the lights to dim and the show to start, while upstairs the owner, Marty Ross, a 46-year-old ex-investment banker, says his prayers knowing that each time the drummer lays a stick on skins, the insomniac in his flat above will reach for the phone.

Miss Gilberto is in shiny black trousers and matching zip-up jogging jacket. She wears white plastic earrings and high-heeled black sandals. At 42 she looks like any New Yorker – young, skinny, wise, foolish and hopeful all at once. She walks in through a door almost as if intruding on the crowded room. There is no sense of an entrance, as there will be no exit. She hardly speaks during her show – no reminiscences, no cosy bouts of chatter. But when she sings it is eerie: her voice floats as it always did over songs that are haunting. It is as if nothing has changed in twenty years.

In her dressing-room between shows she sits on a low sofa glued to television. She can't think of anything to say of the years that have passed. There have been husbands (two or three), houses (seven or eight) and now she lives alone in a Greenwich Village sublet getting used to being single again in New York. One son, Marcelo, plays guitar in her group. Another, Gregory, now 13, chose to live with his father.

When Marcelo Gilberto was a baby, she was at the height of her success. She had left his father, and she took Marcelo with her everywhere. 'They were not very happy times with me, I remember only being very confused and that personally my life was a mess.' For six years she didn't sing at all but lived in the suburbs somewhere being someone's wife ('I liked to clean the house, cook dinner . . . ').

It is disorientating: a voice that is literally from the past, and this slim, elfin woman from the Village who owns no past and is starting again from the beginning. But in a way, how appropriate. Astrud Gilberto is a New Yorker now, and for New Yorkers there are only beginnings.

★   ★   ★

If there are New Yorkers into whose lives a little Luba Potamkin has not yet fallen, it must be said that there cannot be many of them. Her nightly appearances on television, glowing, in chiffon, silk, lurex, sequins, beading, jungle prints and sable, make wonderful viewing.

Luba is one of the stars thrown up by the new wave of

commercials in which those who own the shops, run the companies or make the goods appear on screen to do the selling and lap up the attention. Thus we have grandpa Carvel spluttering and fluffing his lines about Carvel ice-cream, Fred the furrier from Alexander's ('Ann, Barbara, Emily, Susan, I'm still waiting for YOOOOOOOOUUUUUUUU . . .'), Frank Perdue and his chickens and, above all, Victor Potamkin's wife, Luba.

In some 200 commercials, Luba has exhorted New York to buy her husband's Cadillacs. And since everyone knows that Victor Potamkin didn't get to be the largest Cadillac dealer in America through being a softy, it can be reasonably assumed that Luba moves cars.

When she isn't in her penthouse condominium in Miami Beach, where she makes commercials for son Alan's Chevrolets, or in Philadelphia, where she makes commercials for son Robert's Chevrolets, Luba can be found in New York at the luxury Regency Hotel on Park Avenue in the two-bedroom, two-bathroom suite that she calls home.

A phone call to her there revealed the (by now) famous husky voice and a confiding friendliness. 'Guess what, honey? I'm going out at eight so I'll have to start putting on my make-up at five and without make-up, dear, we're not a very pretty girl.' Mrs Potamkin was in New York to grace the annual auto show at which a husband-and-wife boxing team would stage an exhibition fight one lunch-time by way of encouraging the sale of motor cars.

The next morning she was in a black leather pants suit. 'Why, you're just a child. Guess what, honey, Victor is going to be so happy when I tell him. Have some fresh fruit? Let me show you the closets I've built here.' There followed a tour of her wardrobes, Victor's keep-fit machine, the bathroom, the ice-box with diet cookies and her photograph albums. Luba Potamkin is 57. Until Victor decided that no beautiful, young model was as classy, yea, as Cadillac, as his wife, she hadn't worked since they were married.

'I'm a middle-aged woman but I feel like a girl and I have had the most wonderful, celebrated life because of my husband,

Victor, to whom I have been married for thirty-seven years and my fine sons. I adore doing the television commercials for my wonderful husband, Victor, and my fine sons, Alan and Robert. It is the greatest stimulation in life, dear, to do things for your family.' Luba was in full flow.

'When I first met my wonderful husband, he was in the fish business and then he moved into chickens. It was hard then. And it was a different world, dear; we all stayed home and took care of our children. Guess what? My husband is now a very, very rich man. He has millions and millions of dollars. I can hardly believe that he is such a rich man.

'I look wonderful at night, honey, and best on a bed naked. Here, give me your hands, honey. Feel my breasts, can you feel those muscles? I'll show you my exercises. I do this one a hundred times a day and since I've started it, my bust is a quarter bigger. You have no idea what I do. Here feel this. No stomach. Nothing. I'm tight. I'm tough.

'Guess what, my mother is 90 years old and she's a dying woman. It's very sad. My daddy is 87 and he's started to go to Spanish classes. He says that when she goes, he'll find a young Spanish woman to marry. Isn't that wonderful? My family is everything to me. Are you married? What a pity. I would have liked to introduce you to my wonderful son, Alan. I'd like him to get married. Like that if he should get a little bit sick, I'd know someone would take care of him.

'Here, you see this sweater. It's just $3.50 in Alexanders. I'm a funny girl and yet, dear, I can spend a fortune too. See this dress? I am so in love with it, it's really my style. How much do you think it cost? $33. Do you know a woman called me yesterday and said to me, "Mrs Potamkin, I want to tell you how much I admire you and could you tell me which doctor did your facelift?" Here, honey, look, I've never had anything. Still, if I had my neck done like this, see, wouldn't I look like a young woman? What do you think? That's why I always wear low-cut dresses. When they're looking at my cleavage, they don't notice my neck.

'What can I give you? I want to give you a present. Here, you must take this book. It was written by my dear friend Jacqueline

Susann. Hey, I'm going to show you something I showed Liz Taylor. See this lipstick? It has a hairpin in it. You take out the hairpin and it's much easier to put on your lipstick with the wrong end of the pin. That's our secret now. Here, I have something else. It's a note my wonderful husband wrote to me, I'll read it to you. It says: "Luba, I love you. Call me when you wake up".'

There was a final whoop down the corridor before the elevator door closed. 'You know Victor's going to be so happy when I tell him about our little talk.'

Of course she sells cars. Who could resist Luba?

★   ★   ★

Nannette Glushak, one leg in a cast, hobbles along the street. Her cocker spaniel, one leg in a cast, hobbles behind. The juxtaposition of the tubby, willing dog and his ethereal mistress sharing their common misfortune brings a sense of mischief to the grim, wintry sidewalk. Passers-by smile and cab drivers screech to a stop with gallant panache. Miss Glushak, as befits a ballerina, acknowledges the fun with a slight tilt of her pale exquisite face.

It is one thing for civilians, as Miss Glushak terms all the rest of us who are not dancers, to tear ligaments and cartilage in the knee. It is another kind of nightmare for her. If there is a Polish proverb about lightening always striking twice, she is its proof.

Behind Miss Glushak and Sabaka the dog comes her husband, John Prinz, his normally dashing figure hunched with concern. Ballet fans of New York still lament that piece of buckled linoleum on a stage in Los Angeles on which John Prinz's exciting and dramatic career snapped with his achilles' tendon.

To understand what such an injury does to a star of the New York City Ballet and American Ballet Theatre, it is necessary to grasp what being such a star means in this town of balletomanes. John Prinz was part of that generation of handsome, vital young men who brought glamour to dancing. He and colleagues like Edward Vilella went out into the high schools, carrying their glowering good looks before them, telling of what it was like to lift beautiful women, of the athletic muscle that made possible the impassioned embraces. The way they told it, it was as good as baseball.

John Prinz was known to be wild, headstrong, rebellious. The son of an immigrant railroad man, he'd grown up on the rough side of Chicago as the toughest fighter on the block and some of that daring, that defiance still clung. His private world, the one of secret childhood ballet lessons, extraordinary discipline and artistic dreams, was always tempered by this image of sensuality and energy. In short, the message came, ballet was no longer for cissies.

New York became a city of ballet freaks, addicts and groupies. Ballet was no longer just an art form but the epitome of everything that was young, thin, beautiful, driving and very, very sexy. Perhaps the dancers reflected some of this fever; the companies, unsubsidized and aggressive, certainly did. There was no nurturing in the Royal Ballet School, no protection beneath the company's benign wing. 'In America,' says Prinz, 'you're in a state of constant paranoia. Do they like me? Don't they like me? You audition every day. You're in one minute, out the next.'

But John Prinz wasn't the victim of disfavour or infighting. One night he was a star, the next day he was at home on crutches. He spent a year there, reading and thinking. 'My rebirth', he calls it now. He spent three gruelling years of getting back into shape, but by then it was too late. His back was bad, Baryshnikov and Bujones had arrived, he was getting old. In 1979, aged 33, he left American Ballet Theatre. 'When it's over, there's nothing in this country to protect you. No matter who you are, what you've done, no one cares. You're dealing with the world after all those years of nothing but ballet, with people who don't understand and don't give a damn.'

He was not totally alone. There was Nannette Glushak, the dancer from the City Ballet corps who went to live with him at 16 and married him when she was 18 in 1970. She continued to dance, became a soloist with ABT and prima ballerina in Cleveland when her husband was ballet master there. And now she too is hobbling around on her husband's old crutches, somehow laughing at herself and the absurdity of it all.

Strangely, this is not a black story. Prinz has discovered another talent – as a teacher.

'It took me a long while to come around to teaching – at one point I even went to bartending school. You dance all the great roles with the greatest stars and the greatest choreographers do ballets on you and then you go to teach fat old ladies who want to lose weight and say, "Mr Prinz, why don't you pay more attention to me?"

'I think I was a real louse when I was a dancer. I was real bitchy because l was so tired all the time. If I get to the top again in some way, well, I'll be a really different person this time. Nothing can happen to me now, death, pain, a terrible injury, it can't hurt.'

John Prinz carries along the street his small bag with a change of leg warmers and shirts. He's off to teach. Before him hobbles his wife. She's also off to teach. No one looks at him as they once did. Everyone looks at Miss Glushak – and smiles. But then a beautiful woman is always appreciated, even on the streets of New York.

★   ★   ★

One Monday evening at 9.40 Carol Gore was mugged in the lobby of her apartment building. Her money was gone; her person was safe. And there, were it almost anywhere else, the matter would have rested. What is to be done in such a situation except give thanks for being spared? The answer, of course, is to sue.

Responsibility, decided Miss Gore, lay not with her assailant, who had vanished, nor with the police, who would never find him, but with her landlord – for permitting a mugging to take place on his premises.

'I have been advised to sue for damages as high as $10,000,' Miss Gore wrote to the landlord. She went on to say that she would, nevertheless, settle for $1000: $210 that had been stolen and $700 or so for the trip to Sarasota, Florida, to calm her ragged nerves. The reply from the landlord's lawyers duly arrived denying liability.

Shortly afterwards their client paid Miss Gore a visit. He was, apparently, full of sympathy but in something of a predicament:

were he just to pay up, the money would come out of his own pocket. Were she to sue and win, the money would come from his insurance company. The stage was set.

What makes this a particularly New York story is that whoever advised Miss Gore, a rock and roll artist and part-time hypnotist, he was certainly not a lawyer. Miss Gore has no time and no need for lawyers – indeed she has successfully sued one of them for malpractice, having argued the case herself all the way to the Supreme Court. 'I'm very proud of that one; it's one of my major achievements.'

There are those who might point instead to her court-room triumph against the mighty Con Edison as her greatest hour. One summer, when the days had been hot and the air-conditioning particularly expensive, Miss Gore found herself unable to pay her electricity bill ('backed up', as she puts it). She offered to settle in small instalments and took exception to Con Ed's demanding letters.

As it happens, Con Ed was in the habit of calling her each month to arrange an appointment for the meter reader. The inconvenience of having to let him into the building was, she reasoned, a presumption on her time. 'It's Con Edison's duty to get access to the building to do their job, not mine.' She billed Con Ed for services rendered at $50 an hour and, on receiving no satisfaction, filed suit.

She prepared the case herself ('I wrote a terrific brief') and walked into the court-room well prepared for Con Ed's lawyer. He was, she says admiringly, a worthy adversary. 'He fought like anything. He dragged up everything he could to try and discredit me – my marriage, my lifestyle, my morals. He did everything I would have done in his shoes. He was a hell of a good lawyer.' Miss Gore was awarded a $250 cash settlement and Con Ed was ordered to stop harrassing her about the unpaid bill.

It should not be thought that this stalwart came easily to the world of legal tools, briefs, precedent and procedures. She, too, was once an innocent. Some years ago she and her then husband, a Marines career officer, had their $12,000 van stolen in California. 'It was a real special rock and roll van: plush interiors, queen-sized bed, refrigerator, sound system, swivel chairs.' They sued the insurance company for compensation and lost.

'I didn't blame the lawyer for not being a good lawyer. I blamed myself for not seeing that and I vowed then I would make it my business to learn everything I could about the legal business.' Mindful of this vow, she took a job in a law office when she later moved to New York.

'I realized that New York is a city of lawsuits and I saw quickly that anyone living here is embroiled in them for ever. You need to know landlord–tenant law just to survive so I bought a book on it that I read from cover to cover. It's all a matter of knowing how to be in control of your life.'

It was, therefore, all the more distressing to her to find herself temporarily out of control on that Monday evening. 'The fact is I'm a very aggressive, outgoing person; I have this fearless walk. I don't invite anyone to bother me. I'm not a victim personality and I couldn't deal with that helpless, victimized feeling.'

Attempting to recover the money, albeit from a third party, was one way to regain her sense of power. 'I like my landlord and he likes me. Suing someone has nothing to do with liking or disliking.' She filed her claim and looked forward to her moment in court. 'They'll give me $500 – you always have to ask for double what you want.'

And so it was that one Thursday she took off her rock and roll costume and carefully arranged herself in tweed suit and formal blouse. 'You have to be aware of the statement you make. The court must be able to look at me and see an honest, middle-class person with integrity.'

The lawyer for the landlord's insurance company wore a suit with a careworn look about it. ('He's small change,' pronounced Miss Gore.) With him was Frankie the superintendent, brought to testify to the building's security: Frankie presented an unfortunate picture, unshaven and in shirt sleeves. It was not lost on Miss Gore who was, by now, calmly confident.

She told her tale winningly: the horror of the attack, the boutique job lost because she could no longer deal with strangers, the need to escape to Sarasota. Afterwards, however, she rated her appearance as merely adequate: 'Where cases are important, I'm really on my toes but this was just a distraction.'

It was, it seems, a distraction from her new life in Florida as manager of the Kim Steel rock band.

'I'll get my $500,' she said. 'I know I will.' They sent the decision in the mail. She lost. Naturally she wrote to the court protesting in detail this miscarriage of justice.

★   ★   ★

As the train was drawing out of one of the Hamptons, a striking black woman, cool and expensive, entered the carriage. She dusted the seat with a grey leather glove, unwrapped a soft, grey scarf and took off a houndstooth cape. Opening a leather briefcase, she took out *Newsweek*, the *Times*, *Vogue* and a cluster of other fat magazines.

I mentioned how much nicer the Hamptons are in winter without the summer people. She looked surprised, considered me for a moment and responded. During the two-hour journey into New York, we discussed books (she read widely) and the theatre (she went often). She was going to Tiffany to leave a watch for repair and then out to dinner alone at a restaurant I recalled was expensive. Judging by appearances, as is the New York way, I assumed that Norel Baillie was well off, college educated, with a good job.

One day we met again at the house of a friend. Ms Baillie lived there too: as his maid. For $60 a week she cleans, cooks, organizes his papers and his life. The house is exquisite: plump chintz sofas, plants, flowers, beautifully garnished souffles for lunch. Her employer's sense of style she has made her own.

One day last week she came into the city and we talked.

'I was born Eleanor Bailey on October 14, 1942, in Portsmouth, Virginia. My father was 18, my mother was 17. I'm an illegitimate child, need I say. From the hospital I went to my father's mother. My mother didn't show any partiality for me. She didn't keep any of her children – she had nine. My father was killed a year later.

'My grandmother was a bootlegger; for almost thirty years she sold whisky by the shot in her apartment over my grandfather's barbershop. She was rich and we lived well. When I was five, my mother gave me to some of her friends. They asked for one of her children and she gave me because I was the darkest.

'This lady had to be 68, because her husband was 72. They had an outhouse out back, next to the pigs' pen. I don't know till today why they wanted me. From the day I arrived until I ran away in 1954, I had a beating every day, including Christmas. No child could have been that bad.

'The South was still segregated, and there was a development of white people near us. Three times a week on garbage collection days, I had to wheel a baby carriage up there to collect all the thrown-out food that didn't have glass, spit or coffee grounds on them. That's what we ate. I went to a two-roomed school; the first three grades in the room on the left, the others in the one on the right.

'When I ran away, my grandmother took out a juvenile warrant for me. I was had up before the judge and since my grandmother wouldn't have me back, I had to be sent to a training school. She gave me a $20 bill and said, "You'll be a better person when you come out."

'I'd been in the school for two weeks when my grandmother came to see me. She said someone had told her male friend, Captain Charlie, that I liked girls. I was 12 and so green that I hadn't had any kind of sexual encounter but I said, "I tell you I don't now, but by the time you come back I will." So then I had to find someone to teach me.

'They let me out after three years and seven months. I pleaded with them not to release me to my grandmother but they did. I felt that all that hell and damnation I went through was unnecessary and I'd never forgive her as long as I live. I didn't go back to school; I took jobs as a waitress and went to New York for a while as a maid. But I couldn't stand that.

'When I was 17 and back in Virginia, I took up with Addie May. A year later, her mother had me arrested. Addie May was 15. I was found guilty on two charges "contributing to the delinquency of a minor", and "crime against nature" (that's homosexuality). I did my time on this prison farm and when I came out I was so confused, in such a mess that I needed to get away.

'I couldn't go to Bermuda, now could I? So I broke the window of a jewellery store and went down to the precinct and told them. When the judge sent me to the state penitentiary for two years I said, "Thank you."

'I'm not big or aggressive and when I went in I reckoned that I'd better hook up with someone strong. I hooked up with Ruth who was 36 and in for selling drugs. When we came out she went to New York and sent me $500 to join her. I lived with Ruth and then I got married to a drug pusher from Portsmouth for a few months and after that I was just going between Virginia and New York. No matter who I was with, I always took a job.

'I've done it all; I served in a shop, did bookkeeping, did computer programming, worked as a waitress. Few jobs check on your record and the right part of me says I should be self-supporting, earn my way, not live on my sexuality, my looks or my wits.

'In 1973 I went into a drug hospital in Kentucky for eleven months and when I moved back to New York I ran into Addie May again and she lived with me till last year. I used to go back to Virginia until I realized that most of the people I used to know are either dead or in jail and I thought why did I keep running back there?

'I met my present employer through Addie May. She was cleaning people's apartments and I deemed she didn't have to work so I did them for her. When Smithson built this house in the country he asked me to come out and run it for him. I live in self-imposed isolation. I don't see anyone but the two women next-door. I don't have any relationship, sexual that is, with anyone now and sometimes I think if I don't soon I never will. I'm old, really old. I don't feel so chancey now; I get up every morning and say, "Keep cool, fool."

'I think that had I not been black my childhood couldn't possibly have been that bad. Had I been white (since I've always had people browbeating me about how high my IQ is), someone would have invested time and money in me and seen that I got an education. Being gay hasn't been a problem. If I walk into Tiffany's, my gayness doesn't hurt me if I have the money. They wouldn't say "Hey, here comes a gay person!" They might say, "Here comes a black person. Let's hope she isn't a thief."

'Smithson always says I have a millionaire's taste and a pauper's pocket. If I had money, I'd want clothes, jewellery and good food in that order. I'd also like to be able to buy any book or magazine I wanted.

'Happy? No. Underline that, emphasize it, write it in capitals. I suppose I've had moments of happiness but there's never been any on the inside. When I start thinking my mind goes wild and I get a headache. I just have to cut it off, the pain is unbearable. Oh God, if I thought about my life for a moment I could find it really depressing.'

★   ★   ★

Watch them on the bus: middle-aged men fixated on the firm, 19-year-old thighs sitting next to their own fatty deposits. No sign of lust behind those stares, no lascivious fantasies there. Just regret for some, bitterness for others. New York is obsessed with decay – of buildings, neighbourhoods, the city itself and, above all, of the human body. In a country which values enthusiasm (preferably youthful) above experience, where the elders aged 40 clutch their jobs to them, glancing nervously at the 25-year-olds over their shoulder, you can understand the feeling of horror as obsolescence signals its arrival with flabby flesh.

Just such a man was Irwin Yatzkan, now known to his admirers on West 86th Street as Irv the Nerv. There he was facing the down side of his life-cycle when his brother dropped dead of a heart attack and his doctor decided Irwin needed bi-focals. 'I felt,' he says, with gloomy look that once was the Yatzkan trademark, 'like a pudgy old man.'

Certainly he was pudgy. He was 46 years old, completing seventeen years as service transportation engineer with the Long Island Railroad. (And tending the LIRR rolling stock is hardly one of New York's glamour careers.) He would come home from work to his burnt orange and white apartment, nod to his family and flop on to the bed for a nap. The idea that even his eyes were growing old filled him with depression. His doctor put him on tranquillizers for blood pressure and he considerately kept his melancholy to himself. Everyone liked Irwin; he was so quiet and kind you couldn't not like him.

It is at this point that another man might have taken up with a younger woman, desperately wriggled into contact lenses and a new denim wardrobe, and started to have his hair rinsed and styled. But Irwin was already bald and they don't make bi-focal contact lenses. He sank deeper into morose contempt for his increasingly useless body. He also started listening to his heart – waiting in terror for the fatal spasms.

The Yatzkans live on Central Park and no one can live anywhere near Central Park without being aware that a large part of mankind is into running these days. At 6.30 p.m. the well-worn 1.7-mile track around Central Park is in the possession of middle-aged men running not after their youth but for their lives. Faces furrowed with concentration, chests heavy with the after-effects of too much nicotine, they lollop along with extraordinary and unself-conscious earnestness. These candidates for coronaries are running from the Angel of Death.

Irwin, in those days, couldn't jog three blocks. He couldn't touch his knees, let alone his toes. He wasn't in the least surprised when he turned up for a physical fitness test at the local YMCA and was marked 'below poor'. As he signed up for the 7.30 a.m. running class, he reflected that to be able to run a mile was more than he could reasonably ask of his desk-bound body.

The mile gave way to five miles. Three times, then five times, a week he turned up at his office on a grey stretch of Broadway clutching his dirty laundry, looking flushed with triumph. He discovered a passion. His chest grew broad, muscles surfaced in the arms above his small, quiet hands, his paunch almost wasted away. He went out and spent a thousand dollars on clothes for the first time in years. He had become a philosopher, a man of nature. He watched the seasons changing in the Park; pondered the meaning of life as he pounded up to ten miles.

And that's when he decided that he was going to run the New York Marathon – twenty-six gruelling miles around the city's five boroughs. It stiffened his resolve to read somewhere that no one who's finished a marathon has had a heart attack for at least seven years. This was going to be his covenant with life.

Every morning before dawn he was out in the Park. His wife Elaine, a large, jolly social worker, watched the transformation with ambivalent shock. 'I don't feel part of it. I sit back amazed that this sedentary man is now racing round the city. I don't believe it.'

Early one Sunday he went out to join the thousands of runners on Verazano Bridge. Two thousand were first-timers like him; he still hadn't covered more than twenty miles. He provided his growing band of supporters with his projected timetable. Five hours 32 minutes was his estimated time. Drop out? Never. The marathon had taken over his life; he'd finished it a thousand times in his dreams.

Friends and family took to the streets on the great day with banners and posters. And he finished. In 4 hours 51 minutes, Irwin Yatzkan ran 26 miles, 385 yards. He came in before the one-legged runner, the blind entrant, the man in a wheelchair and a couple of thousand others. He did it. That night everyone went to a party for the hero, number X475 Irv the Nerv. There was pastrami, corn-beef, pizza and Irwin wandering around in his shorts almost blinded with tears. He'd heard the roar of the crowd, the cheers and the applause and it had been for him.

'Right now,' he said, 'I feel everyone's older than I am. I have boundless energy, I think I look well in clothes and I've got faith in my body. I'm no longer afraid; I've struck a blow for the life force.'

When Irwin Yatzkan talks now, they all listen. There are eight million stories in the naked city – and Irwin Yatzkan likes his best of all.

Outsiders

There is a man, white-haired, with runny red eyes and bad teeth, who walks along Columbus Avenue every day singing to himself. He wears a brightly checked jacket, a coloured waistcoat and tennis shoes, and sometimes he must be very cold. In his mouth is a canary yellow whistle that he blows constantly and on his nose he has fixed a huge, red plastic ball. He has decided to be a clown.

People are afraid of him. When he stops to do a soft shoe shuffle, tooting on his whistle, mothers draw children to them and hurry on. School children giggle and run away. Lithe dudes scoff but quicken their step. He continues his show for the empty sidewalk and then skips on merrily, waving his bare, weathered hands, while his big red nose bobs up and down.

No one gives him money; nor does he ask for any. Who knows what magical land he thinks he is inhabiting? He never speaks – just chirrups his whistle along the upper West Side. Occasionally a tiny child escapes to stand and clap; he beams at such appreciation and adds a complicated turn or two to his untidy dance.

It is the fear of him that is hard to understand. New York is full of sidewalk crazies who crawl along the streets, muttering obscenities, reeking of their sense of menace. No one gives them a second look. But this harmless old man, dancing along in his dreams, chortling with good will, produces a feeling of panic and embarrassment. It is all right to be crazy and angry; it is not all right to be crazy and benign.

There is another, more famous such Pied Piper who is to be found every afternoon in Central Park by Fifth Avenue. He is dressed in patches of scarlet, emerald and royal blue, wearing a pointed hat and pointed shoes. He travels around with a small battered suitcase in which he keeps scarves, whistles, bells, toys and stuffed rabbits. As the spirit moves him, sometimes near the sea lions in the Zoo, sometimes along a peaceful stretch by the boating lake, he unpacks his case and embarks on a busy dance, waving, jingling, piping and singing to the delight of small children who have learned to look out for him.

He, too, never takes money, no hat lies by his feet as a gentle reminder. Nevertheless sometime in all this merry-making a policeman will come to move him on with brusque impatience. The authorities of Central Park have even taken him to court – he has no licence to entertain. How strange that he should be deemed as threatening while around the corner by Bethesda Fountain drug dealers stroll openly offering their wares for sale. It is as if they have a rightful place in the city. The strange, lonely man with his songs and laughter is the outsider.

Along the streets of New York, whatever the weather, the lonely people sit on benches, watching the others go by. Some talk to themselves, others to stray birds or dogs. Some shout out their anger and bitterness so loudly that their voices rise above the cars and echo down the blocks. And no one seems to notice.

The benches along Broadway are full of outsiders, sitting alone, each with a careful space separating them from the next, and they sit this way for hours. They are not all old. They are not all sick or drinkers or troubled. They have nowhere else to go. In summer they dress too warmly, in winter they wear too little.

It is as if in their loneliness they do not notice the passing of seasons. Unkempt and odd-looking because there is no other in whose eyes to see themselves mirrored, their attempts to talk or to smile at those passing by so busily meet wary disapproval.

Down by 81st Street on Broadway an old man sits singing all the cheerful songs he can remember from across the years, crooning his heart out the day long. Sometimes there is a response. A tourist usually, who hasn't learned the New York ways, will smile and stop to talk. And the old man stomps his feet with pleasure. But mostly those who pass pretend he isn't there, veering slightly away from his harmless celebration.

One day he will no longer be there. As he lived alone, so will he face dying alone. And who will he sing to then?

★   ★   ★

In the beginning the elevated railway ran along Columbus Avenue on the Upper West Side and steam locomotives clattered deafeningly overhead spewing soot over the already shadowed street. Since rich folk wouldn't live near railroad tracks, working-class families did and as their buildings grew dark, their faces grew wan.

Poverty, said the rich folk, smug in their overstuffed, one-family brownstone dwellings, is a sin. It brings noise, filth and disease and our hearts shall be hardened against those who dwell in it. Thus was the ground laid for WSURA, Amendments 4 and 5, Community Board 7, The Site 30 lawsuit, the J-51 red herring and the latest court battle between low-income families of the United Tenants Association and property owners of Continue.

It is impossible by now to do justice to every nuance of the tale of the West Side Urban Renewal Area, the once-heralded master plan to reduce the blight of a rotting neighbourhood. Suffice to say that over $200,000 have so far been raised and spent in legal costs by the newly-arrived co-op and brownstone-owning members of Continue (Committee of Neighbors to Insure a Normal Urban Environment) to stop city-funded low-income housing.

It should be understood that the very inclusion of the term 'normal' is in itself a feat of the imagination: it is so little used in Manhattan these days as to have all the clarity of Middle English. Those nostalgic words 'noise and filth' have become familiar again though, while Continue's chairman, a quiet, clean-shaven stockbroker, Eugene Halpern, is especially keen on the term 'middle class' and the image of it fleeing from the said n & f, leaving behind the well-known 'wasteland' roamed by low-income 'undesirables'.

The saga got going in the seventies when two hundred families, evicted by landlords foreseeing renaissance and high rents, took refuge in abandoned, city-owned buildings. In time, the city accepted the squatters, set rents, issued leases and, a few months ago, agreed to turn over twelve buildings to the firmly-established United Tenants Association to own and manage.

The UTA was jubilant. Advertisements for responsible super-intendents and qualified maintenance men soon appeared in local papers – *The Westsider*, the Hispanic *El Diario*, the black *Amsterdam News*. After eighteen years of neglect, rehabilitation was under way. The sound of plasterers and smell of paint was as magic to the UTA and a relief to all West Siders anxious to see these majestic old buildings preserved.

Not, however, to Continue. 'The land giveaway to the UTA squatters is the biggest swindle in the history of New York,' declared chairman Halpern. (Perhaps this is the moment to point out that many Continue members bought their brownstones from the city ten years ago for $20,000 and that the current price tops $250,000.) Continue went to law. The deal, they said, was to be stopped.

On the morning of yet another hearing, the officers of UTA gathered in the Empire diner on West 86th Street. They were a despondent group. Continue would, as always, be represented by Morris, of Demov, Morris, Levin and Schein – name enough in West Side property circles to send shivers into a mere amateur association. UTA had had a lawyer for only twelve hours; the afternoon before the Puerto Rican Legal Defense Fund had called to offer its services.

And here is what stops this from being another gentrification squabble – the size of the stakes involved and the racial implications that everyone tastefully overlooks. For Halpern's middle classes read white, for low-income read Hispanic and black. That is the ugly divide. Do they know, those 4,000 middle-class families belonging to Continue, of the pain inflicted in their names? Of the distress caused by the slurs and innuendoes? And would they care? No, say those who grow up in bitterness.

Perhaps that breakfast group at the Empire diner would have been less gloomy had UTA president Lucila Velez been there.

Velez, a spunky, generous woman from the Dominican Republic, was one of the original squatters. She and her three daughters live in a fourth-floor apartment on West 88th Street. Her home is crowded but spotless and the front parlour is always immaculate. Outside her barred and locked door, the stairs are menacing, the hallway dirty and dangerous. The city cannot give permission for entrance locks until Continue's court case is settled.

But Lucila Velez couldn't be there. Laid off as a teacher's assistant during the fiscal crisis of 1978, she nurses an old man paralysed by a stroke. Her daughter, Ruth, aged 20, came along in her place. Where the mother is hardy and reconciled to the world, the daughter cannot accept that she and her friends have to go to court to justify their existence.

'I've lived in this neighbourhood all my life. Why can't they leave us alone? They say low-income persons are pollutants – don't they realize that we're not all bums, pimps, drunks or garbage? They say we're filth. How can anyone say that about my mother? If you're hungry she'll bring you home and give you something to eat. If you have no place to sleep, she'll give you her bed. Sometimes, even I have to reassure myself that it isn't true what they say, that we're not bad people. We want a safe neighbourhood too, a safe hallway, a door with a lock downstairs. We get frightened – just like them.'

A few months ago the Velez family was sitting in the kitchen when Ruth heard a strange knocking. It was the sound of flames beating against their walls in the empty apartment next door.

'Arson,' said the fire inspector.

'Life,' said Lucila Velez.

'Our enemies,' said her daughter.

The case continued.

★   ★   ★

In New York affluence and poverty are often only a street apart. West 86th Street is an avenue of large, guarded, comfortable apartment buildings. One block over, 87th Street is a desolation with boarded-up buildings, overcrowded walk-ups; nowhere to raise a family and yet many do because they have to.

Those who are lucky and privileged shrink from the proximity, or any reminder of it, of those who are not. They turn away from all that it suggests and involves and give instead to cancer research, heart disease foundations or public television – worthy causes but, in some way, safe.

Consider for a second the varying successes of those who beg on the streets. The music students on Fifth Avenue running through the Tchaikovsky violin concerto claim to net a couple of hundred dollars over a good weekend. A notice asking for support to finish a musical education and an open instrument case brings approval and a fluttering of notes (how can you give a nice, middle-class violinist less than a dollar?).

The blind, legless man, wretched in every way, selling pencils whose notice pleads for support for his family, who holds only a cardboard box – he is usually ignored or at best thrown a quarter. Stand next to him for a while and see how many look away from him and how many give only a dime. What are they turning away from? Certainly not his look of reproach.

Nearer to home West 86th Street has recently been worked over by an enterprising panhandler. He was a young man, well dressed, whose line was that the police had towed away his car and that he had not the money to go and reclaim it. Some kind souls gave this unfortunate 50 cents for the bus fare. Others handed over enough for a taxi. When he made the mistake of approaching the same man twice, the word got around and he vanished. Everyone seemed to think it was a great joke.

Louie, on the other hand, is a ghastly sight. He is tall, mangy, dirty, stick thin. He has wandered the block for as long as any can remember. Quietly, almost politely, he begs: 'Can you spare a quarter for a cup of coffee?' He says it over and over again in a voice that did not start life in the gutter. He walks all winter, often he is soaking wet. He has never harmed anyone and no one knows how he got to this state. No one knows and no one gives – except for those who can least afford it. Olga the Newslady always did; Harold the Pharmacist does, if he thinks no one is looking. On the other hand, no one tries to harm him. He is not pushed away or asked to move on. It is simply as if he is not there.

★   ★   ★

West 84th Street between Columbus and Amsterdam Avenues is an ugly block. On one side decrepit buildings hint at rats and menace. On the other, the local high school is a jagged, metal scar with bars at the windows and chain link fences. But halfway down the street, behind an elegant 10-foot railing, forsythia is in bloom and the ground is scattered with hyacinths, tulips and crocuses.

The Japanese yews are neatly clipped. A weeping willow hangs over wooden picnic tables, lovingly cleaned. There are Russian olives, poplars, maples, clump birches and a magnificent Thundercloud plum. Someone has been turning over the rich soil with peat moss and staking the rose bushes.

At first, the garden is a mystery. It cannot be private property. If it were, it would be hidden away behind barricades, yet still strewn with litter or damaged by those enraged by its peace and privilege. It is everything that is missing that is so perplexing – no graffiti, broken bottles, destruction for its own sake. Where are the warning notices, the 'Keep off' signs?

One day, a tall thin man appears, dishevelled, grey-faced. In John Simon's tow are some tough, buoyant black youngsters, raised to the streets, now setting to work on a metal dome centre-piece around which roses will climb. In one corner, railroad ties are being neatened in preparation for the vegetable planting. Last summer's harvest, it seems, yielded a host of tomatoes, peppers, lettuces, squash, corn, carrots, radishes, beans and aubergines.

Don't people steal them? 'People come in and pick them,' says John Simon. 'Sometimes they come in and pick them and sometimes they sneak in but I assume they're taking them to eat and isn't that what we're growing them for?'

It is easy to be deluded into thinking that when something is not in vogue here, it does not happen. Do-gooding was a trend of twenty years ago, currently much debunked. Self-help is another word for leaving the poor alone. It is neither fashionable nor expected, therefore, for a nice, middle-class boy from Pleasantville, N.Y., graduate of the Sorbonne, Caius College, Cambridge, and York University to be running a community project for public school failures and rejects.

John Simon's Dome project is, in essence, a village school created in the basement of a friendly church. Its teachers live in the neighbourhood, work within it week-long and year-round and care for its villagers. This nearby garden is but one expression of that care. Two blocks away is Central Park, ravaged, mauled. In five years not one plant has been harmed at West 84th Street. 'People don't feel our garden belongs to someone else. Little kids come in and we get them to plant something and then it belongs to them.'

The neighbourhood high schools are mainly black and Hispanic. Its teachers, mainly white, are often afraid to walk the streets in which its pupils live. Classes are large, illiteracy rampant. In a year 11,000 crimes, often violent, were committed within the city's public schools. It is of this system that John Simon takes the rejects.

His successes have won scholarships to prestigious private schools, others have gone on to college. His failures are in prison or dead. But every year youngsters who would not have had a chance are given one. Classes are small; the school functions evenings, weekends and during the long hot summers. It opened as an experiment in 1973 with five students. It now has 65 and operates as a special programme within the city's system so that its students get high school credits.

Conventional schooling is only part of it: the Dome is a neighbourhood centre. After hours other youngsters pour in for basketball, photography, mime, tutoring, gardening – classes and activities that often offer the only alternative to hanging around the streets, admiring the drug dealers with their cars and fancy clothes, in a neighbourhood where most don't have jobs and those who do sweat for $25 a day.

Simon works eighteen hours a day, earns $15,000 a year to keep his wife and two children and hasn't taken a holiday in nine years. It is not an obvious life for one who took an upper second in English at Cambridge. 'It wasn't what I had in mind but the problems are so enormous that everyone gets sucked in. I have an idea – I'm trying to make it happen.'

The West 84th Street garden was part of that idea. New York City, from whom the Dome rented the abandoned site, announced that it would shortly be putting it up for auction for private development.

★   ★   ★

In the dusty, narrow lanes of the Lower East Side, it is still possible to imagine the harsh and crowded life of the early 1900s – the world of walk-up tenements, slums with no air, water or fire escapes, fetid sweatshops where young bodies were maimed, grew old, toiled for $3 a week in oppressive conditions. Enough remains of this ghostly presence for visitors to wander through and sense its history, secure in the knowledge that this will never happen again.

Doubtless those same visitors never notice the trucks stopping and starting on their routes along the bustling streets, delivering bales of cut fabric, collecting thousands of newly sewn and pressed garments. Who spares a second glance for the tired faces of immigrant workers scurrying from doorways at dusk, as much prisoners and victims of the sweatshop as their forefathers were in the 1900s?

Ten years ago there were probably no more than 200 garment factory sweatshops left in New York City. Today there are at least 3,000. In tiny spaces, always uncomfortable, often dangerous, more than 50,000 people work long hours for $15 a day that may be paid late or may never be paid at all. They are immigrants, usually penniless, lonely, afraid. To whom would they complain? Those who are here legitimately can find no other jobs. Those who are here illegally fear being turned over to the authorities.

Once it was cheaper for Seventh Avenue to send abroad to those who laboured for its prosperity. As wages rose in far-off places such as Taiwan and shipping costs soared, it made more sense to put the work out to jobbers at home in the city. Fabric went out, garments came in – what happened between was no business of those who asked no questions.

In 1977 the average sweatshop owner in Chinatown could get $6 for putting together and finishing a dress. Today an owner is lucky to get $3.50. The newer Korean contractors, burgeoning in Astoria and Queens, may be paid as little as $2.10. In part, this is because the city continues to swell with aliens without official papers and therefore no protection. Mostly it is because the sweatshop industry is substantially controlled by organized crime.

The key to sweatshops is trucking and the cost of ferrying goods to and from the midtown fashion houses. There are probably 500 shops in Chinatown today, each with thirty sewing machines that between them produce some 6,000 garments a week. It has been estimated that a trucker could charge six cents a garment and make a decent profit. The average charge is twice as high. The weekly overcharge for Chinatown alone must come to some $180,000 – over $9 million each year.

Why don't sweatshop owners change trucking companies? 'I'm allergic to pain,' said one. 'Our shop doesn't have fire insurance,' said another.

Many of the owners are 'married' to the truckers for the life of their shop. It is the truckers who own the lofts or arrange leases, who provide the loans for sewing and steam-pressing machines, who find the orders from Seventh Avenue jobbers and collect the payments. And if these same truckers then charge 24 cents for moving a dress, 'fuel and service' charges of an additional 15 per cent a week, or even charge for deliveries never made, what is to be done but pay or shut down? As it is, one third of the shops in Chinatown close each year and each year more open to take their place.

There is a feeling in America that those who are not involved in crime will not have to live with the brutality of its consequences. Those who use drugs must accept the reality of drug dealers. Those who seek a dishonest penny deserve the company they keep. It is a form of puritanical snobbery; crime, unlike random violence, does not infringe on the lives of those who are honest and hardworking.

But what of the 50,000 workers who exist in conditions that were condemned a hundred years ago? What of those who earn perhaps 75 cents (less trucking charges) to make up a blouse that sells in a store for $25 or $20? Others who idly flick through racks at Gimbels or Sears Roebuck, who laugh at garment workers' union advertisement on public buses – perhaps they do not see the chain of which they are part.

A recent report by a New York state senator gave details of the connections between the major sweatshop trucking companies and organized crime. One company is owned by the sons of a late Mafia don. The director of another was killed by a burst of gunfire from a car shortly before testifying to a grand jury. In an unofficial strike by the drivers of one such company, a union official was beaten with a lead pipe and another man was stabbed. The strike collapsed after one and a half days.

Since the report was published, the mayor's office has fined one sweatshop owner $400 for infringement of building codes. The Attorney General's office has arrested others for similar offences. The Labor Secretary, no less, came down from Washington to lead a sweatshop raid in a flurry of accompanying photographers and reporters. This has caused him no little embarrassment – it seems that his media event was staged in a fully accredited union factory. And meanwhile, on the streets outside, the trucks continue to roll.

★   ★   ★

The city has a gaunt look. The buildings are stark; they jab at the heavy skies. On the streets, New Yorkers, stripped of summer's colourful disguises, have their differences pointed up. Eastern European faces hollow out; elderly Koreans and Vietnamese suddenly seem as frail as cobwebs. And in the wintry hush, the babble of the city's languages carries through the clear, biting air – a whisper of English, as often the soft rise and fall of Spanish.

Tito the Relief is sweeping the pavement outside his building. This is not a sight to relish: his hard, young face, tired and stubbly, is whipped by the wind that cuts through his grey cotton uniform. Those who don't know him warily walk past and the prejudice of a city is betrayed in those tentative footsteps.

'We've got a strike against us just being Puerto Rican,' he says. 'They think we all carry knives, we're muggers, we know nothing. We've got a love for this country, you know. It gave us a new chance of life. I got a sister who's going to become a computer expert. My brother's a staff sergeant in the army. I've got another brother who wants to be a cop. We work hard; we got dreams.'

Tito dreams of being a lawyer. ('I'm fascinated with the criminal justice system.') Four nights a week, after he's finished work, when he's taken out the garbage, mopped the stairs of the twenty-storey apartment building, swept the sidewalk outside, washed the lobby and basement through, when he's done all that, he gets on his bicycle and pedals across town to the Benjamin Franklin High School for his classes.

First he must graduate from school with an equivalency diploma. (As one of ten children he left school early to haul boxes in the fruit market. 'Family's got to live and we need money.') Then, and maybe that'll be next year but maybe not, he'll try to register for college – night classes, of course – and that may take another five or six years. His daughters will be almost grown up and law school will still be before him. In the meantime he earns $207 a week as relief man, he's 26 years old and he has a family to keep.

His father had dreams too. Working in the sugar-cane fields around their small home town in Puerto Rico, he pictured a better life in New York. One of his children had died of a hole in the heart, another of pneumonia; in New York, he thought, it wouldn't have happened. He would become a master chef and give his family a life of hope and security.

He died of heart failure aged 52. For the last thirteen years of his life, he worked the elevator in an apartment building. It was the only job he could find after eight years as an army cook, eight years away from his family. When he came back from service in Korea, his children no longer recognized him.

When Tito's father died in 1976 the son inherited his job. The Puerto Rican team who looked after the building also looked after their own. 'My father never wanted me to work here, he always wanted me to better myself, but I can't complain.' And if the new superintendent, who is Cuban, rides him hard sometimes (for it is only to outsiders that all Hispanics seem the same), it is the residents who mind – Tito the Relief keeps his head down and minds his own business.

He's the one who smiles at the older residents who can't afford to tip. He charms the small children: 'Hello champ, howya doing?' But does he sense the irony of these privileged offsprings just starting at their private schools who, at this unknowing moment of childhood, want to grow up to be Tito the Relief or Raphael the Elevator with his shiny buttons?

When Tito goes home at night to his wife, Regina Michele, and his daughters, Devora, four, and Rena, two months, in their three-room East Harlem apartment, does he think of the sixty-two families whose garbage he takes out and whose floors he mops? 'Everybody is meant to lead the life they lead and, believe me, compared to some, I have the best. I've got some greedy kids, but I can afford to feed them. Once in a while, I get to save. About four months ago we got enough together to buy the kids some clothes. Now and again, we get to go out.'

He lives in two of the many worlds of this city. As the pale dawn creeps over the high buildings, Tito the Relief carries his bicycle down to the streets to ride the long cold distance between those worlds. 'I feel Puerto Rican, that's my nationality even though I came here when I was one year old. We still keep our own culture, our dances and our festivals. I think we have a rough deal just being Puerto Rican but that's the way it is. At least I keep up with the Catholic faith. You got to believe in something when you get tense.'

Music scores

A celebration took place recently on West 57th Street. A sizeable chunk of cultural New York turned out to honour one of its heroes. He has been called 'the father of modern American chamber music'; Robert Mann, founder and first violinist of the Julliard Quartet, will shortly be 60. As an early birthday present he gave himself the pleasure of hiring Carnegie Recital Hall to play a dual recital with his 22-year-old son Nicholas.

It was a family evening. Wife Lucy and daughter Lisa took over the box office. The sold out sign soon appeared. It is the greatest compliment when musicians turn out for one another. That night the New York musical establishment appeared in force. But so did writers, journalists, the head of this, the president of that; it was an event of obvious affection.

As the house lights dimmed Nicholas, romantic, elegant, walked out with impressive poise. Bounding behind him, jacket baggy, hair awry, face genial and tousled, came Huckleberry Finn. If the evening had a significance beyond the music itself it was the sense of life and the commitment to it that Robert Mann exudes.

In a cosmopolitan milieu he is the traditional American – reared in the unbroken West and still somehow of it. Mann was born in Portland, Oregon, the son of a Polish Jewish fur trader turned grocer, tailor and lemon grove farmer. 'My father was a wonderful man who had many successful failures.' During one of the times as a tailor, he made a suit of clothes for an old Norwegian cabinet-maker, who paid him with a hillbilly style fiddle that he had carved. That was his son's first violin. It has been to war with him and still goes back-packing with him across the Rockies each summer.

When he was eight the family moved to Tillamook, on the Oregon coast. There he learned to fish, climb, go mushroom hunting and cast horseshoes at the county fair.

'We used to build rafts and pole for miles over flooded rivers. Tillamook was in a valley about five miles from the sea, outside a rain forest. We had about 150 inches of rain each winter and over the years there the outdoors washed in on me. Each year there was a run of smelt and we could literally pick these small, silvery fish out of the river with our hands because there were so many of them.

'An alcoholic Belgian violinist came to Tillamook because he felt he'd raise tulips there. He was my first teacher. He was the first dead man I ever saw – he was shot dead in some drunken argument and that was the end of my teaching.'

It was the depression, the thirties, the era of union struggles and union violence. It was a beneficent world that he grew up in but not a kind one, either among men or out in the wilds. But it was large and teeming with life.

When Robert was 13 the family returned to Portland, and he to a local youth orchestra that had been taken over by a Russian immigrant: 'He was a mad, wild personality, devoted to the idea of being a dictator of the soul. We played every Russian piece we could find – no one has heard of these things now – but what I remember most is the camaraderie of that orchestra. As a teenager I was learning operas, Haydn symphonies, chamber music, madrigals, but also going off camping with friends, reading Ulysses, discussing everything under the sky. And I was also taking violin lessons from one of the finest musicians I've ever known. "Your son is not a *Wunderkind*," he told my father. "But if he practices, he can perhaps become a good practitioner and earn a living." In other words, he knew me for the lazy son of a bitch I was.

'Obviously a person will remember with a vividness things that are meaningful but even so I cannot deny that things have changed since those days. And if I do anything in my teaching it is to try to remember and realize some of the breadth that Oregon and the people I knew there gave to me. Everyone's leading from too narrow a base nowadays – we see wonderful young musicians but it's a veneer, a lacquer over a non-substance.

'And yet I definitely loved the idea of Nicky becoming a musician. I feel the music profession is the greatest life in the world. And I love playing together; it's an organic thing. We've done it for years – I was his first teacher.'

In the olden days, sons always joined the father's guild. Instrument makers, orchestra members – there was a pride of generations. In this country, such continuity is rare and thus wondered at and highly prized, but it is easy to understand the special appeal of the Manns. The delight of the son in the closeness of the father; the joy of the man who founded a quartet that is thirty-five years old this year, and who has fathered a love for chamber music in generations of Juillard School talents and now shares that with his son.

It is strange though that there is no competitiveness, no rivalry, between them. America's most famous quartet player and the young Julliard violin student stand on stage as equals. Only the beam and the hug at the end betray the deep pride behind the music-making.

My son, my son, it is an unusual story for Manhattan but, traditionally, a very American one.

★   ★   ★

The New York City Housing Authority is not a name that smells like a rose. Almost inadvertently, the city has become the largest 'slumlord' in town. Nothing that a few hundred million dollars couldn't put right, but as things are the noble idea of bringing heat, roofs, ceilings, hot water, plumbing and wiring to thousands of slum apartments is so much daydreaming.

In 1976 the city came up with a new gambit: instead of waiting three years for landlords to default on taxes, the city would foreclose after one. This stern tactic was intended to frighten delinquent landlords into paying up. Needless to say, no such thing happened, and perhaps the Housing Authority can now guess why: less than half such apartment rents get paid.

As the first heavy snow of winter seeps into neglected

buildings, there is neither money nor labour to tackle this awesome slum legacy. Under the one-year rule 9,500 buildings with 35,000 occupied apartments have become beneath the city's paternal wing, and 700,000 tenants now call it 'landlord'. It is not a term of endearment.

But the NYCHA is people too, and sympathy for those of them that wince at their reputation moves me to tell the story of Janet Wolfe. Ms Wolfe is well-known to musicians carrying instruments who find themselves waiting for cabs on West Side street corners. A small, attractive woman with absurdly silver hair hurls herself with excitement upon the unknowing.

Like a firework, she shoots questions: 'Do you play? Do you live around here? What are you doing next week? Do you want to play for my orchestra?' She fumbles in an overstuffed shopping bag. 'Take my card. Oh, there's a cab. We'll share it so we can talk.' Her card conveys the unlikely information that she is the manager of the New York City Housing Authority Orchestra. And thereby hangs a tale.

Sometime in 1972 Simeon Golar, patient chairman of the NYCHA, finally revolted against the image of his housing projects as grisly hang-outs for rock 'n' roll and muggers. 'Henceforth,' he announced, 'we also hope to provide our people with food for the soul. Man does not live by shelter alone.'

It does not need intimate knowledge of 'the projects', as they're called, mostly in the ghettos, to see that a tenants' symphony orchestra playing to its neighbours was not a guaranteed success. Enter Wolfe, divorced, mother of two daughters (*cum laude* Princeton and Brown), who was, as she says, 'a rich child and a poor woman'.

She knew nothing about starting a symphony orchestra but once roomed with Leontyne Price, adores a challenge and is, shall we say, more than mildly eccentric. (Wolfe on fund-raising: 'It's simple. I ring up a man and say: "Listen, if you give me enough money, you don't have to sleep with me." And they usually say, "How much is enough?"')

The orchestra stumbled into existence. 'At our first rehearsal we had twenty-two clarinetists and one viola player. I didn't know much about music but even I knew that it wasn't a balanced orchestra.'

Today, it plays at least twenty concerts each summer, mostly in parks or outside 'the projects'. There are six concerts in the winter, an annual benefit performance at Lincoln Center (so far well reviewed) and constant invitations from prisons and hospitals.

'I won't do Sing Sing in winter any more because they always make us stand outside in the cold while they search us for weapons. The first time we went to play in a jail, the warden said to me: "My boys don't like this kind of music. We had the Rochester Philharmonic here a while ago and my boys walked out." I was so mad. "My boys", how do you like that? So I said, "Walked out? I thought you tied them to the seats?"

'But do you see, I knew we would be different. The Rochester Philharmonic is all white and nearly all male. Our orchestra went on with all those beautiful women we have playing and then Karl Hampton Porter, our conductor, came out. He's black and he's proud and he just stood there and the men loved him for what he was doing. We had a special request from the inmates for us to come back.'

The orchestra is mostly black or Hispanic. Karl Hampton Porter, its conductor, is four times married, a dude, founder of the Harlem Philharmonic and Harlem Youth Symphony (both now defunct for lack of city funds). Older members play for nostalgia; younger ones play to learn.

The Saturday morning rehearsals at the Fulton Senior Citizens Center certainly have a different vitality from those of the New York Philharmonic. Five newly-arrived Russian immigrants, veterans of major Soviet orchestras, gabble together. Stanley Hunter, a retired policeman with twenty years service in the 40th Precinct, tunes: 'I always wanted to be a violinist but when I was young, it was hard to get a job in music if you were black.'

As the strains of Tchaikovsky waft over the room, Janet Wolfe rushes across Ninth Avenue for sixty-five coffees. 'This orchestra is the only surviving community orchestra in New York. That must mean something. The trouble with this city is that people are so afraid of each other. One night we were playing at a really rough housing project and two kids turned on their transistor. I told them to turn it off and one said: "We niggers want to listen to our music." I was so angry, I said, "Well, you niggers can put on your music when we niggers have finished ours." The kids grinned – and stayed for the whole concert.'

Janet Wolfe, of course, is white. Will the day ever come when one can tell a story like this without having to explain who's white and who's black?

★   ★   ★

Violence, like everything else here, is subject to fashion's whim. There wasn't too much of it about for a bit, probably due to the mild weather, but pushing subway passengers in front of trains is suddenly with us again. Looking on the bright side, the fad for pouring gasoline into subway token booths, thereby setting the imprisoned attendants on fire, lasted but a moment. And splitting travellers apart with a meat cleaver hasn't even caught on after two recent appearances of gouging the odd eye.

It is all part of death's rich pattern and accepted with admirable phlegm by New Yorkers. This is not a particularly dangerous city. Who fears the chances of being maimed by some maniac compared to the statistics about obesity and cancer? Against the threat of a nuclear reactor leak or the crash of a truck transporting nuclear waste to eternity, violence is but a mischief, if, alas, an inevitable one.

Decent folk take care. They keep their doors locked and their backs to a safe place. Thus, along with the 'no fault' divorce, we now have the 'no fault' mutilation: killing as a two-sided relationship. Prostitutes, for instance, ask to be strangled by hanging around with undesirables and not insisting on credit card business. Careless subway riders provoke attack by their very defencelessness. The unguarded back is as primitive an invitation as the bared throat. Certainly, homosexuals cruising Central Park for partners must accept the possibility of ending up dismembered in the bushes.

If, then, there is one thing that riles gay rights activists, it is the portrayal of homosexuals as inhabitants of some nether world of leather, s & m, sodomy in the back rooms of bars, and flirtations with brief sex and murder. The Gay Men's Chorus is, in part, an attempt to set the record straight.

To those who are not of it, the gay community of New York present a tough and lofty self-containment. Its ideal is a stylized macho: its uniform is that of the construction worker. Short of hair, moustaches neatly clipped, T-shirts tight over big muscles, heavy key chains jangling, feet shod in bulky leather workboots, the gay men's image speaks of strength and a rough confidence.

Their world seems detached, secretive even. The regular press rarely mentions their presence except in terms of who slayed whom. Gay Pride Week came and went this month and the city's newspapers, so quick to feature each and every obscure celebration, looked aside. The life of exclusively gay bars, baths, shops and softball leagues happens as a thing apart. And most assume that they would have it so, that the invisible walls around their community are of their building.

But New York is not San Francisco. Each year an equal rights amendment to bar discrimination against homosexuals in jobs and housing is presented to the city. Each year it is defeated. There is a community of gays but no constituency. No politicians look to their vote. No figure in the city's running has declared his or her homosexuality although everyone is always declaring themselves to as many minorities as possible.

Gays are attacked by electric preachers weekly. The rise of the Moral Majority, with its insistence on all that is 'normal' and 'clean', cannot be ignored. Reagan's Washington is not Carter's, where there was a White House aide to liaise with gay groups. In all, this is not a comfortable time for the gay men of New York. Homophobia is a word that they use a lot nowadays.

And so it was that at Alice Tully Hall in Lincoln Center, 150 men in elegant grey and burgundy tuxedos filed on stage for the first of two sold-out concerts. The New York City's Gay Men's Chorus was making its debut in the home of the Metropolitan Opera and New York Philharmonic. There was a certain piquancy about this. It caused no little hurt when, for a concert of Bruckner's Te Deum, the Philharmonic wrote to all the city's choruses in its search for male voices except this one.

Much thought had gone into those tuxedos, it should be understood. $15,000 had to be raised by raffles, benefits, brunches and parties for their purchase. At one time the 'Bucks for tux' drive achieved an importance on a par with the four-times-weekly rehearsals. But the electric preacher who regularly on television refers to 'evil and poisonous faggots with lace at their sleeves' has clearly never seen a collection of New York gay men honed in gyms and health spas. One hundred and fifty construction workers would look about as appropriate on a concert stage.

It had to be just right. This was no songfest for friends and admirers. Posters put up all over Manhattan had made that clear. This concert was a bridge to the community in the widest sense. It was of great satisfaction, then, that all three city newspapers sent critics (the *New York Times* even dispatching a senior music critic who wrote of 'an impressive debut . . . choral singing of quality' with tributes to its 'musicianship' and 'dignity'). Past slights were forgotten when the Metropolitan Opera House called next day with an invitation to sing there in July. Alas, the pieces would be in Czech and the chorus rehearsals are not yet organized for such exotic fare.

The chorus rehearses regularly in a small, stuffy hall on West 57th Street. Its music director, Gary Miller, is a former schoolteacher – thin, earnest, quivering, passionately dedicated, especially after his attendance at the recent gay men's chorus conference in Chicago. There are sixteen such choruses around America but the first and best known, naturally enough, is that of San Francisco – founded three years ago and veteran of two national tours.

San Francisco is thought to have a much younger sound than New York. That, thinks Miller, is the difference between the cities and the gay experience in each. 'Many here are frustrated actors – they came to New York thinking they were all going to be stars. Their voices are better trained and they're older but they love what we do here because it gives them a chance to perform and to get together in a relaxed way.' As the chorus was formed last August, standards are still not as high as he would like – only 50 per cent of its members read music, for instance – but no group could work harder.

Partly, this is because of the sense of proving something. 'We want people to know,' says Miller, patting a profusely sweating forehead, 'that gay men are just as normal as any other men and in our spare time we get together and sing. I spent eleven years teaching music in public schools and in all that time I could never let anyone know that I'm gay. There are people who've had to give up the chorus because they were afraid someone at work might hear about it. There is a great fear of the Moral Majority and this administration and we're trying to say, "Look, we're gay but we do other things."'

Much of the rehearsal was given to a setting of Thomas Jefferson's writings. 'The God who gave us life gave us liberty at the same time; the hand of force may destroy but cannot disjoin them.' At the Lincoln Center concerts it was dedicated to two gay men killed last November. They were machine-gunned in an attack on a gay bar in Greenwich Village.

Postscript: On 23 September 1978, in his apartment at 513 East 82nd Street, Edward Mallony, 22, was stabbed to death with a kitchen knife by a man he had met in a Greenwich bar. Last week a Manhattan court sentenced the killer, Richard Schreiner, 30, to five years' probation. The judge noted that since his arrest Schreiner appeared to have reformed.

Trust in God

There is a great deal of talk at present about what constitutes an Ordinary Person. According to television and sundry magazine articles, the archetypal Ordinary Person of New York is a creature known as the Mouseburger – a phrase that originates, not too surprisingly, from Helen Gurley Brown of *Cosmopolitan*. The Mouseburger is a woman who was not sent to earth beautiful, brilliant, rich or well-bred but who, nevertheless, through a combination of hard work, diet and deadly discipline, succeeds in becoming almost all of these.

It is an image guaranteed to produce laughter, albeit hollow, from the truly ordinary. It does, however, say something about New York's picture of itself as an island of Mammonites, thirsting for power, fame and fatless muscle.

Let us, then, have a quiet celebration of all those who do not live amid fanfares and alarums, peaks and nadirs. Their days pass. The detail of their lifetime is carefully and thoughtfully assembled. In this most secular of cities, there are still those who give thanks for their daily bread, whose values are still His, whose passages are unobtrusively marked by His love and sustenance. Christina Pogoloff is one, wife of the associate rector of All Angels' Church on the West Side of New York.

She spends her days caring for her husband Steve, her small daughter Elizabeth and their home at the top of an anonymous brownstone – the old rectory, once the focus of the parish, now lies buried beneath a high-rise luxury apartment building.

In England, the church is part of the established order – it is, after all, the Church of *England*. Here it is just another leisure activity: some run, some read and some believe. The church is poor and badly attended; its clergy are badly paid. In a city where there are no vocations, only careers, there is little respect for those who are part of His dominion.

But this is how it seems to outsiders. To the rector's wife, All Angels' is, as she puts it, 'like having a wonderful home to come back to'. In a parish scattered across the city, divided by the subway, there is no outward role for her to play, no daily rounds of visiting. But the telephone rings constantly and she spends hours on it – listening. It is the greatest of gifts in a city where people have to be paid $60 an hour to do just that.

When she was a child growing up on air force bases, she remembers her mother going about her housework singing hymns. There were Bible stories at night and church on Sunday. That was the way most American families lived in those days. In today's New York faith is not an accepted way of life. 'There are very few cradle Christians here, born and raised in the church. It is something most people have to find their way to now.

'We get people at All Angels' who've run the gamut of every twentieth-century fad – yoga, est, aerobic exercise, Zen – before they come to us. A lot of them discover that what they've been looking for all the time is a relationship with God. And, of course, a lot come just because it's a warm place, there's a sense of community – and New York's a harsh place to live without friends.'

There was a time, before Steve went into the ministry, when their lives were very different. As a social worker, he earned a good salary and his job as houseparent in a foundling home brought him respect as well as satisfaction. Christina wrote scripts for a public television station and they lived in a large house in the Pennsylvania countryside. It was a sylvan dream compared with the daily round in an urban parish, trying to raise a child on Steven's $16,000 a year.

'New York is a very seductive place,' she admits ruefully. 'It's very hard to live here and not feel the lure of making money. All around you is the life that you could have with it and there have been times when I've thought what I should really do is go out, leave Elizabeth and do whatever I have to do to make the big pot of money.

'It's a tension and it haunts me. I want to set myself apart from the whole secular world and on the other hand I want Elizabeth to have the best we can afford for her. It's a problem every Christian parent faces in America. In some way it's easier to raise children in New York – they grow up with very few illusions about what life can do to people. You see wealth here but also poverty, need and broken people.

'When you look back over history and you see all the atrocities committed by the church, all the persecution it's suffered at the hands of others – you ask how can it still be alive after two thousand years. I feel the same way about New York – I look at All Angels' and feel wonder that it still survives. And yet in New York there are so many hungry people looking for some kind of meaning and that's why I feel so grateful for our lives. As long as we have His love, our days are full of meaning and of His purpose.'

Lest it be thought that all there is to see in New York bears the stamp of money, remember also Christina Pogoloff – ordinary person.

★   ★   ★

Somewhere in this world some serious-minded Zen Buddhists must be enjoying the joke. It was not so long ago, after all, when everyone who was into being-here-now and enlightenment went Zen. Two meals of cauliflower cheese made a macrobiotic diet. One reading of Lao Tsu constituted the eternal Tao. Three good acid trips meant Nirvana.

It was a spiritual package: a quick trip to the Ganges or up the Himalayas. A few yoga classes, a guru or two, a child named Harmony or Rhama Bliss, and thus thousands of years of Eastern teachings were trivialized. Thea Porter dresses, the Cream, flowers, Inner Tennis, sunsets, astrology, *I Ching*, Buddha – all were colourfully put together and, in time, rendered indistinguishable. The East, indeed, had its day.

Now it is the turn of Christianity to suffer the indignities of fad and fashion. Everywhere joyful souls are being saved, born-again, instantly redeemed, wearing lapel pins, sporting bumper stickers and handy potted digests of the Bible in pamphlet form complete with winsome drawings of lambs, sunsets and flowers. The hippies were into loving; the Christians are into being loved. (Christian, to all intents and purposes, has come to mean born-again. It may not amuse the Catholics but they hardly count as Christian at the moment.)

All of which brings us to the matter of the Revd. Rex Humbard's 4,700 coloured lights. Those who are not aware of Rex's Cathedral of Tomorrow in Akron, Ohio (beloved by even more television viewers than Robert Schuller's Crystal Cathedral in *The Power Hour*) will not know of the magnificent 100 ft high cross hanging above the 5,000 cinema-plush seats of the church. This cross is studded with brightly coloured bulbs for which, each Sunday, a lighting programme is carefully worked out 'to emphasize the theme of any church service'. Thanks to television, any complexities of His message have become as easy to find as a well sign-posted airport. 'To me,' says the man from the Rex Humbard Ministry, 'Resurrection would be all white.'

Rex's grandchildren help to simplify matters even further. 'I'm a big P for potentiality/because God loves me' goes the Sunday show-stopper from the Humbard Family Singers – Rex, Maude Aimee, his wife of thirty-nine years, their children Rex jnr., Don, Aimee Elizabeth, Charles and grandchildren Rex the Third, Donna Sue, Melissa ('Missy') and the rest. It is all utterly wholesome; not a thorn nor a drop of blood anywhere. While Rex preaches of the spiritual and financial blessing of His love, it is hard not to be distracted by the level of hairdressing.

At times, actors recreate touching letters. 'Dear Rex, my brother died two weeks ago.' An elderly chap shuffles to the window, watches the rain drops and turns his eyes upwards where 'his brother has gone to be with the Lord'. At the show's end, Rex prays over a book containing the names of the Prayer Key Family – those who 'pray daily, fast weekly and pay monthly' to support his ministry. (Actually fasting has been 'de-emphasized' – too many people couldn't handle skipping one meal a week.) This, however, is the only reference to fund-raising – it being Rex's opinion that 'there will soon be a backlash'.

There are now over seventy electric preachers, buying airtime for their shows, demonstrating more or less (mostly less) tact in their drive for contributions. Humbard, one of the first to use television in 1952, is still one of the biggest. His message is simple: redemption is instant, painless and You are Loved ('Rex Humbard Ministry. You are loved,' chirrups the switchboard operator in Akron).

Since he moved his show to a tourist garden in Georgia, filling the screen with dappled sunlight, rippling brooks, placid lakes and joyous flower beds, he has come to seem as refreshing and inoffensive as those old cigarette ads showing mountains and waterfalls. 'Rex's main characteristic,' says his spokesman, 'is ultimate sincerity.'

It is those who have followed him on to the air, surpassed him in histrionics, that now attract attention. Those shouters, threateners, purveyors of greed, hatred and frenzy, have sequestered Christianity unto their heaving bosoms. It is as if they own Him, selling His salvation in tiny and expensive pieces. They and their supporters are now a political force. Opponents point with distaste to the fortunes they amass, while traditional liberal ways of thinking shrivel before the fire of their attack. The more publicity they receive, the more awesome seems their power.

Yet the number of people watching religious broadcasting has not changed in many years, although the number of preachers has quadrupled. Even so, this is a vastly lucrative business. The Rex Humbard Ministry income is 'privileged information'. A guess of $55 million a year was described as 'a bit high' by a spokesman. But when the East was in, did not a whole galaxy of maharishis grow fat on the pickings? And where are they now, these erstwhile spiritual superstars? The greening of America, as it turned out, lasted but a while. Will its red-necking last much longer? There is only the hope that each dog has his day and that, in America, this day grows ever shorter.

★   ★   ★

New York's churches are most usually noticed in their absence. These stolid, late-nineteenth-century fortresses are remembered best, and most kindly, when one is elsewhere. For the rest, it is as though they are invisible.

It is not only that great Roman arches and delicate Byzantine leafwork do not sit comfortably with their more basic and recent neighbours. It is that, for the most part, they are perforce thoroughly uninviting – huge padlocks on doors that open rarely, and by appointment, do not create an image of a family of faith welcoming all unto its heart and soul. 'Keep out,' say the barricades, shrinking before vandals and Goths, and most people do.

The West Park Presbyterian Church, circa 1890, on West 86th Street, is no exception. Its rough-hewn red sandstone facade recalls another era when its worshippers were white, middle class and thoroughly sure of what they were about. The church's most obvious use these days is to shelter in its massive porch those shivering souls who wait patiently for the elusive M7 uptown bus.

In some ways the church is an insult to the poor among whom it now finds itself. It is hard to see a simple faith that protects the weak reflected in the grim edifice that devours over $50,000 a year just to keep it standing. Its parish of sturdy, Protestant burghers has now become a bustling village of Dominican immigrants, Roman Catholic by and large, and lingering Jews from Europe. It is an anarchic neighbourhood – in contrast to the austere church with its republic of elders and Scottish tradition.

Churches such as this wither in the city for lack of relevance. They are sold to real estate developers while older members, still living in that other era, rail at the odd notion of giving away the profits to the poor. Indeed, West Park itself was the result of such pragmatism when, in 1911, West Church sold its 42nd Street home for a million dollars and moved uptown to merge with Park.

Even though this year's Thanksgiving dinner was cancelled for lack of funds and the Wednesday afternoon Open House for the elderly is $2,000 in debt, these are but pittances. West Park has, in the last few years, begun to reach out into its community. It has brought in enough friends of all faiths, or none, to give it

meaning even to those who would regard its Sunday worship as
no more than a quaint, minority interest that just happens to
make its home in West Park, along with the Grey Panthers and
the West Side Gays and Lesbians.

And so when notices appeared in the usual places (the fish
market, tree trunks, the drugstore's notice board) to the effect
that the West Park's women's association were holding their
annual fair, it received more careful attention than the customary
'$1,000 reward for one bed apt'. Hint of a bang-up dinner for
three dollars set, it must be said, many a meagre-pensioned eye
agleaming.

For newcomers it was not easy to find a way in. The majestic
front doors stayed shut and it took time to uncover a side
entrance buried among notices about the Hispanic ministry and
the Taiwanese Sunday services. A narrow staircase set off by a
huge, bleak poster announcing 'Nuclear weapons are a sin'
(about which more later) led upstairs to a huge, panelled hall
with *eau-de-Nil* decoration, harsh lights and the warm bustle of a
neighbourhood enjoying itself.

The hall was a mass of hats. Every imaginable size, colour and
shape of head-covering bobbed over stalls laden with wares –
woolly helmets, jaunty berets, purple pompoms smothered with
sequins, neons and fairy shades, feathers and angora. These hats
were like beds of summer flowers waving above dull, worn
clothes that many of their owners were currently trying to change
as they rummaged through the donations. 'Come and get it while
it's hot,' called Claudia Bell, the clothing stall's undisputed star,
'from California, Chicago, Broadway. Coats, dresses, you name
it.'

The cake stall was already out of chocolate pudding (60 cents a
slice) and there had been a run on the sewing circle's
hand-embroidered hankies, to the satisfaction of the retired
librarian, Mrs Florence Currie, who was now trying to push her
circle's dainty pillows.

At one end of the hall, the dinner guests were assembled for
the three-dollar feast of chicken, beans, potato salad, apple pie,
cornbread and coffee. There were exquisite Hispanic ladies with

long painted nails and the one good (surviving) piece of jewellery, ageing white widows eating well with the concentration of those who do so rarely, large black matrons with quick smiles for those who were alone.

Young children ran around, sleek West Siders looked for bargains, handsome young men, spiralling upwards, came so that their grandmothers could show them off. And what struck the outsider was the jumble of it all – ages, colours, rich, poor: here were they who come together so infrequently sharing the church's celebration. In a city that is so divided, the much-used term melting pot is an ironic misnomer, but here it was for once.

High above this hubbub hung the home-made banner for the Presbyterian peace-making mission which is housed in West Park's library. The Revd. Jan Orr-Harter, aged 27, moved through the crowd with her gentle shyness. As the church's assistant pastor, she also runs the peacemaking mission. Nothing points up the dismal state of the peace movement in America as clearly as the modest attempt in this poor neighbourhood to create the beginnings of one.

It is here, where cuts in housing, schools, hospitals and public transport affect lives that are already harsh, that the reality of military aggrandisement means something. 'Why is it sometimes forgotten,' asks the Reverend, 'that people who are poor are just as afraid of being blown up as those who are rich?'

★   ★   ★

On any summer Saturday, in any historic village or beauty spot around New York, the buses and charabancs stand in car parks waiting for their customers' return. Slowly they straggle back: some walk gingerly as bunions cut into new summer sandals, others roll on heavy and swollen legs, still others stand straight with the pride of a best frock. Some wear hats; others carry gloves. A few have menfolk trailing behind, outnumbered and resigned. Summer is the time of the church outing.

The church is the one thing that binds together poor black women – apart, of course, from debts, overwork and the fear of falling ill. Wearied, for the most part, by the daily round, they have no time for those few political organizations that might worry over them. There is only His solace and the hope all the trials of hardship are His will. It is daunting, this faith, but in the shelter of His church, they find the only logic to otherwise incomprehensible lives – and the only escape from them.

Watching the women climb into the buses, having seen the sea, ridden the ferry or toured some old and beautiful house, there is a longing to know more of them – of their sadnesses and also their sustenance. This is the story of one: Pearl Jane Lindsay Hawkins, seamstress.

'I get up every morning at 5.30, have a cup of coffee and get to work in a small shed in our garden. I don't like bugs and bees so I don't go outside for anything. I like the trees though – I hear the Lord in them. Sometimes my husband or one of my sons will come in to sit and talk for a while but I like to be alone. That's why I do furnishings – nobody has to come for the fittings. In dressmaking, there's too many people. I love sewing: this was my calling. I think that pleases Him.

'I was born in Culpepper, Virginia, and my mother died when I was three and a half years old of high blood pressure and childbirth. We were brought up by a great aunt. As you grow older and look at things, she seems very nice but at the time she was strict and mean. I loved my father because he was a good man, a religious man and a trustee of the church. But he had to go to Washington to find work so we only saw him at weekends.

'When I was 14 I went to look after a general's widow, Mrs Holabird, who had a fine house in North Carolina. I loved that place and I loved her. Once we went away to a hotel. I remember everything about it – the bathchairs, the bandstands, room service. I've never stayed in any hotel since then but that was really fine. I was just like one of the family to Mrs Holabird. I always had to go in to see her before I went to bed – she said, 'I want to see your face every night before I die.' She had stroke after stroke after stroke. I had her to myself in the house for five or six years after she couldn't speak but finally they put her in a nursing home and I cried so to leave her. Sometimes I think being with her was the best time of my whole life.

'The family gave me $500 when I left and I married Mr

Hawkins. We moved to Boston because two of my brothers and my sister were there. That's when I had my sons, Alan, he's 30 now, and Donald, he's 27. We had an apartment with our own private entrance and I didn't ever work when my children were small. I would never let my sons go and play with any child whose mother wasn't there. When Donald was nine he came home and said, "Mom, I have the best home in the whole wide world." It's a different story when you come up in the world with no mother. My mother left six young children when she died.

'They took Donald from me as soon as he was 19. They took his name out of a pot and drafted him. I nearly died. I aged fifty years. I cried night and day. That's the truth. I never drank, I never smoked; I worried for my boys but I left that for God. And then they took him from me.

'He went into the army in November and then I got a letter from the government saying he'd be home December 19 for Christmas. I didn't even know where he was. The 19th came, nothing. The 22nd, 23rd; nothing. I was so frightened I got hold of the Red Cross and didn't let them say anything, I just told them to find my boy. On the 24th they phoned to say he'd been in hospital with pneumonia for seventeen days. I didn't see him and I had tears streaming down my face all the time.

'They took him to South-east Asia, it was the Vietnam war. He was so quiet when he came out of the army. He'd just walk around and not say anything until one day he said, "Mom, I saw things there I should never have seen." I couldn't do anything, just pray and hope the Lord would take care of him, but the truth is I've always felt bad that they took him.

'A few years back, a cousin of my husband left us this house here in the country. I come out in the morning to the birds and the sunshine and I love it. In a way, I'm happy but in a way not. I'd be happier if my sons were working – there's nothing for them here or anywhere. We gave Donald money to go to Boston but he couldn't find a job there either so he came home. My son Alan was a computer operator for IBM but he was laid off since last year. There are no jobs anywhere with things like they are for those boys. I always say coloured boys are the first to be laid off and the last to be hired.

'I love to work. I work all the time. I sit here and gain weight and sew and think of the Lord.'

Other New Yorks

On this island of blown-dry, moisturized, therapy-supported, credit-saturated Manhattan executives, who shall speak for the family man from Brooklyn? And when the talk is of New York, Harlem, the wasteland of the South Bronx, muggers, disco studs, rapists of 80-year-olds in backstreet tenements, who shall remember the men leading ordinary lives of quiet thoughtfulness and hard work?

At 5 o'clock in the morning the East River lies still. New York, this Caliban of concrete, is at peace, its aches and darknesses, noises and hatreds laid to rest for a brief moment.

Down on the eastern tip of the island great black braziers burn in the streets. Men pushing trolleys rush past and around them, stopping for a second to hold their hands to the flames. Melting ice streams over the sidewalk. The cold and damp eat into the bones. The Fulton Fish Market has been awake for an hour.

When we talk these days of America as a land of abundance, what comes to mind are washing-machines, tumble dryers, colour TVs, bathrooms, liquidizers, cars, snowmobiles. But here, laid out on endless slabs, is a rare reminder in New York of that original abundance – are there a million fish on sale this morning?

All the fish of many seas; catfish from Carolina, striped sea bass from New England, scallops, grouper, bluefish, swordfish, huge orange fish from the south, the prehistoric sturgeon. No wonder the early Americans attacked this rich continent with such savagery and recklessness. They must have thought the abundance was limitless.

The men who buy and sell here know what the poisons and dumped wastes have wrought of the seas and rivers. Theirs is not an intellectual, or even articulated, knowledge. It comes from living close to the source. Caleb over there, slashing through the side of some deep-born monster, is the son and grandson of fishermen. His grandfather was a whaler.

Now there is no whaling and the fish comes to market, not on boats tied to the quay nearby, but on trucks bearing the licence plates of many states. The sea is no plaything to Caleb, but an ailing wasteland.

Jim is 75; he's been boning fish in Fulton Market for fifty-two years. When the shad run, as they do now, he works seventeen hours a day, slicing away the 365 bones of each fish. He works with pride and enthusiasm, showing off each new fillet to himself before wrapping it.

Across the road at Dirty Ernie's, the breakfast crowd gathers for eggs and fried ham. Watch the hands of the man behind the counter as he slaps the toast with butter, hurls the coffee into cups and tackles the washing up bowl. All this with a kind of gusto that is peculiar to America.

The image of hard, manual work in this country is a positive one, bound up with the memory of those pioneers cutting their way through forests and across the mystery of unknown plains. Why else would all those cerebral executives rush to weekend ranch houses to build their own shelves and cabinets? There's a basic instinct to keep in touch, keep faith if you like, with those who came long ago to build houses and cabins and force a living from the land.

And yet how paradoxical that here, where there is no stigma attached to manual work, there is no concept of a working class either. Scan television in vain for any feeling of the working man's life. The sweat of his brow is lost in the glow of the market place. Presumably men's deodorant won't sell in the middle of a programme celebrating the smell of labour.

But it is more than that. For generations men were relieved to have any children that survived. They were more than content to have children who grew up exactly like them. Fishermen raised fishermen; farmers raised farmers. But in this land of hope, it's no longer enough for children to grow up like their parents. They must do better. These men in Dirty Ernie's are the sons of labourers, but they are the fathers of college graduates.

They work through the cruel winters and claustrophobic summers that their children should be better fed, better educated, better dressed. And when they grow up they will also be better travelled until, eventually, they will go away and not return.

George Morfogen, who started this whole train of thought, has two daughters. One is an executive secretary in Manhattan; the other works for a television station in Los Angeles. George gets up in Sheepshead Bay at the far point of Brooklyn every morning at three. He creeps out, so as not to wake his wife, and drives to the market. He changes his clothes in a friendly seafood firm's office and then sets off on his rounds buying fish for the Oyster Bar in Grand Central station.

He's a popular man; 'a decent man' is how they talk of him in the market. He would have liked to be a lawyer but his father was taken ill and needed him in the restaurant. His younger brother, whose education wasn't interrupted, is now at the top of Time-Life books.

'Do you ever feel resentful of your brother's worldlier success?' I asked.

'No, I don't feel that way. I never clutter my mind wondering whether someone has done better than I. The heck with it; life shouldn't be like that.'

This was a song in praise of George Morfogen. And men like him.

★   ★   ★

There is much to be learned about the neighbourhoods of New York from the various messages left on the local notice boards. West 86th Street, for instance, swaps information through functional, clearly printed notes pinned inside the door of Sloan's supermarket. Dog-walking services, sacrificed Mediterranean dining-room sets, ground-breaking productions of Bach and Strindberg, suicide counsellors – clues to everyday life around here.

Down in SoHo the notice board stretches along a whole wall of an artists' supply shop. Here each message is soaked in intimacy, garlanded with flower sketches and the handwritten notice betrays a deliberate attempt to acquire a style that's heavy with self-expression: 'Hello! I need a place to live and do art. I'm very serious about art and am easy to live with. Walter.' 'Learn the violin without all the tension and agony' (there's a contradiction in terms). 'Horoscope: natal solar and lunar returns progressed etc.' And in place of the solemn announcement of Brahm's Requiem: 'Pink Satin Bombers – an evening of faggot theatre at the Performing Garage.'

SoHo (South of Houston Street) is loft land. It's where the new loft people come 'to get into their own space'. The artists and their groupies who spent the sixties getting into acid and millionaires' guest cottages in the Bahamas spent the seventies in 3,000 square feet of derelict warehouse and factory space talking of two-by-fours and eco-architecture. It's called 'pioneering in the urban wilderness'.

The psychedelic era spawned a beads-and-saffron look. The pioneering costume is designed around hiking boots, plaid hunting shirts and goosedown back-packing jackets. (All this to pick up some unrefined sugar from the corner store.) The old log-cabin has come to West Broadway of all places. The former frisbee throwers, looking for something more purposeful to do with their over-developed upper arm muscles, bought a box of tools and moved to SoHo.

Spring Street, centre of this latter-day Old West (alternative space people do not take the small view of their place in the world) is given over to tiny boutiques selling costly cheesecloth for the smarter pioneer. At the Spring Street bar, singles' centre and gathering place, a coffee costs $1 and gives the opportunity to overhear such snippets as: 'For the first time in my life I've got reviewed properly and it's weird to know that people really understand the meaningfulness of my contribution.'

Not so long ago (1970), SoHo was a bleak, black area of cast-iron buildings in which Orientals bent over sewing machines, seaming neon satin jackets for the mass market. Now the buildings are crammed with artists, their loft beds, spotlights, part-Burmese cats, electric typewriters and a quaint way of referring to those still present Orientals as 'cottage industry'. (It sounds pleasanter to the liberal than 'sweatshop'.)

There's a thick *Village Voice*-style newspaper – *SoHo News*, in which artists in search of their *real* voice tell about Sufi ecstasy and alternate best sellers (highly recommended: Vacuum TrapEzoid $20). And even the tired old *Village Voice* has got into the act: organizing the First Ever, Largest Ever Loft Expo in the original Mercantile Building in Tribeca.

Tribeca (the triangle below Canal Street) is the even more forbidding area into which the loft people are penetrating in their frustrated search for the ultimate urban wilderness. All those early SoHo and NoHo (North of Houston Street) alternative space people have moved away from the organic food restaurants and the tourists to the harsher, unrenovated and therefore more genuine world that backs onto Wall Street. Here they can find 2,000 square feet of pure potential into which they can move their chip-board room dividers, sleeper sofas with eleven different relaxing positions and answer-phone machines (no loft dweller would want to miss calls from their publishers/ galleries/psychiatrists).

A loft-dwelling acquaintance, who forsook the academic London life for a three-times-a-week shrink and the search for his feminine feeling self, goes to his dance class in Tribeca. Four floors up in a dank, decrepit building, his teacher Pamela helps her regulars to come to terms with the flowing beauty of their stiff, urban bodies. Outside the door of her loft are steep, threatening stairs and total ugliness. Inside the huge space is the dance studio, cushions, plants and Pamela's hypnotic voice.

Her artist husband Perry is off working as a carpenter – he was laid off from his public college teaching job during the fiscal crisis. Later, after the class has gone home bright-eyed and ready for multiple orgasms, Pamela and Perry send out to the local Greek restaurant for souvlaki sandwiches. Occasionally they go out.

Most loft people go out only occasionally. Some of them have been known to spend weeks in the beauty of their own space. These are devotees to the inner path. This is the new order; to live in seclusion, laying aside worldly cares. It may not last long.

★   ★   ★

Manhattan sometimes seems to be the figment of eight million imaginations. Seen from a crowded bus on a steamy wet winter's afternoon, it owes much to some giant blob in a Rorschach test. As the M3 bus jolts its way along Madison Avenue from the fifties up towards the nineties, each fantasy stares out through the window and fulfils itself.

There are those riders to whom this street is one large speciality cheese shop. All other windows are obscured from them. Watch these enthusiasts crane to compare the condition of Chaume or the texture of Roquefort ($6.99 a pound each) from block to block. Hear them in Madison's E.A.T.: 'And can I trust your Brie?' Who else would need to trust a cheese?

Their blue-collar grandfathers traded peasant goat cheese for American processed and were proud to do so. Their parents acquired the refinement of vacuum-packed 'domestic' Swiss. But the Burberry and Berlitz generation is constantly searching for the ultimate Saint-Albray and remembering some magical summer in Paris. And occasionally, at dinner, they produce the cheese of their forefathers, only now they call it feta and chevre and talk of it ponderously as an artifact.

For them pride of place on Madison belongs to a hushed spot up in the eighties. The Cheese Pantry. No mere purveyor of the products of a lactating cow this. More of an art gallery than a shop, each of the few hand-picked imported offerings is displayed and lit with the veneration given by a dealer to a newly-acquired Rothko or Man Ray.

Talking of which, it cannot be coincidence that lately more habitues of the M3 have been viewing Madison as a continuous gallery. Collectors have taken note that a Man Ray work depicting giant red lips floating in the sky over a landscape recently sold for thirteen times the painter's previous record.

In a trice table talk is of the Rauschenberg missed, the Nevelson lost, the simply pulsating example of Abstract Expressionism just acquired. Citibank takes a two-page advertisement in the *Times* offering to lend money for acquisitions of art. Those who have just got out of Resorts International gambling stock (on margin, naturally) or off-loaded nine-room co-ops (on second mortgages, of course) are now paying 18 per cent to borrow money for visual investments. Thus the M3 has its share of passengers squinting nervously over the windows of a thousand galleries.

That Madison is also crowded with clothes and shoes boutiques is of less interest now that these same tiny, silk-tossed spaces are filled with foreigners lapping up all the bargains. News that Miami Beach is packed with vacationing Swedes does not go down well among these seasoned travellers who do not like to be done unto as they long did unto others. So they talk of the joys of home, switch on the videotape and sulk over the Perrier.

Madison is Perrier frontierland. They're beyond drinking it here because it tastes good. They use it. Two glasses a day is the ever-slim's calcium substitute for 99 per cent fat-free skimmed milk (in itself a substitute for 4000 I.U. vitamin D2 enriched homogenized, i.e. real, milk).

As a result along thirty blocks of Madison there are no less than eight branches of Gristide Bros., the top persons' order-by-phone charge-account supermarket out of which cases of twelve quart-bottles of Perrier can be seen exiting on the burly shoulders of delivery men. Perrier drinkers do not schlepp boxes on their shoulders. They did that two generations back and thousands have been spent on schooling to prevent it happening again.

Madison is, though, famed for its stationery stores: personal-ized, custom-ordered paper, envelopes, postcards, visiting cards and notepads headed 'From the desk of . . . ', conjuring images of senior vice-presidential efficiency from a note that was in fact scribbled on one corner of a dressing-table.Notelets fan out across the East Side filled with thoughts and unfamiliar handwriting.

West Siders, on the other hand, never send notelets, they compose letters: pages and pages of strong, characterful typing across foolscap lined legal pads and duplicated before posting since every idea, thought, phrase or autobiographical anything must be kept and filed for the Novel.

From Madison Avenue invitations are dispensed; crinkly,

parchment, best quality printed everythings – to dinner, to drinks, above all to $100-a-person benefits. But it is the Madison Avenue handwriting that is the give-away. It's the new plastic surgery, the result of a semester's calligraphy course. It's another step in the make-over process. Learn italic, gothic, copperplate, but be sure that it betrays no more individuality than a mouthful of capped teeth swilled daily with Scope mouthwash.

'Daddy, Daddy what did you do in the recession?'

'Gave up taxis, rode the M3 home, took down the photograph of me with the Empress Farah at Aspen, put back the one of me with Betsy Bloomingdale, sold the co-op for a quarter of a million to an Italian, sub-let four rooms on Madison at 91st for $1,400 a month from an Iranian, put money into liquid money funds at 10 per cent and sent your Mommy to night courses in calligraphy to get us off the hook for giving up our $360-a-seat subscriptions to the Metropolitan Opera.'

★   ★   ★

As the A train rumbles off the island of Manhattan into Brooklyn, the conductor holds on tightly to the door of his small cubicle as if ready to bolt himself inside. The eyes of the nodding old snap open. Women try to hide their handbags in the folds of their coats. The harsh lights, stark black and red graffiti, deafening clatter of the train – this is New York in all its ugliness.

The cavernous stations, dark, dirty, some desolate, some uncomfortably crowded, go by monotonously. The haunted quality of the neglected streets above reaches down into this long, seemingly never-ending tunnel. And then suddenly it is over. The little train that only seconds ago felt like some huge, all-enveloping monster mounts into the sunshine and chatters across the wide expanse of Jamaica Bay, small and friendly against the stretches of sea and sky.

On one side planes soar from Kennedy Airport. On the other, in the distance, is the magical skyline of Manhattan. As the A train pulls into Broad Channel station and the doors open, there is the sound of gulls, the slap of fresh sea air and an almost eerie sense of country quiet. It is curiously unreal – it has been a 75-cent journey from one world to another. Broad Channel, with its rickety clapboard houses, white churches, sailing dinghies and sober Irish community, is a village that owes nothing to those skyscrapers standing out on the horizon.

A short walk along the causeway across the bay suggests the natural splendour that must once have been here long ago when deer, box turtles, bears, mink, racoon, fox, coyote and wolf roamed the lands around. Comforting, though, to know that a biologist has recently been rooting around Kennedy Airport over there collecting springer peeper frogs to bring to this peaceful new home. He had a good haul, too, of box turtles from a wooded patch of Long Island slated to be a shopping mall. Here, within New York city limits, there are over 9,000 acres of lovingly preserved wilderness: the Jamaica Bay Wild Life Refuge.

In the car park one or two hardy types in lumberjacket shirts and woodsmen's caps are gathering telescopes and tripods. Of the millions crammed into the city around, no more than 100,000 visit the refuge each year. They swarm to the Bronx Zoo, a similar subway ride away, for there, of course, it is the humans that are in control. This refuge belongs to birds and animals; here it is their comfort and well-being that matters. There is only the thrill of perhaps spotting a white-rumped sandpiper resting on its journey from South America to the Arctic and of knowing that somewhere out of sight herons are nesting in the rookeries.

Outside the simple visitors' centre a large, rumpled man with long sideboards and droopy moustache is digging into the inhospitable soil to plant hardy black pines – winter cover for the owls. He has that New York look of having slept in his clothes. He takes a long, needy puff on a cigarette, tucks the butt back into the packet and goes back to work. David Avrin, aged 31, is the National Park Service Ranger in charge of the refuge.

'In this sort of work, you feel like you're doing something positive for mankind. It's not like making bug spray. People need places like this; it's dangerous for them to live in a city and completely lose touch with the wild. Working in a park is a nice way to live – people feel very good about you and they're generally happy to see you. It's not like running the complaints department at Sears.' The birdwatchers tramp past. 'Morning,' they call out.

Avrin grew up in the New Jersey suburbs ('a small house with a little front yard and a little back yard'). His father was in the dry-cleaning business and not much of a gardener. The son learned about the outdoors as a boy scout and on summer holidays in the mountains. At college he discovered wild-life biology and went on to take a master's degree in wild-life management. He came here three years ago, not certain that an urban refuge was quite what he understood by 'the wild'.

In some ways, he feels now that Jamaica Bay matters even more than the vast untouched reaches of such as Yellowstone Park. 'Imagine New York without something like this.' In the visitors' centre is a 'see and touch' table full of curiosities to tempt the inner-city schoolchildren brought out here for trips. There are shells, nests, birds, bones. 'It really hurts to see how afraid some of them can be of this place. They've been brought up to believe that everything natural is bad. The first question they ask is "Are there snakes?"'

He points out with pride that he's never had a case of damage or vandalism. Along the sandy paths winding round the fresh-water ponds and out past the marshes, small handpainted signs ask visitors to keep away from nesting areas, to stay off fragile beach grasses or just not to walk on the lawn. 'People pay attention and if one strays off, there are always twenty others to set the offender right. I was riding around on a bicycle one day and this old lady with an umbrella jumped in front of me, barring my way. If she hadn't seen my ranger's uniform, I'm sure she would have taken a swipe at me.'

He goes through to the Over Look, a sandy knoll above the bay, to see how the day is going. The red maple is beginning to bud, the robins are up from the south, Canadian geese are coming in – the subtle signs of a changing season, invisible in the city, are all around. In the bird log M. and J. Greenblatt have just recorded a sighting of a downy woodpecker in the North Garden. Earlier, Mr A. Tepper noted more than a hundred geese over West Pond. The peaceful community of birdwatchers is swapping its special moments.

But even here, lost in the enchantment of a fresh spring day, it's never possible to forget that man and nature share a joint existence. It is not only the sight of the Empire State Building across the way, the roar of jets from Kennedy; there's the knowledge that these still waters are too polluted with metal for swimming, that clamming has had to be forbidden.

Besides, there's the constant reminder of the city dump opposite the Over Look. Once flat marshland, now it's a mountain of garbage that has covered the refuge sandbars with clumps of hideous plastic. By law, the landfill is not supposed to permit anything to blow around. The city authorities of New York, caring little for the nesting areas of tern and glossy ibis, pay no attention to David Avrin's anguished calls.

When the north-west winds of winter die away and the south-easterlies come up again, the park ranger and his loyal band of birdwatching volunteers will set off to clear up the careless debris. 'There have been over 320 species of birds sighted here and that's something to feel very strongly about. When I first came here, I had my doubts but now I think this is the real thing. Solitude and peace and all that stuff – it's precious anywhere but especially in New York.'

★　　　　★　　　　★

On the first hot, humid day of summer, when the air is so wet that it almost is impossible to breathe and the sun turns tinted hair a faint shade of orange, the ladies of New York vanish from its streets.

They linger in air-conditioned apartments and scurry between icy stores where they do battle over skimpy T-shirts in which they will later freeze. The sound of their summer greeting is of high-heeled shoes clicking impatiently across marble floors and white patent bags snapping shut.

The slow and heavy gait of a thousand Jamaican cleaning women is bemoaned endlessly in telephone calls from rose-strewn sheets to which the ladies retire with lunch trays of iced tea in Porcelaine de Paris. Those for whom winter passes spikyfast in the making of lists, appointments, order and plans recoil from the indolent time of summer.

The pace of this city is forged in its chilled seasons – rushing and bustling, invigorated by the challenge of a harsh climate and harsher people. It would make sense for New York to live on two time clocks – one for the urgency of its winter months, another for the stupor of its heat. It is, however, part of its tradition to make no allowances for weather. For those who can afford heat and air-conditioning, protection from its reality, weather simply does not happen. It is a rude noise made at a polite dinner table.

Watch the New York ladies when forced momentarily into the stifling air. Feet swell in ungiving shoes that were bought in another of those icy stores. Hair sags, faces draw. Linen skirts crumpled from damp taxi rides, they still try to maintain a perfection that is beyond reason. Steps never slacken, bodies rigidly deny the very existence of languor. They run the obstacle course in full dress. All is armour. Ungracious anger becomes a shield.

It is no wonder, then, that there are those who believe it is beyond endurance to summer in the city. Packing the Pourthauld sheets and dainty china, they move out to cottages by the sea, taking with them the fragile aura of nurtured chintz, organdie place mats and total order.

Even there they continue to deny the existence of any element that is not of their making. On a shoreline permeated by salt and damp, they keep the air-conditioning rumbling to preserve the French provincial velvet-upholstered dining-rooms, the airiness of plump sofas and fresh flowers, the rustle of swagged silk drapes.

As dawn breaks over the thirty-mile coast of Long Island's south shore that is the Hamptons, the air is filled with the sound of automatic sprinklers drenching carpets of newly laid and patched lawn. Woosh, woosh, the sprinklers turn inexorably as if the words water shortage had never been uttered. And should this relentless wet send up mushrooms to dot the immaculate green, emergency calls go out to landscapers and horticulturists to attend immediately.

Once a month the trees around the summer cottages are sprayed with poisons lest gypsy moth caterpillars drop on to spotless white patios. Too bad, alas, that birds and butterflies perish also. Every handy Hampton larder has canisters of outdoor jungle bombs to demolish flies, moths, bees or spiders that might land on drinks and barbecue parties. Nature is no more welcome in the country than in the city. It is just another challenge to meet and set aside.

The ideal between the months of June and September is to weave one existence that, by sheer inconvenience, stretches across two homes. Those who dine nightly with acquaintances in Manhattan travel each weekend to Southampton or to Water Mill to entertain the same acquaintances. The owner of the Summerhouse, a ladies lunching spot on Madison Avenue, has bought a Hampton inn in which to welcome her regulars in their weekend exile. Habitués of Saks Fifth Avenue have a small version that opens for their summer pleasure in Southampton. Elizabeth Arden sends two beauticians from Fifth Avenue to its summer salon. Last year there was a bit of bother when one had to be sent back for slow waxing – there is nothing leisurely about leisure.

It is called 'resort living'. In fact it is Manhattan with pruned and pristine trees and aquamarine pools around which the ladies do not lie since all decent suntan lotions carry grim warnings of premature ageing effects, wrinkling and cancer. The miles of beach, needless to say, are used only by early-morning joggers and off-duty mothers' helps who are college girls from suitable families.

All this takes a considerable income to maintain. In cottages around the Hamptons, two, three and four telephone lines with outlets in every Jacuzzi-endowed bathroom connect to stockbrokers and offices. Weekends are but a hiatus in moneymaking. Well organized ladies do not sensibly allow incomeproducing husbands to pass summer mid-weeks alone in Manhattan among the dust-sheets and possibilities. On Monday mornings they take off the candy-coloured Lily Pullitzer resort wear, climb back into the white linen skirts, activate the various burglar systems and drive back to the chill of city living.

By two o'clock on Friday afternoon, on a once-again jammed Long Island Expressway, the ladies in their air-conditioned cars turn to husbands in seersucker suits and Brooks Brothers short-sleeved shirts and remark how divine it will be to get back to the country.

Home from home:
Quogue, Long Island

On the flat, soft, white sands where Indians once fished and, later, whalers set out on their years' long voyages, the children of the Incorporated Village of Quogue are engaged in the usual business of digging, building, flooding holes, damming sandy fortress walls and stopping awhile for peanut butter and jam sandwiches. The timelessness of childhood hangs over the beach and laughter rises to meet the call of the gulls.

Somewhere, about eighty miles to the west, lies the city defying imagination in this world of unlocked cars, of soft lavatory paper gracing the public conveniences and nameless adults meeting over white, old-fashioned sunhats. 'Hello, you must be Sarah's mother. I'm Andrew's father.' Only occasionally is there a whiff of unpleasantness – the mother who let her two-year-old run naked soon received a duputation of scandalized ladies pointing out that infants too are subject to the Public Attire Ordinance forbidding bare buttocks.

The Village fathers have recently seen fit to extend this same Ordinance to bare chests in public places. Residents received a stiff note from the Clerk's office, a small, rose-entwined cottage, asking joggers to observe the law and 'to bear in mind the effect in a mainly residential area'. If there are any who are amused by such genteel modesty, they know better than to express it out loud. The great fear of Quogue is that it will end up like Westhampton, sin city, five miles down the beach, where scanty singles prowl and electric nights last till dawn. As it is, more than one brazen and hairy-chested jogger has been berated by outraged ladies behind the wheel.

Like Cranford, Quogue is in possession of the Amazons. If there are husbands, they pass the week in that nearby Drumble travelling out on the Friday night parlour car, being met at the station in estate wagons tumbling with beach umbrellas, infant seats, buckets, inflatable pools and all the accessories of a family summer. Week long, it is a village of spinsters, popping out for left-over meat loaf and lemonade in one another's one-acre zoned cottages, each with its second mortgage.

Quogue is a plump land: thickly padded loungers cover sun decks, gallons of Miracle Gro round out newly-planted evergreens by the score and one-piece bathing suits cover the overweight on the beach. It is the very comfiness of it all that stands out. No lean and stalking predators along this waters' edge. And who would notice them? Eyes turn down to watch small lives take shape. It is a place where men are daddies and mummies, for a while, can forget those chilling words: 'one-parent families'.

But it may not last, this special state of grace wherein Quogue lives apart from reality outside. There will be no endless summer on these quiet and protected sands. Those who complacently accept it as more than a moment in time have surely forgotten the meaning of its Indian name: 'the land that trembles under-foot'. Each winter the ever more hungry ocean batters the eroding dunes and washes across the marshlands on which houses still continue to rise.

There are now 900 homes in the village – 900 septic tanks oozing barely-filtered waste into ground where the fresh water table is but a few feet down. Those same Long Island residents who oppose the opening of a nearby nuclear power station live in houses wrapped in vast stretches of glass, with meagre insulation, devouring energy regardless of cost or supply.

And then there are those shut out by its invisible walls. In a way it is surprising that it has lasted this long and as yet unchallenged. They know it, too, those who come here from their city winters with all those right-thinking *New York Times'* editorials tucked under an uneasy heart. Why, in the name of private property, should so few have a share of all this?

The beach is public property below the high-water line – not exactly the high-water line, perhaps, the winter tides have been known to splash right up into the village behind. Certainly, a large part of the beach is public property. Access is not. Even the Quogue Village Beach carpark is private with a guard on duty in summer to inspect passes and stickers issued by busy Mrs Beckwith the Clerk. There is no public thoroughfare, no right of way and New York state law forbids trespassing to get to what rightfully belongs to all.

That no pioneers have set off across the million-dollar driveways and into the courts is, in part, Quogue's good fortune and, in part, a measure of how unutterably boring it works so hard to be. There is nothing sexy about a beach where no one may play a radio, sell a hot dog or install a space invaders machine, where all there is to see is wall-to-wall, well-padded mothers comparing library books and notes on Dr Spock and where a streaking two-year-old is news. It is for this that house prices doubled in two years – for the make-believe that even now life may be dull and full of small pleasures.

★   ★   ★

At the centre of the village of Quogue, set back from the road, is a ramshackle building, its front painted deep peach, its ceiling either peeling or, in places, simply missing. In this quaintly shabby setting sits Alice Eisenberg, queen of Quogue's antique world.

Outside, her sign warns: 'Antique wicker – not tired old things'. Inside, as befits the purveyor of twenty-seven roomsfull of wicker furniture to Gloria Vanderbilt's summer cottage, Alice Eisenberg surveys the sold tags that adorn her stock. By the time she shuts for winter and leaves for Palm Beach, it should all be gone – her 'tutti frutti early Victorian look', her 'Great Gatsby 1920s' rocking chairs for $485, love seats for $625.

Mrs Eisenberg, fifty years in the trade – forty of them with her husband until he died – is the star of the village's old things business. No one pays much attention to Gretch in the shack across the road, for even in summer Gretch opens only two days a week and then not always. Besides, Mrs Eisenberg is a specialist: her spartan store is graced only by wicker (there is currently no look more fashionable) and only in its most distinguished and pricey form. But these are not pieces merely in good condition: they have been restored to look as new.

Thick white gloss paint hides the spots of time, new seats banish the impression that another ever rested here. And still, the occasional customer, choosey beyond satisfying, worries at the slightest imperfection – a chip on an 1850s rocker, a flaw in an 1890s table. Nothing must be allowed to age. The condition of being old is of value; the question of looking old suggests only someone hasn't been trying hard enough.

Antiques are the whitewood of America. No one even pretends that they are more than a beginning. They are to be scooped off and delivered for stripping, painting, covering, upholstering, refurnishing – all with the single aim of turning them as far as possible into something that could have walked off the floor of Bloomingdale's.

It is not surprising, then, that the fun of bargain-hunting and searching out that special object is reserved not for shops but for yard sales. Every weekend handwritten signs appear on trees all over the county announcing and pointing the way to yard and garage sales. Here is the true treasure hunt: the leftovers of a family's years together hung out for sale on bushes, trees, washing lines and tables.

Chairs, curtains, a cot for $20, a motorbike for a hundred dollars, three plastic glasses for a dime, the fur coat inherited from Aunt Mimi for a song. A history of a child's growing is all there: the first squeezy balls, the push bikes, comic books, adventure stories and the baseball bats. The family's memories are on sale. These are the personal antiques Americans really prize: here they can see, feel and touch those whose past they are buying.

Holiday areas like Quogue have the most frivolous sales, of course. Those who rent homes for the summer will spend thoughtlessly on their temporary comfort. When September opens and the leases are up, yard after yard is festooned with outdoor furniture, air-conditioners, spare bedding, kitchen gadgets, plastic dinner sets for twelve, not to mention a summer's collection of *People, New Yorker, Time* and hardback books. Those who stand behind the tables – uncomfortable in this station of life – happily accept $2 for items tagged $20, lest it be thought they need the money. Often, one suspects, it was only embarrassment that stopped them putting the whole lot out for the garbage man to take away.

But these are not true yard sales whose bitter-sweetness lies on those tables on which a few rusty spoons stand next to mother's jewellery that she never wore, on which Christmas decorations jumble beside a quilt that grandma sewed. Americans do not hoard; they move too often to acquire the habit. But when they do save across the years and put it all out for sale in the front garden, it is as if these yard sales become the nation's true antique shops, trustees of its memories and its past.

★   ★   ★

Every small town has its heroes. They are usually tall men with broad shoulders and a long, sloping walk straight from the hip. Heroes don't talk much. Instead, they have self-respect. Just such a man is George J. Mathys of Quogue.

At 5 o'clock it is still dark. The first trucks rumble out of the yard on Old Country Road next to the railroad track. There is the sweet smell of pine trees and after-shave in the air. Big George is up in his office. Behind his desk is a photograph of the 750 lb tiger shark he landed a while ago. It was a bitter three-hour fight on the rod, but he brought the monster in.

His mongrel, Timmy, at his heels, George goes down and climbs into the cab of his twenty-ton truck. There are 150 stops ahead before he'll be back in the yard. He works alone, sitting upright and easy, as befits an asthmatic who has worked twelve hours a day for sixteen years to build his own business. He put up the huge shed behind him and earned every cent to buy the $100,000 worth of trucks and $150,000 worth of metal containers he owns. Every hour of his working life he sees as a blow for private enterprise.

Since garbage is viewed by the local authorities as an intensely private experience, there are seven garbage collection firms around here. None is bigger than George's Sanitation and no one gives better service, he feels. For $10 dollars a month ($12.50 if he has to go round back), George empties dustbins twice a week. 2,700 homes, 300 businesses, 500 summer only accounts. His customers never have to complain at potato peel strewn across the yard or paper scattered across his track. Big George operates with pride.

Today he starts on Dune Road, the tiny streak of land between the bay and the Atlantic ocean where old fishermen's cottages start at $200,000. There's a nine-mile drive to his first customer on the end of the spit. Joe's Live Lobsters is not the most invigorating of beginnings. The spoiled fish have been in the sun for four days. Still, it's not as bad as the duck farm on his Wednesday route – rotten eggs.

There are twenty customers between here and Westhampton Beach, eight miles down Dune Road. Corporation trucks service a whole road. George has to hop around the town, a dust-bin here, a welcome throw-away trash bag there. Officially, a Village of Quogue Ordinance forbids garbage to be left at the kerb for collection. Time after time, George must back his heavy truck up a 70-foot long, 10-foot wide gravel path searching out the garbage, tastefully hidden from view.

His father did a good job as a truck delivery man, back in Greenpoint, Brooklyn where George grew up. When he died he left nothing, not even a car – just enough insurance to bury him. At 17 George went to work as a $75-a-week milkman to support himself and his mother.

'I'd go out at two in the morning delivering milk and be in the dairy till late at night washing bottles. I wound up working twelve hours a day, seven days a week. For eight years I worked without a day off.'

The local garbage man was Bud, and he wasn't too much of a worker. Whenever George dropped off milk, he'd hear, 'If you see that garbage man, tell him to get over here. My cans haven't been emptied for a week.' One day he bought a small pick-up truck and the next time he heard this lament he offered to do the job himself. Now he has ten trucks and as many men working for him as he can hire – and there's the rub. Even for $300 a week and a smart uniform with his own name on it, a man doesn't want to empty garbage and work George's hours. So the boss is out on the routes himself.

At four in the afternoon, it's time to make for the dump eighteen miles away, before it closes for the day. Goerge keeps his yard spick and span; he hates to have garbage overnight. He hasn't stopped for lunch. What with the smell and his asthma, he doesn't feel much like eating. But George isn't one to complain. Heroes don't. You'd never know from him that he's tired to his bones and can hardly breathe. No more than you'd hear him complain because the Quogue dump was closed two weeks ago after public pressure. Or that the Concerned Citizens Committee is picketing the new one.

This gold coast of the Atlantic has a straightforward way of dealing with rubbish. The authorities dig a big hole in the ground and everyone drops it all in – garbage, old food, raw sewage from overflowing cesspools, the lot. The stench is overwhelming. It's not helpful to think of the drinking water-table only 20 feet below the bottom of this pit of untreated refuse. And everywhere the angry cries of a million gulls.

At five George finally turns into the yard to hear that a truck has broken down and his new man is still halfway through his route. George will be out till nine finishing the new man's work and here till midnight fixing the truck. But first he slips upstairs to shower in his powder-blue bathroom and change into his Gucci moccasins. He sits wearily behind the desk on which stands a bronze plaque engraved: 'George J. Mathys, President.'

It's hard being an old-style hero in modern America, especially one who was raised on the old myths.

★   ★   ★

Quogue Village Hall has been host to pirates, mermaids, Indians, fussing mothers and flying children. Once again the Quogue Junior Theatre Troupe brought the summer social season to a close with its production of *Peter Pan*.

To be frank, it has not been without its problems. The pirates wouldn't concentrate on their choral ensemble. Wendy couldn't fly gracefully. There was a strong feeling among her admirers that vivacious Elizabeth 'Titch' Timperman was wasted as Tiger

Lily. And rehearsals were marred by a gaggle of two-year-olds crowing resentfully from the back. With the entire subteen population of Quogue employed in Thespian pursuits, the village at a stroke lost its babysitters.

These slender and long-legged 10-year-olds, showing unaccustomed nervousness as they hover on stage, are among the village's most voracious and determined entrepreneurs. Racing about on their ten-speed bicycles from job to job, they have been known to make up to $100 a week in season mainly by the ploy of playing one mother off against another.

Their rates seem beguilingly low: 75 cents an hour for 11 years old and under, $1.50 at 13, $2 at 14 and, by way of encouragement, everyone knows of Willette Hautmann earning $200 a week at just 17. But those who at nine talk knowingly of 'my newborns', who can skilfully feed, change and dress a couple of toddlers, also know how to wheedle the odd $5 or $10 a day from mothers anxious not to lose them to their dearest friend next door. Babysitter poaching has destroyed many a friendship.

It is taken for granted that middle-class American children set to work as early as possible. They are, after all, in training for an adulthood of acquisition. In summer those who do not go off to camp, to engage in building an old boy/girl network for later, embark on the pursuit of money.

Babysitting is the most thoroughly useful occupation bringing, as it does, a chance to pick up a rudimentary knowledge of interior decorating, social ease and the real estate market. It is taken as a bad show if babysitters are not allowed to bring with them their five- or six-year-old sisters since they too must start somewhere.

It is also to be expected that the sisters will hustle an hour or two of paid employment for themselves. In Quogue, for instance, a merry trade is plied at 50 cents an hour by those old enough to turn on a tap. The watering of newly-planted trees and bushes, by which each new house is automatically surrounded, is a first-rate business for a six-year-old. It involves only standing still and pointing a hose but, such is the discomfort of new plants in this sandy, unwelcoming soil, watering may provide a steady thrice-weekly income.

Thus it is not uncommon for two small children to be taking away $50 a week from some unsuspecting householder who thought she was providing pocket money to eager young innocents. When it comes to money, there are no innocents. A generation brought up to know the cost of every toy in Manhattan and which has learned a proper respect for venality from prime-time television – such a generation is not into Bob a Job.

Out here in summer, where a policeman goes on duty for a rest and expends his energy on the main business of moonlighting, it is quite safe for the small set to bike around. Most of Quogue's babysitters, however, live in Manhattan all winter and would, one might think, find their money-making activities curtailed there. Not a bit of it. The smallest apartment building, after all, is but a vertical village. Somewhere in the safety of a doormen-guarded building is a mother waiting to be parted from her money.

But like all high-powered people, the babysitters need a vacation. And all this week in Quogue Village Hall, Peter Pan and all the darling Darlings are stumbling through their parts while bewildered toddlers in the back rows cry out with indignation at their desertion.

The land trembles

Examination of the litter bins at the Quogue Village Beach is a disappointing business. Here, in its leisurely waste, should be the many and varied facets of small town life. How dull it all is. Endless, soggy copies of the *New York Times* from which the beach absorbs the same picture of the world. ('Did you hear about . . . ?' 'Yes, I saw that.')

There are polystyrene cups galore, gathered by assiduous, born-again environmentalists. Doubtless these white bits of eternity were chucked overboard by the ghostly fishermen of the dawn. Those who were truly born by this shore care less for the niceties of plastic flotsam than for the havoc wreaked by development. A quarter of a million dead fish surfaced the other day in a nearby inlet; they had been suffocated by the waste of new homes around it.

Those who have built their all-natural-materials, cedar-sided contemporary vacation homes do not litter. Disposable nappies are thoughtfully tucked in Ziplock plastic bags. Empty Perrier bottles by the score fill the bins that will later be taken away and dumped into that gargantuan hole on which gulls and other scavengers feast by the thousand.

It is a curious contradiction: those who come here to seek nature's beauty and abundance, lavishing upon it their sentimentality and aesthetic sensibility, live cheek-by-jowl with the evidence of their careless destruction. And in those beach litter bins, this contradiction becomes ever more clear. Amid the paper and plastic are the gifts of this rich, glacial earth – peaches so plentiful that they can be discarded after a sandy bite, half-empty baskets of sweet strawberries, blueberries, grapes, apples. An orchard can be tossed away, so generous is the land around.

Along the roads between the villages and towns of the Hamptons, peaceful farm fields stretch hazily into the distance. Corn, potatoes, cauliflowers, cabbages, tomatoes – vegetables and fruit grow easily in a soil that has been tilled for generations. In the heat of a summer's day, with the stillness of an old and continuing way of life stretching across the flat lands, it is easy to forget the acres being eaten away each year.

The town of Southampton, for instance, has lost over a fifth of its farmlands in five years. The local newspapers post the losses: '96 acres for sale for subdivision.' They ask $90,000 an acre with water view now in Quantuck Bay Farms, a choice development across the Quogue bridge. They have left the great farm gate in place leading to the secluded pools and patios – so nice, the feeling goes, to keep bits of the past alive.

Potato farming may not survive, of course. The pesticides that fought the Colorado beetle poisoned the wells of the new homes nestling in pastoral bliss. Those who drink bottled spring water by the crate are the first to cry out at contaminated tap water. Farmers do not make appropriate neighbours; those who choose to build expensively over-looking vistas of trembling cornfields do not expect the inconvenience of tractors ploughing at dawn. The police stations are getting quite used to irate city folk calling to complain as day breaks.

But as long as the farms keep their place as part of the postcard scenery, as long as the farmers' problems do not intrude on the rural retreats, they are all treasured. It is quite possible and, in some pockets of the Hamptons, quite chic, to go into the fields to pick vegetables for almost nothing a pound. Most, however, prefer to patronize the roadside farm stands which, together with the 'dear little antique shops', are part of local lore.

These farmstands, with their boxes, bins, crates and trappings of a harvest festival, also suggest that they are run by those who till the fields. In fact, few are farm-owned; few even sell local fruit and veg. The crafty entrepreneurs behind the stand, with just enough soil rubbed into their business-like hands, prefer to drive to Hunts Point Market in the Bronx, bringing back wares from California and the south-west. It's often cheaper; it's always easier. They prosper nevertheless.

Some are more honest than others; some more beloved. Nick the Original Fruit King, covered in tattoos, blinking through thick glasses, proudly caressing his handwashed and dried stock, draws customers from miles away. Nick, born and bred in the dingy streets of Brooklyn, lives for his fruit. He has a passion for vegetables. 'I've been in this business for fifty-eight years since I was eight years old, earning 25 cents a day, selling fruit from a wagon. I've been on my own since I was 15 and got my own horse. I love this stuff: fixing it up, playing with it, selling it. It's got all the different colours – green here, you've got red here, yellow there. It's all I ever did in all my life. I didn't want nothing else.'

On a summer Saturday maybe a hundred people crowd around his displays – hand-picking cherries, tweaking basil, prodding romaine. Over some bins hangs Nick's finest accolade – a hand-written notice that reads 'LOCAL'. Thick ears of corn, fat lettuces, thin ones, beans, broccoli, fleshy peaches, huge scarlet tomatoes – Nick's great, rough hands gently cradle them all as he gives each piece of fruit a softer resting place, each vegetable a more gallant showing. How easy it is to take all this for granted.

★   ★   ★

No one cares more articulately than a New Yorker: theatre, conservation, energy, the minorities. You name it and the New Yorker cares about it – which brings us to the plight of the American Indian. Feeling guilty about the Indians was a sixties thing in New York. *Bury My Heart at Wounded Knee* has lost its place on today's bookshelves.

Maybe it was the skyrocketing prices of Navajo jewellery, maybe it was that New Yorkers moved on to diamond tear-drops, anyway Indians are over these days. And perhaps that explains why no one out here in the Hamptons remembers the existence of the Shinnecock Indian Reservation. There on the map of Southampton, it is clearly marked: Indian Reservation. 800 acres of prime real estate, bounded on three sides with water-frontage. $35 million worth. At least.

Turning right off the highway, an unmarked road leads to the

Presbyterian Church, physical and emotional centre of the reservation. Its founding was written into the original 1640 treaty between Chief Nowadonah of the Shinnecocks and the colonists from Massachusetts. The Church quickly taught the Indians English (so they could learn the Bible), baptized them and put them into clothes. As late as 1950 every child living here went to the one-roomed church school. Its minister is the only non-Shinnecock allowed to have a house on the reservation.

At 11 o'clock on Sunday morning the Reverend Matthew Henry Thies, formerly of Brooklyn, Newark and Detroit, is pulling on his shoes, fastening his dog-collar and tucking his old-fashioned stomach into his shirt. His jowls hang down wearily; he was up until 3 counselling an alcoholic. It's hard to imagine what the Indians make of this German minister who sits in his run-down Victorian manse quoting Hegel, Freud and Bismarck.

Out of the 350 people living on the reservation, 187 are faithful church members, but in the end, Revd. Thies buries them all, out in the grounds by the bay. 'There's no organization to where we put them, we just bury them wherever the spirit moves us.' There are three roads on the reservation and 115 houses. Since the land is owned by the tribe ('A big kibbutz,' explains Revd. Thies), no one can get a mortgage to build. That explains the mobile homes, the shabby older houses.

Anyone who can prove a blood tie to a Shinnecock is a Shinnecock. Would-be Indians come by every year. They're taken along to the old people who either do or don't know them. If they don't, they're not Shinnecocks. A few years ago, a marina development company offered the tribe a $450 million deal to rent a strip of their waterfront. The tribe refused; they had visions of being tied up in court for years by all and sundry claiming to be Shinnecock.

Simple, some might say. You either are or aren't Indian. Not exactly. It becomes clearer in church. Revd. Thies walks up the aisle, the congregation rises. Here is the result of three hundred years of inter-marriage. In the beginning, they married the white colonists. Over there is 87-year-old Alice Phillips, a Cuffee. With her elegant pink hat, carefully washed frock and immaculate white gloves, she looks like a frail Victorian lady from an English sea-side town. Over there is a Hunter; she can trace her line to Chief Nowadonah himself. She's black.

Although not one full-blooded Shinnecock still lives (nor has for years), there's an elaborate hierarchy on the reservation. There are white Indians and black Indians. They're highly touchy about who goes back furthest and whose blood is Indianest but they're still a tribe – although the Shinnecocks have refused to go to any American Indian meeting ever since the terrible time that the Iroquois called the Shinnecock 'niggers'. They have the one thing that other tribes didn't: they have land.

In 1954 some sharp builder put up a model house and dug foundations for twelve others on the Shinnecock side of Montauk Highway. The tribe was poor; few of its members had a college education. Most of them worked as domestics for the rich summer folks in Southampton. They were used to being subservient; presumably they would simply accept this latest humiliation. This was no reservation as such, either. No federal agency had rounded them up and granted them land. They were here because they had always been here.

A local lawyer in the district took it upon himself to go to court on their behalf. The case took six years but in 1960 the Supreme Court handed down the decision that this 800 acres south of Montauk Highway is all Shinnecock land. The jubilant tribe dug up the concrete foundations and hurled them into the sea. At low tide you can see them still.

But here, on the reservation, all that seems remote. Only the cars and the television aerials suggest the world outside. A horse wanders around unfettered, nibbling at the long grass. The tribe is still arguing about who should cut it. On a corner the young radicals gather round their bicycles. They're the ones who are giving themselves Indian names (not always authentic), searching for more Indianness, rebelling against the Victorian Christianity of their parents and grandparents.

Over the road, in an old house overlooking the bay, Courtland Cuffee, 73, sits mulling over the changes. Here for the first time is the outward expression of what being Shinnecock means. That extraordinary Indian face with the granite features gives almost nothing away.

The only time he left the reservation was to serve in the army during the war. American Indians then could choose to serve in white or black regiments. Why did he choose black? He shrugs. 'I'll tell you why,' a quiet voice from the kitchen, 'because of me.' His wife, Muriel, part Indian, part white, part black. 'There are parts of my own family that won't accept me because of my mixed blood. I have always had trouble knowing who I am so I've always said I am black. And I have always felt inferior. Because I am.'

Beneath the black skin are the fine bone structure of an Indian and the unhappiness of one for whom an identity has always been a problem. Does her husband understand any of what she feels? 'No, for him it's simple. He's Shinnecock.'

On the wall is a plaque from the Southampton Highways Department: 'To Courtland Cuffee for service 1926–1968'. How did he feel laying roads for forty years on lands over which his ancestors once roamed freely? Courtland Cuffee, Shinnecock, shrugs . . . his eyes glare a fraction more and his head goes up almost imperceptibly.

★   ★   ★

The leaves are turning in Quogue. As far as the eye can see from the steps of the deserted Quogue Village Beach Hut, there are layers of orange, red and gold across the distant hills. The shower, water fountain, garbage bins, telephone and soda machines have been dismantled and taken away. The beach has been given up to the elements. The winter ocean is Quogue's minotaur.

Fall storms move across it. Heavy rains clean the beaches of debris. In the morning the sun shines on the Atlantic, pursuing its impartial climb up the dunes towards the fishing huts and majestic 'cottages'.

Schools of blowfish, herring, fluke, flounder, bluefish and striped bass are gathering for the journey to their far-off wintering places. The plover have already left. Occasionally there's sight of hawks from Canada and Maine passing by. And all over Quogue there are the sounds of fall: turf nutrient being scattered, pools being drained, oil pumping into fuel tanks.

In summer the time to bicycle down to the village is in the early morning before the relentless thud of tennis balls spoils the quiet. Now there is only quiet. And cycling around at five in the afternoon, the rich smell of woodsmoke celebrates the departure of summer's Sternolog population.

The weekend amateurs hate to burn wood in their open fireplaces. It makes a mess, brings crawling creatures into the house, oozes over spotless brass endirons. How much more convenient to burn odourless blocks chemical-drenched for fast ignition, wrapped in clean paper. All that's needed is a match and a handy fire extinguisher. 'Do not use water in case of emergency,' it states ominously on the package.

But the Sternolog set is back in Manhattan. At dusk the Quogue air is sweetened by all the fragrances of real winter fires: honest pine, strong and lusty oak, occasionally a whiff of something more elusive – ash, perhaps, or sycamore? In the 1890s rugged woodchopper camps dotted the wilderness of Long Island. On the North Shore thousands of cords of wood waited for spring and the small sloops that would ferry them down to New York City. Now the air hums with electric saws and each garage and porch has its neat stack of winter logs.

The first pilgrims arrived in a country that had over 900 million acres of forests. A little over 5 per cent is left. A village like Quogue, desperately trying to protect itself from creeping suburbia, hugs its trees tightly. The worst insult a local can pay a neighbour is to allege that he has cut down trees unnecessarily.

Imagine the social standing of the man around the corner on Old Depot Road who wiped his front yard clean because he didn't like having leaves on his lawn. That each fall he erects a fence of chickenwire to keep out the leaves of others completes his betrayal.

The nights in Quogue grow longer. The ocean mist rolls in across clean and empty streets. The village truck has vacuumed from them the carpet of leaves, so now the dark roads gleam with moisture under the occasional headlight.

It is the time of year when those residents of the Suffolk Pines Adult Mobile Home Park who have not left for their second trailers in Florida begin to walk more hesitantly. The central heating units in the Park have begun their nightly chug. The grandchildrens' rooms have been closed up for winter and the summer snapshots in their cut-price frames have been moved on to the colour television sets.

It is not a bad life in the mobile home park. Most of the residents owned houses in Quogue that they built or bought for a few thousand dollars and sold for $50,000 or more. The 50-foot trailers have built-in washing machines, dryers, washing-up machines, central heating, air-conditioning, a tiny garden and that vital second bedroom for the summer grandchildren until they get too busy to visit.

It may not be smart to live behind Strebel's laundry and three-minute carwash on Montauk Highway, but such considerations count for less on small, fixed incomes. There may not be the choice of entertainment of New York City, but neither is there the loneliness nor the expense. No fear of landlords cutting off the heat by way of encouraging the rent-controlled tenants to move. No hiding behind locks and bars.

Quogue's summer life is rigidly structured: income level mixes with income level. Large cottages near the beach do not dine with small ranch houses near the highway. When winter comes around, the democracy of middle and old age settles down again. Clara Blaufeld, the glamorous former opera singer in her late fifties, has a beautiful house on Quogue Street, but she has always been generous with others in more modest circumstances.

To one she offers a trip into the city for a special concert; to another, a celebration supper in one of the few restaurants that stay open all year. There is no feeling of awkwardness or envy. All of Quogue rejoiced when she lost nine stone at a costly clinic down south early this year. Her achievement was everyone's.

It is this sense of confidence, of effectiveness that sets the older residents here apart from those in the city. One does not give up, wait helplessly to be pushed around and then to die.

The older residents are gentle, kindly neighbours. They live with the seasons, acutely aware of the lapping of time, the power of nature. Each November they say goodbye to their gardens and long farewells to the outdoors. This is a very special time for the regulars on Quogue pier, a small bare spit jutting out into the bay. This is where the older residents who can no longer afford boats, and are too stiff to climb into them, come for the last two weeks fishing of the season.

Fishing for the summer residents is a social affair, all about directors' chairs on yacht decks and talk of marlin landed in Mexico and salmon outwitted in Scotland. The regulars on Quogue pier, with their old trusted rods, cannot afford the fish shops. What they cook is what they catch. This is a serious business.

The bay stretches for miles, the still brilliant sun glints over it for a few days of perfect beauty. Bill used to be a long-distance truckdriver; now he is retired and cycles everywhere. Antonio ran an Italian restaurant with his wife who died suddenly four years ago. He has a crab basket hanging over one side of the dock and while he waits, he walks up and down busily offering recipes for flounder in tomato sauce.

He and Bill discuss their worms dug up for the day's fishing. Then his craggy beaming face drops as he tells of his new wife, a widow of 56, who has just revealed that she married him for security. Each time Bill turns sympathetically from his rod to listen to this woeful tale there is another bite. He will go home tonight with twenty fish.

Maybe there are sixteen men down on the dock – casting, crabbing and taking their farewell. They worked for forty years. Some had businesses, some clung to jobs they could hardly bear. In their old waders and jackets, each with an individual and battered hat keeping the sun away, they share together the enthusiasm of the moment. Soon even the flounder will go out to sea, the dock will be deserted and the gales will drive across the bay.

★   ★   ★

If there is one fact known to middle-aged, American suburban males it is that they suffer their greatest number of heart attacks while shovelling snow. All that unaccustomed exercise, all that aggravation and sense of helplessness before the elements – every twinge represents a moment of terror. This may explain the brisk business being done around the village of Quogue by small tough boys who have yet to acquire the American phobia of coronary mishaps.

The eastern end of Long Island is suffering its bleakest winter for fifty years. In the new contemporary boxes bought for the languor of summer resort living, the effects are now being seen of building with green wood, huge stretches of glass and occasional insulation. Central heating systems, sputtering to keep up, spew hot air at enormous cost – thereby ensuring that doors buckle, fireplaces spring loose from the floor and walls crack. And yet the frozen glades are still aloud with hammering as more such boxes rise between the gaunt trees.

Who can they be for, these new $250,000 houses? Realtors insist that the only surviving market at the moment is for something – anything – over three-quarters of a million. The place, they say, abounds with buyers wandering about, cash in hand, looking to put a million or so to rest in a handsome estate. Greeks, French, South Americans, wherever the monied feel uneasy, they dream of a heaven in little man's America.

But the other houses, those five-bedroomed, four-bathroom affairs with pool and tennis courts, who can possibly afford those nowadays? As it is, many homes are closed up for the winter because owners can no longer meet mortgage repayments *and* pay heating bills. So Quogue is an eerie place. From the roads a line of snow-covered pools stretch in the distance. Around them is the ghostly presence of the over-stretched middle-class lingering in hot-weather loungers and barbecue tables heaped higgledy-piggledy by the storms.

Now and again a family appears across the snow-drifts, gathering armchairs joyfully left out in the euphoria of summer. Small city children in designer down suits wobble like miniature spacemen across the unaccustomed spaces, shrieking with surprise as snow touches impeccable mittens. Parents clamber around overwhelmed by the reality of second home-owning – broken windows, frozen pipes, buried entrance ways. A day trip to wonderland turns to misery as a call for help raises only the answering machine and its announcement that Mr Builder is in Florida until next month.

This is the time that the only happy person in Quogue is the house-sitter. Sprawled on the sofa, drinking gin, a log burning merrily, thermostat set at 72°F – and all this paid for by another – he is indeed a contented man. Since he is probably living in a house that is up for sale (all houses in Quogue, by definition, being up for sale), he knows that in such wretched weather no one turns out to view, so that the scattering of his dirty underclothes far and wide will be of no consequence.

The housesitter is he who, in September, portrays himself to the chicken-hearted home-owner as responsible, tidy, experienced and newly separated (the latter suggests that he isn't renting a lovely home himself only because he hopes by his lowly plight to move his wife to a reconciliation). Furthermore, he mentions that he is friendless, a non-smoker, teetotal and delighted with the small bedroom to which he promises to confine himself. ('My needs are very simple.') January is the moment of reckoning.

It then becomes clear that he is lazy, messy, imaginative in the wrong ways ('I would have shovelled the snow but decided that the ice below would create too treacherous a path'), invites acquaintances to stay and is firmly ensconced in the master bedroom, slightly out of sorts because the supply of French bath oil has run out.

Since winter has set in with all its threats, he feels confident enough to demand that the cable television be reconnected and no longer even pretends that he expects to 'contribute' to the bills. In order for the owners to enjoy a short break in their own home, they are forced to offer instead their empty apartment in Manhattan for his convenience. (It will, almost certainly, have been his idea: 'It seems so obvious.')

Never mind that back in September he pencilled their visit into his diary saying, 'I like to get away to the Caribbean in January so that'll work fine.' Possession, as they say, is nine-tenths of everything that counts. In the end he's quite glad that they come. At least the house gets cleaned, the drink restocked, his mouldy left-overs are cleared out of the fridge and in the general cleaning up doubtless someone will find that shoe he mislaid a month ago. He will have had a marvellous holiday in the city and called once or twice to be sure that all is running smoothly and, incidentally, to find out how to use the videotape machine. ('Do you have more movies anywhere?')

On his return he will peruse the long, seething list of instructions left behind for him. If he has any real pride in his role as house-sitter, he will be forced to telephone Manhattan to explain that he cannot wrap garbage in plastic bags as per the request on ecological grounds. ('You probably don't realize that plastic never decomposes.') He will, however, promise to do something before he leaves about the maggots in the dustbins. Naturally, it will be beneath him even to mention shovelling the snow.

★   ★   ★

There is no subject dearer to the heart of an upwardly mobile American than real estate. It has everything: romance, sex, status, fantasy, the security of deep love, the fever of grand passion.

It is a virtuosic display: 'It's a 10-acre parcel, the bank would roll over 50 per cent, the owner would take back 40, so for 10 grand upfront, I'd clear 100.' It is a harmless dream: 'They want a million, I could get it for 600 thou, in a year it would turn over for a million two.' At the very least, it's a painless way to escape: 'We've been in it for five years; time to move on.'

Nowhere is this more apparent than in the Hamptons. In the time of the white heat, the last six weeks of summer, the air is loud with the sound of front doors closing behind panting buyers and the roads swish with realtors, clients captive beside them, eager to sell to those wanting water view for $200,000 or some cosy wooded retreat for over three.

It is called 'making music'. It is not a home that is being sold but an image of hedonistic happiness. A house costs $145,000 to build, the land is worth $80,000 – the asking price is $350,000 firm. The difference is music. Drive along any road; the houses for sale are the ones with geranium urns newly installed outside. Why geraniums? They're scarlet, hot and bold and they do not shed – dying leaves do not make music.

During the weeks of the white heat, owners must endure certain inconveniences. Garbage bins must be shut away in basements and sprayed twice daily with Chanel No. 5. Hedonism knows not the bother of smelly trash. Living-rooms must be glacially air-conditioned to soothe and seduce and in them owners must, nevertheless, be found half-naked and languorous, suggesting that this is a house in which sex is always spontaneous and never less than ecstatic.

At the first sound of a car, housework must cease. This haven of sensuality is to seem chore-free. (It is the opposite of selling an over-priced ski lodge where it would be essential to be caught poking a log fire and checking a pie in the oven.) One person must be deputed to leap into the pool and smile, another to jump into a bubble bath and purr. During these weeks, no fat friends may be entertained.

Bathrooms are the true battlefield. All medicines are to be thrown out. Those who allow a cabinet to be opened on bottles for the relief of acid indigestion, wind or constipation deserve to lose the sale. Better by far, along with the geraniums, to invest in jars of Vitamin B complex, Floris bath oil and a vibrator or two.

Pity the poor owners who built their home three years ago before the bathroom came into its own – never guessing that the Jacuzzi would become standard, forgetful of mirrored walls for the lean and glistening. Introspection and self-indulgence are where the money is: those who are into jogging, aerobic jumping, dieting, therapy and Smokenders want a bathroom to be an experience. They want marble, they crave mirrors, they need skylights for a oneness with the heavens.

Do not ask why prices held for so long in these shaky times. What does a mortgage mean to those who put no price on gratification? They come from all over America to Manhattan; in tough offices, five days a week, they quiver with ambition and insecurity. On weekends they want it all: self-indulgence, escapism, sensuality, the rewards of their imprisonment, the illusion of their freedom. It's no longer money; it's numbers.

And in this world where a five-bedroomed sale means at least $20,000 in commission, realtors swarm, imprisoned in their own fantasies. Enter James Paul Malvey: choreographer of romance and real estate. It started with his slogan: 'You are where you live.' In tasteful weekly advertisements in the *Hampton Chronicle,* he brought the music-making into the open. Below a picture of Rodin's *Creation of Man* ran his simple message: 'The value of fine art forever increases; a truly fine residence may enjoy a similar appreciation.' Beneath a Chagall: 'A house doesn't create an owner's image. It confirms it. Westhampton Beach $350,000.' Matisse: 'In a world that demands so much of you, take time to be kind to yourself. $325,000.' Gone forever was the news: 'W. Beach, 5 beds, 1 acre, cathedral-clgs.'

James Paul Malvey, the son of a subway train driver from Kilkenny, has been in business for one year – commission: over $100,000. How exquisitely ironic that one who was a monk in the Order of Christian Brothers, who, for twenty years, gave his life to vows of poverty, chastity and obedience, should so thoroughly understand the worldliness of all this.

For ten years he worked as a missionary, teaching in a black South African township. Until his advertising campaign this year, his greatest success had been in founding the first black marching band in Kimberley, instruments courtesy of a defunct New York City police club. He left the order when he was recalled to America: 'I didn't feel that children in this country needed a teacher who was dedicating his whole life to it.'

So here he is, after a brief spell in the men's gold jewellery department of Tiffany ('It was very useful. I realized I was the same as everyone else. They were no different from me – they just had money'), off-loading real estate, moving into million-dollar negotiations and relishing the satisfaction of a useful job well done.

'When I was a brother, I believed that was where I should have been at that time of my life, as I believe this is where I should be now. This is real. This is not Monopoly. This is as much part of life as Africans working in mines.'

One morning James Paul Malvey woke up to find the bottom had fallen out of the housing market.

★   ★   ★

The condition of being anywhere near solvent, of not charging up to the limit on every available credit card, of not knowingly writing cheques on empty accounts – in short, the condition of not drowning in debts – is known in America as being a financial conservative.

Quogue, needless to say, is not a village of thrifty souls. Where there are second homes there are also first mortgages, second mortgages, bank loans, $15,000 borrowed from a passing aunt and astounding conjuring tricks whereby income swells into outgoings that bear no relation in size. One Quogue hero filed a tax return last year showing an income of $61,000 and taking a deduction of $29,000 of interest charges alone. Only America could so reward the state of being in debt.

The idea is not to pay off debts but to service them. They are not a liability but an asset. Ownership is an attitude of mind. If the thing coveted is in one's possession what does it matter whose money was used for its acquisition? Putting one's money to work actually means using somebody else's.

It is worth understanding a typical Quogue house sale. Ten percent down in cash, say $20,000, is easily found by using next year's taxes which can, after all, be worried about next year. A Manhattan bank enthusiastically grants a first mortgage of $80,000, a local bank within moments hands over a personal loan of $25,000 and an anxious seller willingly takes back a second mortgage of $70,000. Why, there's the house and only $4,000 or so to be paid each month and something will doubtless turn up.

Unfortunately for all, the property market has suddenly gone cold. Hardly a house is now changing hands. In these days of 16 per cent loans, the music has stopped. American money, though, is just another thing one goes out to buy, rather like a dishwasher or car, which, being a product, must be available in endless quantities. The problem, they say, is merely that the product has become momentarily too expensive. Thus is the economic plight of a country dismissed with a wave.

Middle-class Americans do not go broke; they get stretched. At a pinch, they get strapped. There is no shame in not being able to service the monthly debts, only irritation at not being able to incur more of them. Who will wait? Who will be satisfied with less? At a pinch there's the time-honoured device of sending off a bunch of unsigned cheques or putting the one made out to New York Telephone in the envelope to American Express. Any sleight of hand helps that keep the bills in the air just a while longer. It is not called owing money, it is being financially creative.

Knowing how to handle debts with panache is a question of having personal style. 'I don't know how he/she does it' does not express disapproval but admiration. The impoverished Quogue householder, dunned and hounded, forced to offer for sale his brand new, marble-lined beach house, will continue to acquire the most elegant of furnishings with which to flatter it. When the house sells, everyone gets paid, everyone's happy and his credit rating will be impeccable.

People do not fight to preserve their homes; they sell their homes to preserve their life-style. Today a house is sold that tomorrow another may be acquired. Where nothing is invested but money, the backdrop may be sacrificed that the accessories may be saved. Those who cannot afford mortgage repayments reach out for the realtors. The matching loveseats and sofas, the scatter cushions and Kilm rugs, the Brown Jordan deck furniture and Bill Blass bathsets go, like some majestic opera production, into store until the next engagement.

In this land of comings and goings and financial alarums, it is, though, worth noting that some stay put in their neat and gentle place. Opposite Quogue Post Office, the parish pump where matters are exchanged of who has how much and who no longer has what, a joyous bank of roses greets the eye.

Here in a small white bungalow has lived Donald Goodale with his wife Mildred for nearly thirty years. His blue spruce have grown tall, his copper beech shades the trusty lawn and his roses commemorate the moment he went to work for the lumber yard in which he passed his life until retirement. His garden is full of flowers as is his home of moments past.

The two empty acres on either side of his house have been planted to please the passer-by and for his own continuing delight. Those used to other ways often ask why he doesn't sell off these two prime building acres. 'I love the space,' says he, 'and is money really that important?'

On the move

At twilight a faint mist seeps over the palm trees on our street. For one clammy moment there is confusion. What is a sea fog doing in this patch of suburban bungalows squashed between two great highways snorting unleaded gasoline?

Against the sound of the distant traffic and splashing of a thousand automatic sprinkler systems, memory stirs. We are but three miles from Santa Monica Bay and the Pacific Ocean where oil rigs will soon also rise.

This is Lotusland, California where answering machines communicate. T-shirts talk, scatter cushions ask, 'How was that for you?' and people are into non-verbal relationships except with their analysts and plants. (Please note that the former now wish to be known as 'expanders' not 'shrinks'.)

Change is always with us in Los Angeles. But this time it is more than usually perplexing. For a city that is the byword for hedonism back East, there is a definite and growing nostalgia for the good old days of Sparta. Self-denial is the new order. Don't eat red meat, don't drink, don't smoke, don't let body hair blemish the glistening new muscles. (It's announced as 'executive waxing': back, chest, shoulder and chin hair removal for men.)

The regime is all. The very word is redolent with militant fervour. Where once there was a kite shop, now there is a martial arts studio. Those who grace Spantex-clad exercise classes three times weekly also take karate. 'Join the tortured and look terrific,' reads the glossy magazine advertisement for a training gym. The look is mean: spare of flesh, firm of muscle. Who, one wonders, are these traditionally sun-kissed, pleasure-loving, fun babies of California drilling themselves to fight?

The New Yorker, ready perhaps to finesse a little hand-to-hand combat if necessary, quails before these magnificent fighting machines of the West. The contradictions of the coasts: the New Yorkers with their big mouths; Los Angelinos and their big biceps. For New York state, a governor who marries a property developer; for California, one who meditates.

Fortunately, in this condition of renewed culture shock, we stay in one of those forgotten corners that fashion neglects to penetrate, where a few old-fashioned paunches are still to be seen and treasured as mementoes of the past. This avenue of tiny two-bedroomed bungalows shelters lace curtains, rose bushes, ageing widows and retired educators from nearby UCLA.

The women walk a determined three miles from 8.30 to 9.30, the men go bike riding in jogging suits from 10.30 to noon. But those are the only concessions to the mood of the moment. The widows still wash and scrub their neat homes as only ethnic maids coming in from some far district of the city are meant to do. (Bussing of cleaning ladies has always been acceptable: it's only bussing of white children that offends Los Angeles.) To be fair, it's perfectly all right to do your own cleaning if it's in the quest for enlightenment: Zen laundry, inner housework, holistic window washing, that sort of thing.

But the old-timers are slowly moving on. Some can't resist cashing in on the market price for their fifty-year-old homes. Others start to fret at the threatening quiet of night. They move into retirement communities for the active elderly: $200 a week, food-for-fitness included and 'as long as he's able to function on his own we'll keep him'.

The newcomers arrive, dragging the businesses behind them. When the pace gets too much on the avenue, it's always worth the walk to watch through picture-windows the body-builders in the new Nautilus Aerobic Center Spa. The Nautilus Sports/ Medical Industries' machines are the pride of the new Sparta. They cut down exercise time: pain and exhaustion can be yours within minutes. See the sufferers grabbing the chocolate-coloured frames, sweating over the tan leatherette upholstery. It is even better than the Rams play wounding football or the

Tuesday night women wrestling in mud at the local bar. This is for real and this is for free.

See those once soft-hearted, slack-skinned boys who, long ago, marched for civil rights. Now they flex hefty shoulders beneath clipped hair; they've grown into hard-hearts marching for no man. The muscle power for which once they admired, envied and feared the street-hardened blacks they have made their own. The middle-class white boys strut around the gym tautly aware of the prize-fighting might they have wrested into being.

See the daddies drop the daughters on the corner of Westwood. Then see those daughters, brought almost to perfection by cosmetic surgeons and orthodontists, reared in cotton wool (even if soaked in amyl nitrite), work out according to the Nautilus concept: hurt me, please. All that money to buy protection from pain or hardship and it comes to this.

Naturally, a dog is a rarity here. One Doberman Pinscher, a breed common as the cockroach in Manhattan, stops a crowd on Westwood. Dogs, like heroes, are now only for the movies. They have no place in everyday life.

The faithful friends have been replaced by machines: cars with names for instance. 'Ralph and I are going out to dinner' means 'I'm driving my VW'. Telephone answering machines talk to you when you get home but don't demand bowls of new soft Purina. And, at last, Nautilus: the machine that lets you experience S & M in the privacy of your own body.

★   ★   ★

On Sunday the centre of Columbus, Ohio, is cold, frosty and quiet. It has the atmosphere of a 1950s postcard of an American city. No squeal of brakes, no war calls from roaming teenagers. Cars gently glide by while, on the sidewalks, families bundle towards church. The bells ring out over empty streets. On Sunday morning in Columbus even Macdonalds is closed.

In American consciousness, this is a nothing town. Not banished into an oblivion as total as that of, say, Bismarck, North Dakota, it still has no role, no character to play in the nation's fantasy.

Portland, Oregon, for instance, is a virgin – highminded, ecologically principled. Detroit is a slob; Miami, an ageing gigolo; Dallas a mean ol' boy. Los Angeles is a nympho, New York a harpy and Columbus, Ohio, is a very nice place to have left behind.

Certainly, on this ordinary Sunday morning, its appeal is not immediately evident. Downtown there are a handful of tall new buildings; the rest are low and bleak. The shop fronts are post-war Scunthorpe. The newspaper headlines could have been written by Disgusted, Cheltenham: 'City's rising homosexual population is blamed for venereal disease surge,' reads one. But Ohio is the heartland where Gerald Ford is still hero, honoured for his college football career and for being a Republican. Columbus is the state capital and the merest glance down the list of major legislation now before the Ohio General Assembly gives a fair idea of its concerns and persuasions.

Senate Bill 233 increases penalties for participating in dog and cock fights. House Bill 557 prohibits criminals from profiting from the sale of books and movie rights about their crimes. House Bill 74 reinstates the death penalty. 893 eliminates the plea of not guilty by reason of insanity. And House Bill 879 requires unmarried girls 15 years old and younger to obtain parental or court permission before having abortions.

Opposite State House, a stone, porticoed building in the square, the Ohio chapter of the Right to Life organization is holding a weekend jamboree at the Neil House motel. It is a crowd that might gather round the hairnet counter of Woolies. There is a smell of French fries and indignation. The first ten women questioned say of course no 15-year-old should have an abortion. A pregnant teenager should have the baby and 'put it out for adoption'. (How revealing is that 'out'.) The talk is of avoiding killing and murder.

A petition is going around against registering women for the draft. 'Americans won't allow their daughters to be drafted,' says a mother of four. 'I wouldn't let them take mine.' And what of the sons? Who speaks for them? No one who's taken seriously in Ohio, that's for sure. No killing in the womb – only on the battlefield or in the wild.

Guns are man's business as birth is woman's. There are half a million eager hunters out there in Ohio, fretting at the poor sport. Under a new programme, the state will pay $2.5 million to farmers for not planting crops. The idea is to provide more nesting places for pheasants and thus more pheasants to shoot (shades of Trollope).

Concern over a dwindling pheasant population (3 million in 1960, 100,000 now), a burgeoning Right to Life association, organized opposition to gun control laws, this is not a town for the queasy conscience from New York. The dilemma for the outsider, however, is that, as a place to live, it obviously pleases those who are here.

Ohio State University at Columbus is America's largest campus. Admittedly its 51,000 student body is known mostly for the muscular excellence of its sports teams, but that's America. Where some universities rest on their Nobel prizes, others rest on their football trophies. When Ohio State played the University of Southern California at the January Rose Bowl, the television spectacle is said to have attracted 6,000 new residents to the California sunshine and 3,000 new students to Ohio State.

A university presence in America means money, grants, theatre, concert series, bookshops, cinemas, restaurants – not just for students but for the community. The successful businessman, too, defines himself by the amount of expensive culture that he and his town can support. Once a city needed a cathedral to feel secure about its place in the world; today it needs a performing arts' complex.

Columbus has its own symphony orchestra, professional theatres, opera and ballet companies, modern gallery and fine arts museum, and that's apart from university imports such as Gilels, *Coppelia*, the Los Angeles Philharmonic. That's why Ann Arbor, Michigan, Minneapolis, Minnesota, and Columbus, Ohio, often dismay the East Coaster who visits prepared to suffer and scorn. Could it be that New Yorkers do not stand closest to heaven?

It is a matter of great pride to the New Yorker that Carnegie

Hall did not become a parking lot. This overlooks the inconvenient fact that Isaac Stern saved it almost by himself and that the
old, now lamented, Metropolitan Opera House simply vanished.

On this Sunday morning, on the West Broad Street side of
Columbus' central square, the strains of Beethoven's Fifth can be
heard through the heavy brass doors of the Palace Theatre. In the
marble foyer under the newly restored 54-lamp chandelier, a
transistor radio rallies the volunteers who are sanding mirrors,
vacuuming and sweeping a red-carpeted staircase, brushing
renovated seats, painting walls and generally readying the
54-year-old art deco Palace for its gala night. The theatre that
nearly became a car park reopens this week.

Directly across the square, a Moose convention has taken over
the Ohio Theatre for the day. This baroque, gilded, damasked,
historical monument was designed by an architect who wanted
to remind people of a European palace (Ludwig of Bavaria?). It
was saved by the community within days of its demolition order.
No one talks of the 'quality of life' in Columbus; they frequently
use the word 'community'.

Standing in the square, listening to the church bells, there is a
moment of painful nostalgia. Ah yes. Bournemouth, '55.

★   ★   ★

The Park Plaza Hotel in Cleveland, for reasons that will become
evident, is now world famous. There is Muzak piped outdoors
into the driveway. From its bedroom windows, it is possible to
gaze upon the full majesty of downtown Cleveland. It is not
exactly a feast for the eyes.

Just over the road from the hotel is a brown-brick building of
some stature. It is the Cleveland Clinic – fashionable new venue
for petro-dollar operations. King Khalid of Saudi Arabia came
here for open heart surgery. Now the hotel lounge is full of lesser
Arab families whittling away the hours between visiting times.

It is a scene familiar to frequenters of London hotels. It is quite
novel to Americans. They look vaguely puzzled as a call comes
over the public tannoy for Mr Al-this or Mr Al-that. But in the
lounge no one stares at the women in black, sitting patiently in
the midst of their large families. Americans on the whole don't

stare. They are too wary of giving offence. They are also inured to surprise – although resigned might be the better word.

It is interesting, however, to watch the Arabs watching the Americans. They are fascinated by their infinite variety. The most sought-after spot in the lounge is directly opposite the bank of elevators. Seven in the evening seems to be the favourite time as guests come down for yet another slow, dark dinner in the restaurant.

Arabs have been known to remark that Europeans, especially the British, all look alike to them. They could hardly say that about the Americans. A few businessmen, anonymous in dark suits, are in the hotel. There are older couples wearing all the colours of the rainbow, of course. But even without these extremes, the elevators disgorge an astonishing mixture. Nowhere in Europe would there be such diversity of styles, skin tones, body language. Who would have thought that there were so many ways to step through a door? And none of this is lost on the lounge watchers. They never seem bored. How could they? It is a constant show, and about the only one available to them.

Cleveland minds very much about its national image. It stands in relation to television much as the mother-in-law did to the music-hall. It is an old industrial town (mostly steel) on a poisoned lake (Erie) with a downtown area from which the middle classes stay away. Visitors hear about the superb fortress-like museum – and then about the bomb explosion that shattered the right leg of Rodin's *Thinker* outside. No wonder the Arabs cling to the lounge. It is dangerous to walk the streets outside the hotel and there is nothing there worth the risk.

Each morning reveals a new mountain of shopping bags in the lounge. Inquiries reveal that Beechwood Place, a new mall in the suburbs, is well worth a visit. The best shopping complexes in this country are its real museums of modern art. The greatest artifacts and creations of the age are to be found in them and no effort or expense is spared in their display. They are museums, entertainment palaces and psychotherapeutic expeditions all rolled into one.

Three minutes away from the hotel, the road climbs into

suburbia; elegant, wooded, dotted with ponds. Shaker Heights, to the right, is said to have the highest *per capita* income in the States. Even the suburbs around New York don't have this impact. Manhattan for all its faults still has a magnetism. Downtown Cleveland has nothing to offer the Heights except work.

Three years ago Saks Fifth Avenue decided to open in Cleveland. Their store is out here in Beechwood Place. There is almost nothing to see from the outside, except rainswept spaces for 5,000 cars scattered over seven acres. Inside is a two-acre, two-storey park with trees and fountains framed in gleaming brass and wood. Careful lighting dapples the whole with 'sunlight'. There are 'outdoor' cafes, tiny tiled alleys, the smell of roasting coffee, the sound of rushing water and 110 shops and two department stores.

What pleasure it is to spend money here. It has none of the inconveniences of real life: no weather, no swollen feet, no pollution, no danger, no stale air or air too fresh. There are no heavy doors to juggle, no short-tempered crowds, no moment when the parcels grow too many – smiling assistants quickly offer to take them to the car.

A small puritan voice inside clucks nervously at so much creative energy being devoted to spending, spending, spending. Is it coincidence that the lowliest purchase from Saks is wrapped in a scarlet box held together with a golden garter? Thrift beware; the end is nigh.

★   ★   ★

As the valley road winds into Aspen, the Rocky Mountains get gentler. They are covered with thick trees and dotted with pastures where wildflowers grow beneath the warm summer sun. But all through town run the swift streams, curling beneath bridges and along paths. Their water is icy for it brings the melting snow down from those fierce peaks that can be glimpsed in the distance.

A hundred years ago the silver miners traipsed over those peaks and the hard years they lived here still haunt old ghost towns such as Ashcroft that are scattered around today's Aspen with its boutiques, condominium chateaux and arrays of perfectly ripened French cheeses.

Standing on the bridge by Castle Creek on the outskirts of town, the new migrants can be seen rolling in past the solar houses and private planes parked at the airport. They come in huge station-wagons, dusty from days on distant highways. Their cars are jammed with boxes and battered trunks.

Some come for the ski-ing, others for a touch of Nirvana. Still others come because here, they believe, is still work to be found – that fool's silver of the present. They all, though, come in search of a better life. Soon, they reason, they will replace the furniture, records, books and bikes that they sold so cheaply in yard and garage sales because there was no room in the wagon, not enough money to get to the promised land out West.

Standing on Castle Creek bridge as an onlooker, it seems a thoughtless way to discard a life, digging up roots, wiping the past clean, moving on. It is usually assumed that they choose to wander and embrace the challenge eagerly.

Myra Langridge drove over the bridge two years ago with four children, a cat, a dog and boxes of clothes. Her husband Roger had driven in three weeks earlier with a friend. The day he arrived he found a job. That afternoon he started work; a week later he rented an apartment. 'Since Roger had found somewhere furnished, all I brought with me from Wisconsin was the children and they were allowed only one or two things that were favourites. It was hard.'

Her husband is now in Houston, her horse is in Wisconsin. She works as a maid cleaning holiday homes; nine days on, two days off. 'Roger is a carpenter and at first he had work but then it slowed down here too. There are so many people moving here from all over the States that they're underbidding all the time. It got so he couldn't afford to do a job here even if he could get one. He left for Houston in February.'

She didn't go with him because they had already tried a year there once. The only job she found was putting body-side moulding on cars in an open lot. 'The day I quit working it was 114° and I could hardly touch the cars they were so hot. I like cleaning; it's easy work compared to the car lot and I like the folks I meet.'

Myra is 38; she's been married for fifteen years. Her oldest son is 14, her youngest daughter is 8. Their best years together were in the early seventies. Her husband had enough work at home in Evansville, Wisconsin and they lived in their own three-bedroomed house amid three acres of garden. 'I grew African violets and begonias in the living-room. It was sunny all day long.'

Construction slowed and for two years her husband travelled two and three hundred miles away from home to find work. Houston was a boom-town, centre of the sun belt. The Langridges sold their house and used the money, all they had, to buy an eighteen-wheel truck. Roger left in it for Texas and a new career as a trucker. A year later he was back to carpentry. His business had failed, the money was gone.

'I found the thought of moving from Wisconsin very scary. I'm basically a small-town person and Houston frightened me. I went because I thought it was the thing to do.' She had been raising quarter horses in Evansville; her first colt, which cost $100 breeding fee, had just been sold for $1,200. When she led her three horses into the 16-foot trailer for the drive to Houston, she thought she could somehow make money breeding in Texas.

'I got into the wagon with four kids, all our belongings and the horses behind to drive 1,300 miles by myself in a blizzard. The first day, we got stuck in the snow. I walked the kids across the street to a motel and shovelled the ice out from underneath the car and then my oldest boy and I fed, watered and exercised the horses in the parking lot. It was 40 degrees below and I thought to myself I don't dare cry so I just loaded up and drove on. The second day I drove in freezing rain, the third there were flash flood warnings and I was on my own – the only time I'd used the trailer before I took off was for a local horse show.'

They lived in a small apartment in Houston; she went to work on the car lot and the children, who had gone to one school in Evansville, were bewildered by the change. A year later she left and drove back to Wisconsin. 'The financial pressure was so tough that my husband's drinking got real heavy. I couldn't take it any more.'

She rented a farmhouse and worked in a factory making metal stampings at $4 an hour. Her husband followed them home and again there was the life of travelling hundreds of miles for work. 'One night it was freezing, Roger was working in Sheboygan, I was short of money so I'd had to buy fuel oil in a five-gallon can. I was standing in the snow pouring it into the tank and I said, "I'm not going to do this any more." My children were so cold, I'd had to move them downstairs to sleep. Roger was always away, I wasn't able to make ends meet and I knew we had to try something else.'

Sometimes in Aspen when Myra sits down for a second and thinks of their first home in Evansville, of her husband miles away and the constant wandering in search of work, her sturdy Midwest reserve gives way and she cries for how things are and how she once dreamed they would be as a 22-year-old bank clerk getting married in her local church. Most of the time, she keeps too busy to think. 'The harder I work the better I feel. I don't have to be fancy; I just need to know where the rent's coming from. I feel like you get married and you're supposed to be the ever faithful and go along but this time I've had it. We've chased around enough as a family. My kids are happy here. Me? I don't go out. I don't drink. I don't smoke. I go to work and go home and take care of my kids and that's my life.'

The resident population of Aspen is 4,000. It is estimated that every year 11,000 more come looking for work.

★   ★   ★

Brits who live in America are notorious for their bouts of homesickness. They suffer it like malaria: intermittently and without warning. Symptoms vary. Some start to talk of a landscape gardened for a thousand years as if all of England were Sissinghurst. Others suddenly pine for Christopher Robin, tepid beer or the Bedser brothers (nostalgia being both sentimental and inexact).

Prone to such attacks myself, it always comes as a surprise to meet those who suffer them not at all. They embrace America as if another past had never existed. They rise to Jones Little Sausages in the mornings as if bangers had never greeted their dawns. Not for them the comfort of Rumpole on Channel 13 nor the chill before the New-All-Action-Eyewitness News.

Lingering by the public park in Aspen one afternoon, I was drinking in the sight of the London Welsh rugby club's fourth team in the field against the Aspen Gentlemen (12-0 to the London Welsh). Over the crowd wafted the magical sounds of Manchester: flat, thick and cheerful.

There by the sidelines, ice-cold Coors' beer cans firmly in hand, stood David Chambers and Simon Smith, formerly of Cheadle, now of Aspen. They were holding forth on the London Welsh, their innate sense of field position, the excellence of their teamwork. Mentioned too were their days as hooker and prop in the fourth team of the Wilmslow Rugby Club ('The drinking team'), their years together at William Hulmes Grammar School, Simon's time at Pembroke College and David's career at Manchester Town Hall. Now they are Aspenites: Simon's a waiter, David mows lawns.

They've been friends for twenty-two years since the Saturday they met on the number 32 bus and went to watch the Cheadle Rovers. They meet now once or twice a week to play chess, watch television and talk of the Denver Broncos, the Middle East and the Aspen development plan. Occasionally, there's an echo from long ago – of F. J. Smith, perhaps, captain of the cadet corps and how he always carried Senior Service for himself, Woodbines to offer others.

David came to Aspen in 1977 for a ski-ing holiday, married and settled down to mow grass in summer, haul trash in winter. Simon came last year, half-way through his PhD on feminist criminology at Manchester; he spent his first season here working as a maid and part-time dishwasher.

'What it boils down to is attitude,' explained David. 'We don't have careers any more. Being a something or other – we're not that. Therefore we're free to do about anything. I might clean out garbage dumpsters this winter or shovel snow. I don't know and it doesn't worry me. I couldn't go back and mow lawns in

England for five shillings an hour, could I? First, I couldn't live on it, and besides there's all that social stigma. Here I'm free to be whatever I want and I can't think of one single reason for going back to England.'

Some come to America that they might better themselves; others that they need no longer work to do so. In the New World, the past with all its expectations is left behind. David's life now is almost a complete contradiction of that of his careful, middle-class parents who put him into computer programming and talked of security and the future. 'People who came out of the war years thought that way – that anyone who had a job was secure. But the whole concept of making money for money's sake – I couldn't take it seriously. I had three years with Honeywell and it was enough. I look on myself as retired now; I work in my spare time.'

He lives quietly with his wife and two children, spending little, going out rarely except to hike and ski. 'We live as the rich live – only free. People spend a fortune to come here on holiday and it's all ours, all the time. You find great peace here – you don't find that in Manchester.'

The rich are profligate; those who are not proud can live well on their leavings. Simon's first pair of skis were retrieved from a rubbish bin. Their clothes come from a charity thrift shop. 'I like to go in when I hear Leon Uris's wife's been there; my best suit was his.'

The soft lawns around the deserted condominiums were not put in for economy – taking care of three or four over the summer yields enough for a family to live. Simon may not find the satisfaction in waiting tables that he knew in his years as a welfare officer in Durham Prison but through the windows as he works he sees mountains and ski-trails.

What is strange is how little Simon found David had changed after his years here. Brits in America are just more foreigners; they adapt either as chameleons, quickly colouring over vowels and other differences, or by clinging to an ever more idiosyncratic Englishness, as if their very identity existed only through this constant and deliberate definition.

David has done neither; he has cheerfully moved from one culture to another almost without noticing. 'It's like licensing a car in another state. What do I miss? Nothing. What do I find hard? That's a really stupid question.'

But even in the new life, it's nice to have just one person who shares old jokes, understands the shorthand. 'It got easier when Simon came. We've been friends for twenty years – that's a long time to know someone. It's good to be here together. Your friends are always what matter. I feel I belong everywhere I live; I always have.

'I don't understand people who worry about where they'll die. Someone asked me if I minded not knowing where I was going to be buried. I said, "My father died in Cheadle last year – he was cremated."'